One City's Wilderness
PORTLAND'S FOREST PARK

Maps Legend

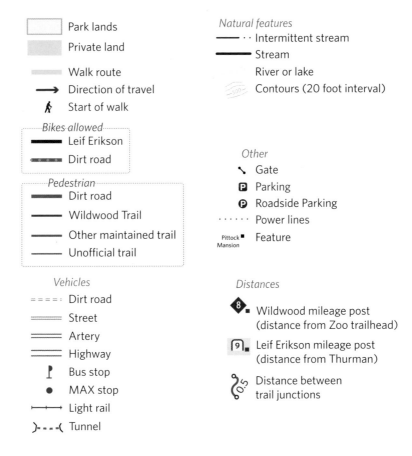

	Park lands
	Private land
	Walk route
→	Direction of travel
👤	Start of walk

Bikes allowed
	Leif Erikson
	Dirt road

Pedestrian
	Dirt road
	Wildwood Trail
	Other maintained trail
	Unofficial trail

Vehicles
=====	Dirt road
=====	Street
=====	Artery
=====	Highway
🚏	Bus stop
●	MAX stop
⊢—⊣	Light rail
)- - -(	Tunnel

Natural features
—··	Intermittent stream
——	Stream
	River or lake
≈520≈	Contours (20 foot interval)

Other
↘	Gate
🅿	Parking
℗	Roadside Parking
· · · · · ·	Power lines
Pittock ▪ Mansion	Feature

Distances
◆8▪	Wildwood mileage post (distance from Zoo trailhead)
[9]▪	Leif Erikson mileage post (distance from Thurman)
⌇0.5	Distance between trail junctions

One City's Wilderness
PORTLAND'S FOREST PARK
Third Edition

Marcy Cottrell Houle

Maps by Erik Goetze

Oregon State University Press
Corvallis

The paper in this book meets the guidelines for permanence and durability of the Committee on Production Guidelines for Book Longevity of the Council on Library Resources and the minimum requirements of the American National Standard for Permanence of Paper for Printed Library Materials Z39.48-1984.

Library of Congress Cataloging-in-Publication Data
Houle, Marcy Cottrell, 1953-
  One city's wilderness : Portland's Forest Park / Marcy Cottrell Houle. -- 3rd ed.
     p. cm.
  Includes bibliographical references and index.
  ISBN 978-0-87071-588-4 (alk. paper)
  1. Hiking--Oregon--Portland--Guidebooks. 2. Forest Park (Portland, Or.)--Guidebooks. 3. Portland (Or.)--Guidebooks. I. Title.
  GV199.42.O7H68 2010
  917.95'49--dc22

                         2010007205

Oregon State University Press
121 The Valley Library
Corvallis OR 97331-4501
541-737-3166 • fax 541-737-3170
http://osupress.oregonstate.edu

In a few years, nearly a million people will be living within
a few miles of the Forest Park... This wilderness within
a city is not a place for speeding ...; here there should be
no need for haste. Its roadways should be sufficient for
leisurely picnickers, nature students, photographers, and
not used so as to inconvenience pedestrians... There will be
requests for facilities for active recreation: play equipment,
play courts... (but) this is not the place for such active
recreational uses. Portland is well supplied with many
and better parks for such uses...It is hoped that soon the
privately owned land within the exterior boundaries will
have been acquired by the City ...thus the feeling of an
extensive, uninterrupted forest sanctuary may be preserved
"far from the madding crowd."

—Thornton Munger (1883 – 1975),
an original founder of Forest Park

Generous gifts from the following donors helped make publication of this book possible. The Oregon State University Press is grateful for their support.

Oregon Parks Foundation

The John and Shirley Byrne Fund
for Books on Nature and the Environment

*I gratefully dedicate this book
to my husband, John,
the love of my life
who makes me see each day with new eyes*

*And to my dear and stalwart hiking buddies,
Becky Sondag, Annie Heminger, and Catherine Thompson
who through sun, rain, sleet, or snow
were always up for still another adventure.*

Contents

Preface to the Third Edition

Returning to Forest Park to work on a new edition of *One City's Wilderness* is like becoming reacquainted with an old friend. You spend time together and realize, once more, the value and meaning this friend gives to your life. Walking Forest Park's trails, studying it carefully, and digging even deeper into its mysteries has made me see the park with new eyes. More than that, it has made me fall in love with it all over again.

After fourteen years, the park has seen changes. Wildwood Trail, the longest contiguous trail in a city park in the United States, has at last been extended to the park's northern boundary at Newberry Road. Several new connector trails have been built. Important inholdings have been purchased to protect the park's corridor. At the same time, pressures affecting the park have increased. Portland's population continues to rapidly grow. Housing developments have burgeoned next to parts of Forest Park. New destructive species, such as garlic mustard, have invaded the region—worrisome additions to the non-native weeds that threaten the park's native vegetation.

But like all true friends, the things that really matter stay the same. Forest Park's 5,157 acres remain overwhelmingly natural and beautiful. Its exceptional numbers of native plants and wildlife and its watersheds are still predominantly intact. The park continues to maintain its high-functioning value—a testament to peoples' careful stewardship and to the vision, goals, and directives of the excellent 1995 Forest Park Natural Resources Management Plan.

Something else, I found, has not changed in fourteen years. That is, the need for a place like this in my life. Forest Park's spectacular beauty and naturalness continue to impart peace and renewal. For me and for many, its wildness refreshes and inspires spirits grown weary from the fast-paced existence of modern life.

To know this park ... to spend time in it ... is to love it. And when you care for something, you want to preserve those values that make it unique. My hope is to help others gain an understanding of this resource and, from that, a desire to protect it.

This third edition of *One City's Wilderness* contains many new things. Foremost, every trail in the park is now described. In twenty-nine hikes, all eighty miles can be covered as an "All Trails Challenge," a fun goal that can be accomplished in however long it takes—six months or six years. There are exciting new maps, filled with information. Included are GPS coordinates and, for the first time ever published, the names of the park's streams, water features, and small connecting trails. You'll find a new chapter on the watersheds of Forest Park and eighty-four color photographs of its native plants and birds. Up-to-date information on the park's history, geology, vegetation, and wildlife, and a complete guide to Leif Erikson Drive, are also included.

So go out and enjoy the park. And while you're there, perhaps take a moment to look a little more closely. Discover for yourself why Forest Park is considered the nation's premier urban wilderness. In the process I think you will realize, as I did, that you have received an amazing gift.

Appreciate it, protect it, and pass it on.

I hope to see you on the trails.

Marcy Cottrell Houle
September 2010

Acknowledgements

I owe sincere appreciation to many people who have been involved with this new edition of *One City's Wilderness*. More than any other book of mine yet, this has been a true collaboration. I feel honored to have worked with so many outstanding specialists and artists on this third edition.

Erik Goetze, an award-winning cartographer, spent hundreds of hours making these maps of Forest Park. His talent, attention to detail, willingness to make changes time after time whenever new information became available, as well as his artistic eye and desire to make these maps as informative and accurate as possible, set a new, high standard for trail-guide maps. There are none out there better than these, Erik.

I am very grateful to the exceptional photographers who graciously donated their photos for this edition. Dr. Gerry Carr, botanist, is a nationally known photographer of plants, and I appreciate all the effort he has made going over the plant checklist and compiling such beautiful images for this book. Lois Miller also spent countless hours in discussing and providing her exceptional photographs of Forest Park birds. I am indebted to her. My dear daughter Jennifer Houle also took many of the photographs of Forest Park presented in this edition. I greatly appreciate her time and artistic eye.

And then, this book would not carry the factual significance it has without the help of many specialists, who generously donated their time to assist. Dr. Susan Kephart, plant systematist and evolutionary biologist at Willamette University, spent hours hiking and talking with me about the plants of Forest Park. Her knowledge was invaluable. She assisted in a large way with the new plant checklist for Forest Park, as did Wilbur Bluhm, of the Native Plant Society of Oregon, who was very helpful in updating the species list. John Deshler provided everything known under the sun about pygmy owls and their population within the Park and his depth of knowledge of

Forest Park birds and mammals was highly beneficial in creating the new bird and mammal checklists. I think his photo of a baby owl will be one of the favorites in the book. Dr. Jerry Franklin, one of the finest scientists I have ever known, graciously lent me the use, once again, of his fine map of the vegetation zones of Oregon and Washington, and also aided in information about the importance of old-growth habitat.

An important new part of this book is information on the watersheds of Forest Park. For this I am very grateful for the help of my husband, John, for his knowledge, and for the expertise of Paul Ketcham, Senior Environmental Program Manager for the Willamette Watershed of the Portland Bureau of Environmental Services. Paul graciously offered his time to explain the park's watersheds in depth and gave me copies of several recent publications, including the City's "2005 Portland Watershed Management Plan and Framework for Integrated Management of Watershed Health." Much of the information in these documents underscores the overall health and intact character of the Forest Park watersheds and the important role they play in the lower Willamette River.

I am also very grateful to Portland Parks and Recreation employees who care for Forest Park. Special thank-yous go to Fred Nilsen, recently retired Park arbiculturist, who spent hours carefully reading the manuscript and gave invaluable help on many things, including the locations of interesting and unusual plants found in the park as well as detailed information on trail mileage. Dan Moeller, City Nature West Natural Area Supervisor for Portland Parks and Recreation, also carefully reviewed the manuscript. Dan met with me monthly for nearly two years to discuss the park in detail. His assistance helped craft this book more than he can ever know. Kendra Petersen-Morgan, Natural Resource Ecologist for Portland Parks, gave hours of her time and expertise regarding Forest Park. Working with these individuals made me deeply appreciative of the work they have been able to accomplish within a limited Park budget. Their dedication is impressive and has made a huge difference to Forest Park.

Acknowledgements

Many other people were helpful in the development of this edition. In particular, I am deeply appreciative of all the members of Oregon Parks Foundation, who have continuously supported Forest Park and this book for over twenty-nine years. My original study and this book would never have been possible if not for them.

I am also extremely grateful and indebted to the Oregon State University Press, in particular Tom Booth, Associate Director, Jo Alexander, Managing Editor, and Judy Radovsky, Editorial and Production Assistant. They are committed to producing outstanding books and have been a true pleasure to work with. From beginning to end, Tom has been a large part of this book and I deeply appreciate his enthusiasm and professionalism and wise counsel.

Lastly, I could not have written this book without the help of my wonderful friends and family who hiked with me month after month, rain or shine. I am grateful that my daughters, Emily and Jennifer Houle, never complained when their mother said, "Who wants to go on a hike in Forest Park?" You have graciously and willingly come along ever since you were born.

Finally, my deepest and most loving thank you goes to my husband, John. He has hiked countless hours with me in this magnificent park. He has patiently explained the watersheds… pointed out the birds I didn't see… spent hours going over maps … discussed endlessly its geology and hydrology and history and wildlife and plants and just about everything else in-between.

Truly, John, this book is just as much yours as it is mine.

Introduction

Forest Park represents an unparalleled resource where citizens can enjoy the peace, solitude, ruggedness, variety, beauty, unpredictability and unspoiled naturalness of an urban wilderness environment; a place that maintains this wilderness quality while allowing appropriate passive recreational and educational use without degrading natural resources; an urban laboratory for environmental research and resource enhancement and restoration; America's premier urban ancient forest.

—1995 Forest Park Natural Resources Management Plan, Portland Parks and Recreation

What is it that makes Portland, Oregon, a leader among the cities of the nation in its livability and appeal? Part of the answer comes from its historical and cultural heritage and its outstanding natural beauty. And the culture, history, and beauty of an area are directly related to that area's natural features—from the watersheds, vegetation, mammals, and birds that characterize it.

Close to the heart of downtown Portland lies a large, relatively undisturbed tract of land that captures the essence of what is natural and wild and beautiful about the Northwest—Portland's Forest Park. One of the largest city parks in the world, Forest Park stretches 7.5 miles long by 1.5 miles wide along the eastern slope of Portland's West Hills. Bordered on the south by Burnside Street, on the north by NW Newberry Road, on the west by NW Skyline Boulevard, and on the east by NW St. Helens Road, Forest Park's 5,157 acres are an example of a natural western Oregon coniferous forest ecosystem. Hundreds of species of native Oregon plants and animals live and range within its borders. From this forest sanctuary, panoramic views of the city of Portland, the Willamette and Columbia rivers, and four major peaks of the Cascade Range—Mts. Rainier, St. Helens, Adams, and Hood—can be seen through the tall fir trees.

From its conception in 1903 and creation in 1948, Forest Park has been a refuge for both people and wildlife, and an integral part of the environment of Portland. It is the cool, green backdrop casting beauty to the city. It is part of the long, forested ridge known by Native Americans as "Tualatin Mountain." This ridge, rising eleven hundred feet above the banks of the Willamette and Columbia rivers, stretches northwest from Portland all the way to Oregon's rural Coast Range, and links Forest Park with the natural habitat of that range. Presently free from urbanization, this forest corridor allows scores of native species of birds and mammals to freely traverse from the more wild areas into the city forest. In addition, the northernmost section of Forest Park has nearly pristine interior forest habitat—land areas that have not been fragmented by multiple roads or developed uses. These areas provide critical breeding habitat for many native wildlife species. What this means is the observer hiking among Forest Park's eighty miles of trails may be rewarded by the sight of Red-tailed Hawks, Pygmy Owls, Pileated Woodpeckers, Ospreys, Bald Eagles, Peregrine Falcons, black-tailed deer, elk, coyotes, and perhaps even a bobcat while breathing the fresh air and enjoying the forest. No other city park in North America can offer such a natural experience.

For its open space, recreational and educational opportunities, and exceptional natural beauty, Forest Park is unquestionably America's premier urban forest. Only minutes from a major, growing metropolis, this extraordinary place continues to remind us of our coexistence with the natural world, and at the same time saves for future generations a priceless part of Oregon's native heritage.

*Rural parks [such as Forest Park] are intended to afford
to visitors that sort of mental refreshment and enjoyment
which can only be derived from the quiet contemplation
of natural scenery ... The fundamental purpose of a
rural park requires the shutting off from the interior as
completely as possible, all city sights and sounds, and the
resolute exclusion of many exceedingly popular means of
amusement ... even at serious sacrifice of opportunities for
those using them to enjoy some of the scenery.*

—John Charles Olmsted and Frederick Law Olmsted, Jr.,
Report of the Park Board, Portland, Oregon, 1903

*Because of its rugged beauty and magnificent outlook,
this mountainside has long aroused the attention of
people interested in intensive outdoor recreation, tourist
travel, forest development, and wildlife protection ... After
consulting with many interested and technical parties the
committee is convinced that the area should be preserved
for public forest-park use. Also it appears to the committee
that such development should be of a primitive nature
rather than as a park in the ordinary sense.*

—Report of the Committee of Five
as printed in the City Club Bulletin, August 31, 1945

History

The Euro-American discovery of the Willamette River in 1806 by Captain William Clark marked the beginning of interest and speculation in the fertile river valley that lay tucked away in a remote corner of the wild Oregon Territory. Twenty years later, spurred by the settlement of a Hudson's Bay Company headquarters in the region, pioneer travel up and down the Willamette River began. Permanent settlements soon dotted the landscape along the lower Willamette, beginning with the small communities of Linnton and Springville in 1843, and in 1845 the establishment of Portland further upriver. Along the plains to the west additional towns arose, and with them the desire of farmers to find ways to transport their crops to the people and shipping docks located along the Willamette River.

One geologic feature stood in their way, however—an eleven-hundred-foot forested ridge known as Tualatin Mountain. Thus, the recorded history of Forest Park was set into motion.

The early settlers were enterprising. Immediately they began to widen routes that had been used by Native Americans and explorers crossing Tualatin Mountain. By 1849, these primitive trails had turned into well-traveled passes, the names still used today: Germantown Road, Springville Road, Cornell Road, and Cornelius Pass. As the area grew more populated, parcels of forest land adjoining the roads were acquired by settlers. By 1859, most of what is now Forest Park had been given away in Donation Land Claims and was quickly being logged. Wood from Tualatin Mountain was used for a variety of purposes—building materials, firewood, as well as fuel for steamboats coursing the river.

The vision of preserving what is today one of the largest city parks in the world began in 1867 with the arrival in Portland of Reverend Thomas Lamb Eliot, a Unitarian pastor educated at Harvard. For over thirty-five years, Reverend Eliot was dedicated to improving his chosen city. His dream was a Portland "enlightened"—a moral,

Macleay Park Walkers, ca. 1900. OHS Photographic Archive, OrHi neg. 25924

humane place—and his labors quickly acquired for him the nickname "the conscience of Portland." By 1888, however, Reverend Eliot began to fear his vision was doomed to failure, seeing the Portland he loved quickly heading in a direction that he felt would cause it to become governed merely by accident or just another crossroad of struggling humanity.

Reverend Eliot increased his moralizing; it accomplished little. Not one to give up, however, he decided to initiate a new tactic, one that over the years would prove more successful than he ever could have dreamed: setting up a park system for Portland. In 1899, at Reverend Eliot's persuasive insistence, the Municipal Park Commission of Portland was formed. He was appointed to its first board of commissioners, and, through his direction, the commission contracted the most important landscape architecture firm of its day, the Olmsted Brothers of Brookline, Massachusetts, to make a park planning study of the city of Portland. In 1903, John C. Olmsted came to Portland to conduct research and made several far-reaching suggestions. In their report, the Olmsteds planned for a circuit of connecting parks looping around the city—today known as the "40

Macleay Park. OHS Photographic Archive, OrHi neg. 91753

Mile Loop." They also strongly suggested that the hills west of the Willamette River, now Forest Park, be acquired for a park of wild woodland character.

> "A visit to these woods would afford more pleasure and satisfaction than a visit to any other sort of park," wrote the Olmsteds in their report. "No use to which this tract of land could be put would begin to be as sensible or as profitable to the city as that of making it a public park."
>
> —Olmsted report

In 1907, voters approved a million-dollar bond issue to carry out the Olmsted plan. Unfortunately, most of the money went to developing existing parks, not to creating new ones. The plan to purchase Forest Park was set aside.

In spite of the setback, advocates continued to press for a forest park. The head of the Bureau of Parks and Recreation from 1908 through 1915 was Emanuel Mische, who actively campaigned for a wooded park running along the West Hills. For years he led people through this forest and publicly wrote editorials, hoping to convince citizens that: "One of the choicest landscape features of this region is the opportunity afforded by developing a parkway along the side hills north of the city."

In 1912, E. H. Bennett, an eminent city planner, was brought out from Chicago to develop The Greater Portland Plan. In agreement with Mische, he also advocated the development of a large reserve spanning much of the area that is now in Forest Park: "A wide stretch of country and the Columbia River are seen from that proposed park on the North," wrote Bennett. "[There are] deep splendid ravines and promontories from which the whole country with the distant snow-capped mountains come finely into view ... The forest reserves are extensive in the large cities of Europe. The great woodland areas are the great life-giving elements of the City."

Even with such repeated accolades, again nothing was done to preserve the land for the proposed park. Rather, several things happened in quick succession that made the creation of a forest park appear more and more unlikely. In 1913, a two-million-dollar park bond measure was voted down. In addition, there was a shift in politics and the organization of the park board was changed by city charter. In 1914, the City of Portland dropped the idea of creating a park and instead opened a wood-cutting camp on Tualatin Mountain to provide work for the unemployed. At the same time, eager developers were becoming hopeful of a great land boom in the west hills of Portland.

Greatly disheartened by the turn of events, Emanuel Mische resigned his position as park superintendent.

For the next several years, a coterie of land speculators, filled with expectations, went to work. Developers proposed and laid out massive subdivisions across Tualatin Mountain; thousands of lots were platted alongside a network of imaginary roads. One of the most prominent realtors, Richard Shepard, also promoted the building of a scenic drive that contoured in and out of Tualatin Mountain's steep ravines at a six-hundred-foot elevation above the Willamette River. Enlisting investors and engineers, Shepard built the road, today known as Leif Erikson Drive, in 1915. But the $150,000 cost of completing it was nearly twice as much as anyone had anticipated. To make matters worse, in its first year, a winter's landslide closed the road, and engineers estimated that it would cost an additional $3,000 to make repairs.

Shepard's dream soon became his worst nightmare. To cover costs for the road, the owners of the vacant lots were assessed. The vast majority, however, refused to pay. Consequently, between 1915 and 1931, hundreds of lots, totaling fourteen hundred acres, were forfeited to the City of Portland for nonpayment of the assessment and taxes. In addition, other land on Tualatin Mountain, after being logged off and subsequently burned by out-of-control slash fires, was forfeited to Multnomah County because of tax delinquency.

Although the idea of creating a forest reserve appeared to have been forgotten after Mische left his office, in reality the vision was still held by many Portland citizens. One such supporter, Fred Cleator, regional forester for the U.S. Forest Service and great lover of the outdoors, vociferously advocated for a wilderness park. Cleator volunteered hundreds of hours of his time building trails and leading groups of the Trail's Club, the Mazamas, and the Boy Scouts in planting trees throughout the area to restore forest cover to the bare hillsides. His cause was given increased visibility when Robert Moses, a city planner of national reputation, came to Portland in 1943 to make the "Portland Improvement" report. A cogent item in Moses's findings dealt with Forest Park:

> *The City has not taken full advantage of its great natural assets such as the wooded hills and the river front. Wooded hills and valleys in and around Portland have in a large measure been overlooked, probably because good scenery and forests are so plentiful in the Northwest. We believe that the steep wooded hillsides located on the westerly border of the City should be in public ownership. ... The wooded hillsides west of the City are as important to Portland as the Palisades of the Hudson are to the city of New York.*

Demands continued to grow that the area be set aside. Yet it was not until 1944, when Garnett "Ding" Cannon, an active Portland businessman and president of Standard Insurance, became involved that the idea began taking serious form. Cannon, an ardent advocate for the creation of an urban wilderness park, asked the City Club of Portland to conduct a study on the park's feasibility. Responding to Cannon's request, the City Club appointed a committee—John Carter, David Charlton, Allen Smith, Sinclair Wilson, and, as chairman, Cannon himself—to undertake the task.

In August, 1945, the committee published its findings in a report. The study strongly endorsed the idea of preserving the natural forest as a city park. One month later, the City Club of Portland voted unanimously to support the creation of a six-thousand-acre municipal forest park "for the benefit of the community." The creation of such a park, the City Club concluded, could provide the opportunity for several important objectives.

Following the report's publication, Cannon took charge and began a program of action. In 1947, he called a public meeting of citizens,

The City Club's objectives, as identified in the report:

1. Provide facilities that would afford extensive nearby outdoor recreation for citizens and attract tourists.
2. Beautify the environs of Portland.
3. Provide food, cover, and a sanctuary for wildlife.
4. Provide a site on which youth and other groups could carry on educational projects.
5. Grow timber, which would in time yield an income and provide a demonstration forest.
6. Provide productive work for casual labor.
7. Protect the forest and exposed contiguous areas from fire, the slopes from excessive erosion, and the roads and lands below from rock, dirt, and other materials washed from the slopes.
8. Eliminate problems of unwise settlement and excessive public service costs.
9. Put idle public land into productive condition.

under the umbrella of the Federation of Western Outdoor Clubs, of which he was president, to formulate a plan to preserve the park. At this meeting the "Forest Park Committee of Fifty," a group of civic, commercial, educational, and recreational agencies, was formed. Chosen as the group's first chairman was Thornton Munger, a scientist recently retired from the position of chief of research for the Pacific Northwest Forest Experiment Station, who was devoted to the idea of a wilderness park for Portland. For twelve years Munger remained the committee's chairman, never wavering in his enthusiasm for or indefatigable support of a magnificent, wild forest in the city's backyard.

Soon the public's attention was aroused; agreement was strong that the park be protected. Using this leverage, the Committee of Fifty petitioned the City Council of Portland to dedicate all public lands in the area for park purposes. In addition, it proposed adopting a policy to acquire private holdings within the designated six-thousand-acre boundary of the park.

On July 9, 1947, the City Council unanimously adopted the resolution. At the public hearing, the council requested that "all city and county and delinquent tax-owned property located on the hillsides .... (be dedicated) to the City of Portland for park purposes." Following the decree, the City of Portland transferred fourteen hundred acres of land from the assessment collection division to the park bureau. Ten months later, Multnomah County, after overcoming several legislative obstacles, transferred eleven hundred acres of land to the city park bureau without cost. Together, with additional gifts of land and other tax delinquent properties, a total of forty-two hundred acres of forest land was formally dedicated as Forest Park on September 25, 1948.

Today Forest Park spans 5,157 acres. Acquisition of the remaining private lands within the designated six-thousand-acre boundary slowly continues. While the Committee of Fifty has changed its name several times, in 1989 becoming the Friends of Forest Park and in 2008 subsequently renamed the Forest Park Conservancy, its mission and goals have stayed the same: to preserve, protect, and enhance this magnificent urban wilderness for both people and wildlife.

The vision of Reverend Eliot and the Olmsted Brothers, and the work of Mische, Cleator, Munger, Cannon and others, at last met with success. Their devotion and the dedication of those who today continue to advocate for Forest Park demonstrate that, despite setbacks, a far-fetched, century-old dream has the power to become a splendid reality.

Geology

Forest Park is a major defining element of the Portland landscape.
Rising to elevations exceeding 1,000 feet, Forest Park is visible from miles
away. The park and adjacent forest provide a backdrop to the city and
add visual relief to nearby urbanized areas. ... The natural resources
and physical setting of the City of Portland's Forest Park are unique. No
other major city in the nation can claim a wilderness-like forest of this
magnitude within its boundaries.

—1995 Forest Park Natural Resources Management Plan
Portland Parks and Recreation

The geologic history of Forest Park has been a continuing drama predominantly characterized by several recurring themes: violent volcanic eruptions originating far to the east that flooded vast areas with thick basaltic lava flows; episodes when land surfaces were inundated and submerged by marine, lake, or river waters; periods of local volcanism; periods of faulting and folding; and, in between, long, relatively quiet periods when land building subsided and surfaces lay subject to erosion.

The oldest recorded geologic event in Forest Park began approximately twenty-two million years ago, during late Oligocene and early Miocene time, when the land area that would one day become the city of Portland was submerged underneath an inland embayment of marine waters. Thick beds of siltstone and shale, accumulating to depths of several thousand feet, were deposited under water at this time. This fossil-rich deposit, referred to by geologists as the Scappoose Formation, is the oldest known formation underlying the West Hills of Portland and Forest Park. Deposition of the sediment ceased, however, when the entire region was slowly uplifted, forcing the seas to retreat. Over the next few million years, the area experienced a time of quiet and stability, and the sedimentary marine beds partly eroded. The calm of the period, however, belied what was about to happen in the east, an event that would, in retrospect, sculpt Tualatin Mountain more than any other in its history.

Sixteen million years ago, in middle Miocene time, intensive volcanic activity affected much of Oregon. Fissures in southeastern Washington and northeastern Oregon began erupting enormous quantities of fluid lava, sometimes pouring out hundreds of cubic miles of molten material that covered tens of thousands of square miles. As the lava cooled, it solidified and formed basalt, a heavy, fine-grained igneous rock. Vast plains of what geologists refer to as Columbia River Basalt stretched from Idaho to the Pacific coast. It flooded the Portland area, entering through an ancient Columbia River gorge, and covered the underlying Scappoose Formation with over one thousand feet of basalt. Today, approximately seven hundred feet of Columbia River Basalt underlie Tualatin Mountain and constitute most of its bulk.

As Miocene time progressed, the eruptions stopped, and for several million years weathering forces attacked the basalt, slowly decomposing exposed surface rocks into clay. During this period, the climate of the Portland area was tropical, and an extensive, reddish laterite crust, which is created under tropical conditions, formed on the exposed basalt.

Thirteen million years ago, another major disturbance rocked the region. At this time, the present-day Cascade and Coast ranges were uplifted and formed, and the basalt land surface of Portland, which had originally been laid down nearly horizontally, was squeezed and folded. This rippling action formed valleys, geologically referred to as "synclines," that were separated by upfolded arches of layered rock, or "anticlines." This is evident in the ridge called Tualatin Mountain, which is an anticline separating two major synclines to the east and west—the Portland and Tualatin valleys.

Between three and ten million years ago, during Pliocene time, the valleys continued to settle and eventually filled to become great lakes of water. The lakes, in turn, were filled with silts, today known as Sandy River Mudstone, that buried the basalt surfaces of the lake bottoms. When at last the basins could hold no more, they breached and joined with a powerful, ancestral Columbia River, which then rushed in to dump its load of quartzite pebbles and granitic rocks (carried all the way from the Canadian Rockies) into the deformed, submerged valleys. These river deposits, known as the Troutdale Formation, overlie the Columbia River Basalt on side slopes in Forest Park at elevations of up to six hundred feet.

As Pliocene time drew to a close, volcanic activity resumed, this time, however, on a regional scale. Dozens of small, isolated volcanoes, generated by underlying source vents, rose up like exclamation points across the land surface of the Portland area. Referred to as Boring Volcanoes, they erupted lava, which cooled to become gray, platy basalt. Several such volcanoes existed along the crest of Forest Park and poured out Boring Lava, a formation still visible in isolated sections along the ridge top and on the western slope of Tualatin Mountain.

The final rock formation capping most of Forest Park was laid down during the last million years of Pleistocene time by the actions of two major forces, the river and the wind, working in tandem. The pulsing Columbia River, working to excavate a major river valley, was continually whipped by the wind, which over time picked up large quantities of yellowish-brown, clay-like silt from the Columbia's floodplain and transported it to the south and west. Today this wind-deposited silt formation, known as Portland Hills Silt, covers the upper part of most of the West Hills of Portland; its greatest known thickness of fifty-five feet occurs on Forest Park's crest.

Geologic sculpting of Forest Park still continues, with other forces influencing and altering its land configuration. Some geologists believe the eastern flank of Tualatin Mountain, a steep, straight, fifteen-mile ridge, is the result of a long fault that lies beneath present-day St. Helens Road. More recently modifying the surface of the West Hills of Portland, landslides have carved the major side slopes and over the past one hundred years have created major construction problems. Portland Hills Silt, overlying Columbia River Basalt, is an unstable formation when wet, and in an area of high seasonal rainfall, such as Portland, it has repeatedly proved to be a poor foundation material. Often landslides have resulted when the equilibrium of slopes blanketed by silt have been affected by excavation or construction. This seemingly detrimental condition, however, while causing chagrin in many an expectant and hopeful land developer, is a significant reason why Portland's Forest Park escaped development in the past and still remains in its lovely natural state today.

The Watersheds of Forest Park

[A watershed is] that area of land, a bounded hydrologic system, within which all living things are inextricably linked by their common water course and where, as humans settled, simple logic demanded that they become part of a community.

—John Wesley Powell (1834-1902)
Geologist and explorer of the American West

Maintaining healthy watersheds is a way of preserving for future generations the natural legacy on which our community was built, and that in some sense still defines who we are.

—From the 2005 Portland Watershed Management Plan

Forest Park's predominantly undeveloped character plays an important role within the city of Portland. Its vast unbroken area of forested land—spanning eight miles from W. Burnside to NW Newberry Road—functions as a sequence of naturally occurring wilderness watersheds.

Eleven significant watersheds drain Forest Park and discharge clean, cool water into the Willamette River and its tributary, Multnomah Channel. Ranging from several hundred to over a thousand acres, these watersheds in order of size include Balch Creek (1,550 acres), Doane Creek (1,037 acres), Saltzman Creek (964 acres), Miller Creek (900 acres), Linnton Creek (855 acres), Springville Creek (695 acres), Newton Creek (447 acres), Johnson-Nicolai Creek (389 acres), Alder Creek (340 Acres), Thurman Creek (301 acres), and Willbridge (275 acres).

Many factors influence a watershed's properties and together determine its quality. Foremost among these are the size of the drainage, its geology, topography, soils, vegetation, ecological functioning, and climate. Within Forest Park drainages, geological features largely preordain observable attributes. The entire park is stratigraphically uniform. It is underlain by a lava bedrock—Columbia River Basalt— and topped by Portland Hills Silt, wind-blown from the historic Columbia River floodplain. Because of this geologic consistency, all watersheds within Forest Park have very similar characteristics. This point is important, for variation among the watersheds is therefore attributable, not due to differences in geology, but to differences in the activities occurring within individual drainages.

> "A watershed is a discrete stream basin that includes the headwaters, main channel, slopes leading to the channel, tributaries and mouth area."
>
> —2005 Portland Watershed Management Plan

Learning to read the watersheds of Forest Park unveils the story of its natural and cultural history. Since the beginning, when Tualatin Mountain became the dividing feature separating the Willamette and Tualatin river basins, water has been the active sculptor creating the relief seen in the park today.

Over thousands of years, flowing water continually incised the thick silt layer beneath the park, stopping only when it reached the bedrock basalt. Ravine after ravine was formed as the streams discharged their burden and shaped and molded the many walls along the slopes of the mountain. The easily erodable nature of Portland Hills Silt, combined with the uplifting of Tualatin Mountain, created a series of stream channels that are predominantly narrow and steep. On the average, the waterways of Forest Park exhibit a 15 percent slope, extending from the crest of Skyline Boulevard to the Willamette River one thousand feet below.

The rapid vertical drop of this eastern slope has also resulted in creeks that are highly linear. In general, Forest Park creeks run directly downhill with little to no meandering. If not for the forest cover, the force and volume of the runoff from these streams could be considerable and damaging. Fortunately, the impact of precipitation is modulated by the natural wilderness features found within Forest Park. Falling rain, which contributes to stream flow, is considerably slowed by its interception by the park's dense canopy of trees. When it at last reaches the ground, rainfall has lost much of its energy—power that could, if unabated, cause substantial erosion and downstream flooding.

The largely uninterrupted blanket of native vegetation of Forest Park, coupled with this high ecological functioning, are major factors contributing to the exceptional health of its watersheds. Much of the park's landscape is not damaged by fragmentation from development or intensive land use. Critical pieces of land, though, especially within some of the parks' headwaters, are still privately held. If these areas are not protected and over time become developed, the future quality of the park's watersheds will be compromised.

Watershed headwaters are always essential areas. What happens in the headwaters affects everything downstream. For this primary reason, a watershed's headwaters require special attention and management. Upstream activities that upset natural hydrologic balance increase in magnitude as water moves downstream. In other

words, downstream flooding, erosion, channel degradation, and transportation of pollutants all expand their capacities for damage if the native headwaters are degraded.

Forest Park's eleven major watersheds still function as they have for hundreds of years and are considered among the most native within the city of Portland when compared with their historical conditions. Throughout the park, streams predominantly act in natural ways unobstructed by artificial features. There is one significant exception, however: as flowing water prepares to leave the park to enter its large repository below, it is met with a major impediment—U.S. Highway 30.

At the abrupt intersection of streams with roads and industry, the natural water course is disrupted. Here, the native streams are captured into pipes and carried for considerable distances until they are at last discharged into the Willamette River.

Until recently, stormwater and sewer overflows seriously impacted the upstream water coming from the park. Leaching into the pipes, this unclean water mingled with the fresh water from the park and diminished its quality. Today, however, efforts are underway to mitigate these adverse impacts as part of an ongoing, larger process to clean the severely degraded Portland Harbor. Currently, drainage pipes at the base of Forest Park are being modified to prevent contaminants from entering and mixing with the park's clean water.

In essence, the healthy character of the watersheds of Forest Park is a visible manifestation of its history. A critical part of that narrative is the result of years of vision, planning, and ongoing management of the park. Securing the park's boundary conditions—from the Skyline crest to U.S. Highway 30—continues to be of vital importance in preserving the soundness of its watersheds. This protection not only benefits the park's plants and animals and the deeply troubled Willamette River … it benefits all of us.

Vegetation

In the long run it is easier to protect existing functioning habitats than it is to create new ones.

—2005 Portland Watershed Management Plan

Citizens need opportunities to escape the urban environment. Forest Park ... offers places of solitude for those who seek them out. These special places ... provide park users with the feeling that they are alone and that they have entered an environment that is dominated by nature.

—1995 Forest Park Natural Resources Management Plan
Portland Parks and Recreation

This will be a show place, unrivalled by any other city, to which to take visitors and introduce them to the lush forest flora of the Douglas fir region.

—Thornton Munger, Chairman, Committee of Fifty,
and one of the original founders of Forest Park

On April 4, 1806, while the Lewis and Clark expedition was returning eastward, William Clark made a side trip up the Willamette River; there he commented on the hillsides to the west and south of Sauvie Island, which today comprise Forest Park: "The timber on them is abundant and consists almost exclusively of the several species of fir already described [Douglas fir, grand fir, and western hemlock], and some of which grow to a great height. We measured a fallen tree of that species, and found that including the stump of about six feet, it was three-hundred-eighteen feet. ... There is some white cedar of a large size, but no pine of any size." As both Clark and Meriwether Lewis often would note in their journals, the trees of western Oregon were impressively abundant and immense.

Today, scientists agree that the forests of the Douglas fir region of western Washington, western Oregon, and northern California are unique among all temperate forest regions in the world. A combination of factors, including the region's mild winters and dry, cool summers, the relative absence of hurricane-force storms, and the genetic potential of its tree species, make the area significant in three outstanding respects:

1. Species of coniferous trees of the region attain a greater age and size than those found anywhere else in the world.

2. In terms of the sheer plant material, these forests have a greater accumulation of biomass (living and decomposing vegetative matter) than any other of the earth's temperate forests.

3. In their native condition, Northwest forests are highly unusual in that they are dominated by coniferous trees.

In order to better understand the massive forests of the Pacific coast, scientists have subdivided the region into specific areas that exhibit similar assemblages of plants and similar microclimates (rainfall and temperature). These vegetation zones are classified and named on the basis of an area's climax, or mature and self-perpetuating, vegetation. In western Oregon and Washington, the Western Hemlock Vegetation Zone encompasses the greatest area. Included within it is Portland's Forest Park. In its natural, undisturbed condition, the western hemlock zone is forested primarily with three tree species: Douglas fir, western hemlock, and western red cedar. To a lesser degree, grand fir, black cottonwood, red alder, bigleaf maple, madrone, and western yew trees also occur throughout the landscape. Shrubs of the western hemlock zone are well developed. Common indicator species are sword fern, salal, Oregon grape, lady fern, red huckleberry, and vine maple. The zone's predominant wildflowers include wild ginger, inside-out flower, Hooker's fairy bells, vanillaleaf, evergreen violet, and trillium.

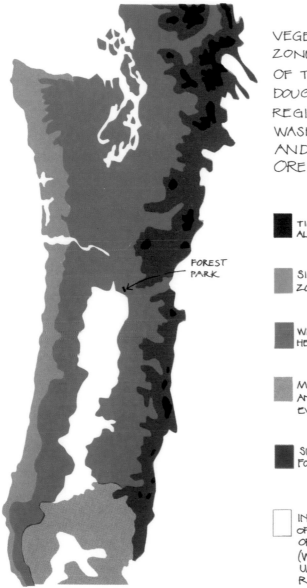

VEGETATION
ZONES
OF THE
DOUGLAS FIR
REGION IN
WASHINGTON
AND
OREGON

FOREST
PARK

TIMBERLINE AND
ALPINE REGIONS

SITKA SPRUCE
ZONE

WESTERN
HEMLOCK ZONE

MIXED CONIFER
AND MIXED
EVERGREEN ZONES

SUBALPINE
FOREST ZONES

INTERIOR VALLEYS
OF WESTERN
OREGON
(WILLAMETTE,
UMPQUA AND
ROGUE VALLEYS).

Because Forest Park still remains in a largely natural condition, it has maintained all of the western hemlock zone's naturally evolved, characteristic plants. However, one change is significant today. Instead of being dominated by evergreen trees, much of the park is clothed with a preponderance of red alder and bigleaf maple trees. A large portion of the western hemlock zone, including Forest Park, has been extensively logged in the past one hundred and fifty years. Evergreen trees have therefore declined appreciably. Hardwood species, mostly red alder, have proliferated as a result.

Under natural situations, red alder is abundant only in streamside areas of the Northwest. In contrast, in areas that have experienced repeated disturbance to the natural vegetation, such as through intensive logging and brush fires, the soil becomes depleted of nutrients. Alder readily establishes itself under these conditions, sometimes choking out all the fir trees, unless the young evergreens have been seeded on the bare soil and gained a foothold concurrently with the encroaching alders. If Douglas fir does not get going at the same time with young alder, it will not compete as well, and may take a long time to grow into a stand.

As a forest grows, it goes through several observable changes. After a major disturbance such as fire, windstorms, logging, mudslides, or disease, a forest transforms and progresses along a relatively linear trajectory. If little disturbance affects it, it may reach, after two hundred and fifty or more years, a climax stage. The series of conditions along the way are referred to by botanists as successional stages.

With an understanding of how succession and disturbance influence the landscape, suddenly the individual trees and shrubs in Forest Park take on new meaning. In addition, by understanding succession, one gains a deeper appreciation of the complete interaction existing between plants and wildlife, because, as will be explained in the next section, successional stages are directly related to the habitats of different species of birds and mammals.

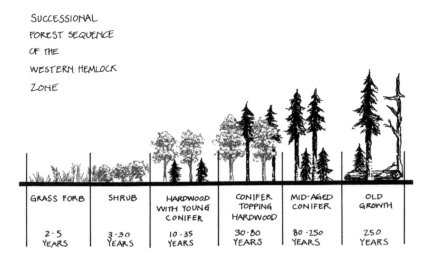

SUCCESSIONAL
FOREST SEQUENCE
OF THE
WESTERN HEMLOCK
ZONE

GRASS FORB	SHRUB	HARDWOOD WITH YOUNG CONIFER	CONIFER TOPPING HARDWOOD	MID-AGED CONIFER	OLD GROWTH
2-5 YEARS	3-30 YEARS	10-35 YEARS	30-80 YEARS	80-250 YEARS	250 YEARS

Six successional stages can be observed in Forest Park. Because of differences in levels of disturbance such as logging activities, forest fires, and tree plantings within the park, they are distributed as a mosaic throughout its five thousand acres.

The first successional stage of a forest, occurring two to five years after the previous vegetation has been removed by logging, fire, or other disturbance, is the grass-forb stage. This pioneering "forest" has a low profile—less than five feet tall—and contains no trees at all. Instead, it is identified by its numerous species of grasses and large patches of bracken fern, Canada thistle, and fireweed. In Forest Park, the grass-forb stage makes up only 1 percent of the vegetation, occurring mostly along the park's firelanes.

When a forest is between three and thirty years old, the shrub stage becomes apparent. Red alder, bigleaf maple, willow, bitter cherry, and Douglas fir trees begin to establish themselves at this time. But more noticeable, perhaps, is the variety of common shrubs that proliferate— thimbleberry, salmonberry, red-flowering currant, Indian plum, and several species of blackberry—ranging in height from two to twenty feet. In Forest Park, this stage covers approximately one hundred acres.

The third successional stage, hardwood with young conifer, is noticeable when a forest is between the ages of ten to thirty-five years. It is recognizable by the presence of young, thickly growing alder and maple trees, twenty-five to seventy-five feet tall, with girths of eight to ten inches.

Alder and maple's reign in a forest does not last forever. When Douglas fir trees reach an age of approximately twenty-one years, they increase their annual growth rate, and by forty years of age, begin to exceed the deciduous trees in height. A forest between thirty and eighty years old, therefore, grows into the fourth successional stage, conifer topping hardwood.

Fifth in sequence is mid-aged conifer. This stage becomes noticeable when a forest has achieved the age of eighty years.

Because much of Forest Park was logged between 1913 and 1940, making the forest approximately seventy to one hundred years old, the mid-aged conifer stage covers large areas of the park. At this age, red alder, a tree that lives for only about one hundred years, is growing old and dropping out of the vegetative scheme. Douglas fir, which has a life span of more than seven hundred and fifty years, is still young and thriving, and forming tall, stately stands. Individual Douglas fir trees can reach heights of one hundred to two hundred feet and have trunks thirty inches or more in diameter. In their shadows grow a variety of younger, shade-tolerant trees—western hemlock, western red cedar, and, on wetter sites, grand fir. If nothing happens to disturb these forests, western hemlock and red cedar will eventually dominate the landscape as the Douglas firs grow old. The forest floor of mid-aged conifer areas is also rich with plants. Sword fern, Oregon grape, red huckleberry, vine maple, and salal naturally flourish beneath the evergreens.

When a forest has escaped any major disruption for at least two hundred and fifty years, the final successional stage of vegetation becomes established. This old-growth stage is self-perpetuating and will continue indefinitely, unless something forces it back to an earlier condition. Past logging activities and substantial fires in

40

Forest Park have reduced old-growth vegetation to almost nothing, but a few patches still occur in isolated locales near Macleay Park, Germantown Road, and Newton Road. These areas are set apart from younger stands by virtue of several indicative structural features. Trees in the old-growth stage—predominantly western hemlock, western red cedar, and Douglas fir—are observably old and huge. Often they are individualistic in appearance, many sporting broken-off crowns. Also present in abundance are large snags (standing dead trees) and dead and downed logs in various stages of decay. These last two features are also apparent in mid-aged conifer stands, but not in the quantity found in old growth. As will be further explained in the following section, snags and downed logs are necessary for many species of wildlife, which require them for breeding and feeding sites. They are also vital to the regeneration of the coniferous forest. Downed logs act as "nurse logs" for hemlock and Douglas fir seedlings, which establish themselves on the nutrient-filled trunks. (Alder rots too fast to become a nurse log.)

Old-growth areas play a critical role in the health of an ecosystem, for their giant trees hold within them rich gene pools containing characteristics such as longevity and the ability to ward off disease. These traits are vital for the welfare and stability of future generations of trees. Additionally, the decaying snags and downed logs in old forests, far from being signposts of demise, in fact help insure that life-giving nutrients are being recycled back into the soil.

While succession can be predictable and lead to a single end point if disturbances are relatively infrequent, more often than not a forest's development is impacted by the numerous factors that impinge upon it. Differences in soil characteristics and climatic conditions, the availability of sources of plant seed, and specific land management actions (logging, tree thinning, or planting, for example) all play a part in how a forest's vegetation will change over time.

When one unravels these secrets bit by bit, the seemingly disjointed parts suddenly unite to explain a fascinating, holistic picture of a living forest, such as Portland's own native Forest Park.

PLANT CHECKLIST

Common name	Scientific name		Location	Dates
CONIFERS				
Douglas fir	*Pseudotsuga menziesii*	C	Woods	E
Grand fir	*Abies grandis*		Woods	E
Pacific silver fir	*Abies amabilis*		Woods	E
Western hemlock	*Tsuga heterophylla*	C	Woods	E
Western red cedar	*Thuja plicata*	C	Woods	E
Yew	*Taxus brevifolia*		Woods	E
HARDWOOD TREES				
*American chestnut	*Castanea dentata*			
Bigleaf maple	*Acer macrophyllum*	C	Woods	3-4
Bitter cherry	*Prunus emarginata*	C	Woods	4-5
Black cottonwood	*Populus trichocarpa*		Wet areas	4-5
Cascara	*Rhamnus purshiana*	C	Woods	5-6
*English laurel	*Prunus laurocerasus*			
*European mountain ash	*Sorbus aucuparia*			
*Filbert	*Corylus avellana*			
*Horse chestnut	*Aesculus hippocastanum*			
*Norway maple	*Acer platanoides*		Woods	
Oregon white oak	*Quercus garryana*		Open areas	4-6
Oregon crabapple	*Malus fusca*		Woods	5-6
Pacific dogwood	*Cornus nuttallii*		Woods	5-6
Pacific madrone	*Arbutus menziesii*		Dry areas	3-5
Pacific willow	*Salix lasiandra*		Woods	5-6
Red alder	*Alnus rubra*	C	Woods, drainages	3-4
Scouler's willow	*Salix scouleriana*		Open, damp areas	3-4
Sitka mountain-ash	*Sorbus sitchensis*		Open Woods	6-7
*Sour cherry	*Prunus cerasus*		Woods	
*Sweet cherry	*Prunus avium*			
Vine maple	*Acer circinatum*	C	Woods	4-5
Western hazelnut	*Corylus cornuta*	C	Open woods	2-3

KEY
* Introduced species
C = Common
Blooming Dates: January (1)-December (12), deciduous (D), evergreen (E)

Common name	Scientific name		Location	Dates
SHRUBS AND VINES				
Blue elderberry	*Sambucus mexicana*		Woods	5-8
Common snowberry	*Symphoricarpos albus*	C	Woods	6-7
*English hawthorn	*Crataegus monogyna*			
*English holly	*Ilex aquifolium*	C	Woods	
*English ivy	*Hedera helix*	C	Woods	
*Evergreen blackberry	*Rubus laciniatus*	C	Open areas	5-8
*Himalayan blackberry	*Rubus armeniacus*	C	Open areas	6-9
Indian plum	*Oemleria cerasiformis*	C	Woods	3-4
Little wild rose	*Rosa gymnocarpa*	C	Woods	5-6
Low Oregon grape	*Berberis nervosa*	C	Woods	3-5
Nootka rose	*Rosa nutkana*	C	Woods	5-6
Ocean spray	*Holodiscus discolor*	C	Woods	6-7
Orange honeysuckle	*Lonicera ciliosa*		Woods	5-6
Oregon viburnum	*Viburnum ellipticum*			
Pacific blackberry	*Rubus ursinus*	C	Meadows, woods	4-6
Poison oak	*Toxicodendron diversilobum*		Dry meadows	5-6
Red elderberry	*Sambucus racemosa*	C	Woods	3-5
Red flowering currant	*Ribes sanguineus*		Open woods	3-4
Red huckleberry	*Vaccinium parvifolium*	C	Woods	4-6
Red-stem ceanothus	*Ceanothus sanguineus*		Open woods	5
Salmonberry	*Rubus spectabilis*	C	Moist woods	3-5
*Scots broom	*Cytisus scoparius*	C	Woods	4-6
Tall Oregon grape	*Berberis aquifolium*		Open woods	3-5
Thimbleberry	*Rubus parviflorus*	C	Open areas, woods	4-5
Western blackcap	*Rubus leucodermis*		Fields, woods	5-6
Western clematis	*Clematis ligusticifolia*		Open woods	6-9
Western serviceberry	*Amelanchier alnifolia*		Woods	3-5
GRASSES, SEDGES, RUSHES				
*Annual ryegrass	*Lolium multiflorum*			
*Bamboo	*Bambusa* sp.			
Common rush	*Juncus effusus*		Damp woods	
Field woodrush	*Luzula multiflora*	C	Open areas, woods	
Henderson's sedge	*Carex hendersonii*	C	Woods, fields	
*Kentucky bluegrass	*Poa pratensis*			

Common name	Scientific name		Location	Dates
*Meadow foxtail	Alopecurus pratensis			
Oniongrass	Melica bulbosa	C	Woods, fields	5-6
*Orchard grass	Dactylis glomerata	C	Meadows	6-8
*Reed canary grass	Phalaris arundinacea	C	Damp areas	6-9
Small flowered woodrush	Luzula parviflora			
*Sweet vernal grass	Anthoxanthum odoratum	C	Meadows	5-6
*Tall fescue	Schedonorus arundinaceus			
FERNS, HORSETAILS				
Bracken fern	Pteridium aquilinum	C	Open areas	D
Deer fern	Blechnum spicant	C	Woods	D
Field horsetail	Equisetum arvense	C	Wet areas	D
Giant horsetail	Equisetum telmateia	C	Open areas	D
Goldback fern	Pityrogramma triangularis		Rocks, open slopes	E
Lady fern	Athyrium felix-femina	C	Woods	D
Licorice fern	Polypodium glycyrrhiza	C	On trees	E
Maidenhair fern	Adiantum aleuticum	C	Woods	D
Spreading wood fern	Dryopteris expansa		Woods	D
Sword fern	Polystichum munitum	C	Woods	E
Western oak fern	Gymnocarpium disjunctum		Moist woods	D
WILDFLOWERS				
Lily Family	**Liliaceae**			
Clasping twisted stalk	Streptopus amplexifolius	C	Woods	5-6
Fairy lantern	Prosartes smithii	C	Woods	5-6
False lily-of-the-valley	Maianthemum dilatatum	C	Woods, stumps	5-6
Solomon's plume	Maianthemum racemosum	C	Woods	4-5
Hooker's fairy bells	Prosartes hookeri	C	Woods	4-6
Oregon fawn lily	Erythronium oregonum		Woods	3-4
Star-flowered Solomon's seal	Maianthemum stellatum	C	Woods	4-7
Tiger lily	Lilium columbianum	C	Woods	6-7
Western trillium	Trillium ovatum	C	Woods	3-4
Iris Family	**Iridaceae**			
Oregon Iris	Iris tenax	C	Meadows, roadsides	5-6
Nettle Family	**Urticaceae**			
Stinging nettle	Urtica dioica	C	Moist areas	4-6
Birthwort Family	**Aristolochiaceae**			
Wild ginger	Asarum caudatum	C	Woods	4-5

44

Plant Checklist

Common name	Scientific name		Location	Dates
Buckwheat Family	**Polygonaceae**			
*Japanese knotweed	*Polygonum cuspidatum*			
Western dock	*Rumex occidentalis*	C	Moist areas	5-6
Purslane Family	**Portulaceae**			
Miner's lettuce	*Claytonia perfoliata*	C	Woods	2-6
Narrow-leaved montia	*Montia linearis*		Woods	2-5
Water chickweed	*Montia fontana*		Wet areas	3-4
Candyflower	*Claytonia sibirica*	C	Woods	3-10
Pink Family	**Caryophyllaceae**			
*Common chickweed	*Stellaria media*	C	Meadows	2-9
Crisped starwort	*Stellaria crispa*			
Buttercup Family	**Ranunculaceae**			
*Creeping buttercup	*Ranunculus repens*	C	Damp areas	5-10
Little buttercup	*Ranunculus uncinatus*	C	Moist areas	4-6
Red columbine	*Aquilegia formosa*	C	Wood margins	4-9
*Traveler's joy	*Clematis vitalba*			
Western red baneberry	*Actaea rubra*	C	Woods	4-5
Western buttercup	*Ranunculus occidentalis*		Woods	
Western white anemone	*Anemone deltoidea*		Woods	5-6
Barberry Family	**Berberidaceae**			
Inside-out flower	*Vancouveria hexandra*	C	Woods	5-6
Vanillaleaf	*Achlys triphylla*	C	Woods	4-5
Bleeding-Heart Family	**Fumariaceae**			
Pacific bleeding-heart	*Dicentra formosa*		Woods	3-6
Mustard Family	**Brassicaceae**			
Angled bittercress	*Cardamine angulata*		Woods	5-6
*Garlic mustard	*Alliaria petiolata*			
*Hedge mustard	*Sisymbrium officinale*			
Slender toothwort	*Cardamine nuttallii*	C	Woods	3-4
*Silver dollar plant	*Lunaria annua*		Roadsides	4-6
*Water cress	*Nasturtium officinale*		Wet areas	5-10
Saxifrage Family	**Saxifragaceae**			
Fringecup	*Tellima grandiflora*	C	Woods	3-6
Golden saxifrage	*Chrysosplenium glechomaefolium*		Wet areas	3-5
Leafy bishop's cap	*Mitella caulescens*		Woods	4-6
Small-flowered alumroot	*Heuchera micrantha*		Woods, rocks	5-6

Common name	Scientific name		Location	Dates
Foamflower	*Tiarella trifoliata*	C	Woods	6-10
Piggyback plant	*Tolmeia menziesii*	C	Woods	4-7
Rose Family	**Rosaceae**			
Douglas spirea	*Spiraea douglasii*		Meadows	6-8
Goatsbeard	*Aruncus dioicus*		Woods	5-6
Large-leaved avens	*Geum macrophyllum*	C	Woods	4-9
Woods strawberry	*Fragaria vesca*	C	Meadows	4-6
Pea Family	**Fabaceae**			
American vetch	*Vicia americana*			
*Hairy vetch	*Vicia hirsuta*			
Giant vetch	*Vicia nigricans*	C	Moist areas	6
Many-leaved pea	*Lathyrus polyphyllus*	C	Woods	4-5
Geranium Family	**Geraniaceae**			
Bicknell's geranium	*Geranium bicknellii*		Woods	5-8
*Crane's bill, Filaree	*Erodium circutarium*	C	Trailsides	3-6
*Cut-leaved geranium	*Geranium dissectum*		Trailsides	6-7
*Herb-Robert	*Geranium robertianum*			
Oxalis Family	**Oxalidaceae**			
Oregon oxalis	*Oxalis oregana*		Woods	3-5
Violet Family	**Violaceae**			
Evergreen violet	*Viola sempervirens*		Woods	3-6
Yellow woodland violet	*Viola glabella*	C	Woods	3-8
Evening Primrose Family	**Onagraceae**			
Enchanter's nightshade	*Circaea alpina*	C	Woods	5-7
Fireweed	*Chamerion angustifolium*	C	Roadsides, fields	6-8
Parsley Family	**Apiaceae**			
Cow parsnip	*Heracleum maximum*		Wet areas	
Sweet cicely	*Osmorhiza beteroi*	C	Woods	4-6
*Poison hemlock	*Conium maculatum*			
Water parsley	*Oenanthe sarmentosa*	C	Wet areas	5-8
Heath Family	**Ericaceae**			
Common pink wintergreen	*Pyrola asarifolia*		Woods	6-7
Indian pipe	*Monotropa uniflora*		Woods	7-8
Salal	*Gaultheria shallon*	C	Woods	4-8
Primrose Family	**Primulaceae**			
Western starflower	*Trientalis latifolia*	C	Woods	5-6
Morning Glory Family	**Convolvulaceae**			
*Field bindweed	*Convolvulus arvensis*	C	Meadows	5-9

46

Common name	Scientific name		Location	Dates
Waterleaf Family	**Hydrophyllaceae**			
Pacific waterleaf	*Hydrophyllum tenuipes*	C	Woods	4-6
Small-flowered nemophila	*Nemophila parviflora*	C	Woods	3-5
Mint Family	**Lamiaceae**			
Great hedge nettle	*Stachys cooleyae*	C	Woods	7-9
*Heal-all	*Prunella vulgaris*	C	Roadsides	6-9
Figwort Family	**Scropulariaceae**			
California figwort	*Scrophularia californica*	C	Woods	6-7
*Common mullein	*Verbascum thapsus*	C	Open areas	5-9
*Common speedwell	*Veronica arvensis*	C	Margins	5-6
*Foxglove	*Digitalis purpurea*	C	Trailsides	7-8
Nightshade Family	**Solanaceae**			
*Bittersweet nightshade	*Solanum dulcamara*			
Arum Family	**Araceae**			
*Italian arum	*Arum italicum*			
Plantain Family	**Plantaginaceae**			
"Common plantain	*Plantago major*	C	Meadows	6-9
Madder Family	**Rubiaceae**			
Common bedstraw	*Galium aparine*	C	Cosmopolitan	3-7
Fragrant bedstraw	*Galium triflorum*			
Honeysuckle Family	**Caprifoliaceae**			
Western twinflower	*Linnaea borealis*	C	Woods	6-8
Sunflower Family	**Asteraceae**			
*Bull thistle	*Cirsium vulgare*	C	Open areas	
*Canada thistle	*Cirsium arvense*	C	Meadows	6-8
*Common burdock	*Arctium minus*	C	Meadows, woods	8
*Common dandelion	*Taraxacum officinale*	C	Cosmopolitan	2-12
Common yarrow	*Achillea millefolium*	C	Meadows	4-7
*False dandelion	*Hypochaeris radicata*			
*Nipplewort	*Lapsana communis*			
Oxeye Daisy	*Leucanthemum vulgare*	C	Meadows	5-8
*Spiny sowthistle	*Sonchus asper*			
Coltsfoot	*Petasites frigidus*	C	Wet areas	2-5
*Tansy ragwort	*Senecio jacobaea*	C	Roadsides	7-9
Trail plant, Pathfinder	*Adenocaulon bicolor*	C	Woods	6-8
*Wall lettuce	*Mycelis muralis*			

Plants of Forest Park

Photographs by Dr. Gerry Carr

FERNS

Deer fern *Blechnum spicant*

Licorice fern *Polypodium glycyrrhiza*

Sword fern *Polystichum munitum*

Maidenhair fern *Adiantum aleuticum*

WILDFLOWERS

Candy flower
*Claytonia
sibirica*

Clasping
twisted stalk
*Streptopus
amplexifolius*

48

Coltsfoot *Petasites frigidus*

Fairy lantern *Prosartes smithii*

False lily-of-the-valley
Maiathemum dilatatum

Fireweed *Chamerion
angustifolium*

Foamflower *Tiarella trifoliata*

Fringecup *Tellima
grandiflora*

Hooker's fairy bells *Prosartes
hookeri*

49

Inside-out flower *Vancouveria hexandra*

Miner's lettuce *Claytonia perfoliata*

Oregon fawn lily *Erythronium oregonum*

Oregon oxalis *Oxalis oregana*

Pacific bleeding-heart *Dicentra formosa*

Oregon iris *Iris tenax*

Pacific waterleaf *Hydrophyllum tenuipes*

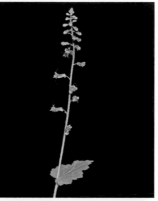

Piggyback plant *Tolmiea menziesii*

Solomon's plume *Maiathemum racemosum*

Star-flowered Solomon's seal

Stinging nettle *Urtica dioica*

Sweet cicely *Osmorhiza beteroi*

Tiger lily *Lilium columbianum*

Trail plant *Adenocaulon bicolor*

Vanillaleaf *Achlys triphylla*

Western starflower *Trientalis latifolia*

Wild ginger *Asarum caudatum*

Western trillium *Trillium ovatum*

Yellow woodland violet *Viola glabella*

TREES

Douglas fir *Pseudotsuga menziesii*

Bigleaf maple *Acer macrophyllum*

Vine maple *Acer circinatum*

Red alder *Alnus rubra*

53

Western red cedar *Thuja plicata*

Western hemlock *Tsuga heterophylla*

INVASIVES

English holly *Ilex aquifolium*

English ivy *Hedera helix*

Garlic mustard *Allaria petiolata*

SHRUBS

Indian plum *Oemleria cerasiformis*

Low Oregon grape *Berberis nervosa*

Red elderberry *Sambucus racemosa*

Red huckleberry *Vaccinium parvifolium*

Salal *Gaultheria shallon*

Salmonberry *Rubus spectabilis*

Thimbleberry *Rubus parviflorus*

55

Wildlife

Portland's Forest Park, in all its native diversity, today allows people the opportunity to observe, study, and interact with the natural heritage of the Pacific Northwest. This is an enviable situation, for [most] urban and suburban parks are devoid of many native, forest-interior species as a result of their combination of small size, increasing isolation from sources of potential colonists, and high level of human related disturbance. In the final analysis, however, the success of efforts to retain natural diversity in Forest Park will be judged on the number of native species surviving, not in just the next ten years, but in the year 2100 … The process of fragmentation (of natural habitat) is, for all practical purposes, irreversible.

—The West Hills Wildlife Corridor Study, Phase One
Multnomah County Division of Planning, 1990

Over one hundred and seventeen species of birds and fifty-three species of mammals can be observed living in or ranging through Portland's Forest Park. This diversity of wildlife, the majority of which are species native to the Northwest, is highly unusual in comparison with parks in the nation's other major cities.

In most large metropolitan areas, urban development has resulted in an insidious but definite decline in the numbers of native birds and mammals. The usual progression of a city's expansion means that natural habitats disappear parcel by parcel, and that large, continuous, wooded areas are broken up by urban sprawl. Under these circumstances, native wildlife species are at a loss to respond. They become trapped within limited pockets of available habitat, cannot find mates with which to reproduce, and are unable to migrate to more hospitable natural areas, which are too far away. What is the common result? Unfortunately, many naturally occurring

This satellite image, showing how Forest Park serves as a wildlife corridor to the Coast Range, faces west to the ocean beyond. Used by permission of Google Maps. Image © 2010 Metro, Portland Oregon. Image US Geologic Survey, Image State of Oregon. © 2010 Google

species fall prey to local extinction. Larger species that have more specialized requirements for breeding and feeding are often the first to disappear—the native hawks, owls, and large woodpeckers.

For this reason, the majority of wildlife species in most urban areas is non-native. Starlings, pigeons, house sparrows, Norway rats, and house mice proliferate in cities, these species finding no difficulty coexisting with humans. They readily migrate from other urban areas as native species decline.

Forest Park, however, makes Portland unique among cities. Because of the park's exceptional size and, at present, its continuous, unfragmented habitat, large numbers of native birds and mammals live within it and thrive. More important in respect to wildlife, the park presently maintains a natural link with the habitat of Oregon's rural Coast Range. A corridor of natural vegetation connects the park's northwestern end to more wild, undeveloped areas. In effect, this acts like a funnel, allowing native animals to wander in and out of the park at will. This attachment to a larger range increases the chances that local mammals and birds will be able to find suitable mates and appropriate habitat conditions, and not suffer genetic isolation and eventual extirpation.

The existence of a wildlife corridor helps to explain the continued presence of the kinds of wildlife today that were also observed by Lewis and Clark in the same vicinity. In 1806, Captain William Clark commented on the animals he noticed in the forests along the Columbia River: "We observe the marten, small geese, the small speckled woodpecker with a white back [Hairy Woodpecker], the blue crested corvus [Steller's Jay], ravens, crows, eagles, vultures, and hawks."

With the exception perhaps of martens, all of the species that Lewis and Clark recorded in 1806 can still be observed in Forest Park. From a biological standpoint, it is critical to remember that this assemblage of Northwestern animals is not random but instead has evolved over centuries of time, owing to each animal's specific adaptations to its habitat. All wildlife species have requirements for breeding areas and feeding sites, and this results in wildlife and habitat being completely interrelated. Wildlife is its habitat. The two cannot be separated.

Another important aspect contributing to Forest Park's variety of native wildlife is the interior forest habitat found in the park's North Unit. This resource, defined as native woodland vegetation occurring in large, unbroken pieces and not dissected by roads, clear cuts, or residential or agricultural development, is becoming increasingly rare. Yet many species of native mammals and birds, particularly migratory songbirds, are extremely dependent upon habitat that occurs deep within the forest, far from the "edge." Many animals that frequent edges of forests—starlings, brown-headed cowbirds, scrub jays, opossums, skunks, and raccoons—tend to be predacious or parasitic upon forest birds. This has wreaked havoc on native wildlife populations. Throughout the northeastern United States and southeastern coastal plains, for example, regional extinctions regularly occur as a result of loss and fragmentation of natural interior habitat.

Forest Park is set apart from other city parks in that it still retains a significant amount of exceptionally cohesive interior forest habitat north of Germantown Road. This feature has been deemed Forest Park's most important asset. Because of its scarcity within urban areas, its value only continues to rise.

> "The high quality of Forest Park's interior forest habitat—large (and) relatively intact ... is unique and supports wildlife not found in any other urban park in the world."
>
> —1995 Forest Park Natural Resources Management Plan
> Portland Parks and Recreation

Because animals respond to the structural components of vegetation, the successional stages of a forest community can be thought of as different habitats for wildlife. Early successional stages of a forest, with their low-growing profile and open conditions, attract animals adapted to these particular things. Later successional stages, which have many layers of vegetation, snags, and downed logs, attract wildlife that require these components. For this reason, a person walking through Forest Park or other low-elevation western Oregon and Washington forests can expect to see different assemblages of birds and mammals depending upon which successional stage of the forest that person is in.

Many wildlife species found in the older stages of a forest require snags and downed logs as sites for breeding, feeding, and courting. In urban parks, however, these features are usually removed in an effort to create "park-like" settings. This policy can have deleterious effects. When these necessary components are taken away, fewer places are left for native wildlife and the diversity of birds and mammals, therefore, is sharply reduced. Forest Park's large wildlife numbers are partially the result of the abundance of snags and downed logs throughout its landscape.

Woodpeckers are especially dependent on snags and require them in varying stages of decay. They use those with sound wood in which to excavate their nesting cavities. They need those that are more deteriorated in which to forage for insects. Woodpeckers are extremely important inhabitants in an ecosystem, because many species of animals require holes in trees for nesting sites and do not have the ability to make them for themselves. Saw-whet Owls, Violet-green Swallows, Tree Swallows, chickarees, and northern flying squirrels, for example, are entirely dependent upon woodpeckers to drill holes in snags for them.

Observing the wealth of plants and animals found today in Forest Park, one must come to the inescapable conclusion that it is an outstanding example of a city park in terms of its naturalness and ecological functioning. Only minutes from downtown Portland, one has the opportunity to observe Bald Eagles and Peregrine Falcons, eight native species of hawks, six species of owls, ten kinds of warblers, five types of colorful woodpeckers, eight kinds of sparrows, and scores of other birds. One also has the chance to see coyotes, beavers, long-tailed weasels, black-tailed deer, elk, black bears, and bobcats.

Why is that impressive? It is because these animals are not in a zoo. Rather, they are living in a semi-wild, natural habitat, all within the confines of a city park. Portland's own Forest Park.

MAMMALS CHECKLIST

Common name	Scientific name
MARSUPIALS	
Opossum	*Didelphis virginianus*
INSECTIVORES	
Shrews	
Dusky shrew	*Sorex obscurus*
Marsh shrew	*Sorex bendirei*
Trowbridge shrew	*Sorex trowbridgei*
Wandering shrew	*Sorex vagrans*
Moles	
American shrew-mole	*Neurotrichus gibbsi*
Coast mole	*Scapanus orarius*
Townsend mole	*Scapanus townsendi*
Bats	
Big brown bat	*Eptesicus fuscus*
California bat	*Myotis californicus*
Hoary bat	*Lasiurus cinereus*
Little brown bat	*Myotis lucifugus*
Long-eared bat	*Myotis evotis*
Long-legged bat	*Myotis volans*
Silver-haired bat	*Lasionycteris noctivagans*
Western long-eared bat	*Plecotus townsendi*
Yuma bat	*Myotis yumanensis*
RABBITS AND HARES	
Brush rabbit	*Sylvilagus bachmani*
Snowshoe hare	*Lepus americanus*

Common name	Scientific name
RODENTS	
Mountain beavers	
Mountain beaver	*Aplodontia rufa*
Squirrels	
Beechey ground squirrel	*Spermophilus beecheyi*
Chickaree	*Tamiasciurus douglasi*
Northern flying squirrel	*Glaucomys sabrinus*
Townsend chipmunk	*Eutamias townsendi*
Pocket gophers	
Mazama pocket gopher	*Thomomys mazama*
Beavers	
North American beaver	*Castor canadensis*
Murids	
Black rat	*Rattus rattus*
Bushy-tailed woodrat	*Neotoma cinerea*
California red-backed vole	*Clethrionomys californicus*
Creeping vole	*Microtus oregoni*
Deer mouse	*Peromyscus maniculatus*
Dusky-footed woodrat	*Neotoma fuscipes*
House mouse	*Mus musculus*
Muskrat	*Ondatra zibethicus*
Norway rat	*Rattus norvegicus*
Red tree vole	*Arborimus longicaudus*
Townsend vole	*Microtus townsendi*
White-footed vole	*Arborimus albipes*
Jumping mice	
Pacific jumping mouse	*Zapus trinotatus*
NEW WORLD PORCUPINES	
North American porcupine	*Erethizon dorsatum*
OAPROMYIDS	
Nutria	*Myocastor coypus*

Mammals Checklist

Common name	Scientific name
CARNIVORES	
Dogs	
Coyote	*Canis latrans*
Red fox	*Vulpes vulpes*
Bears	
North American black bear	*Euarctos americanus*
Raccoons	
Raccoon	*Procyon lotor*
Weasels and allies	
Long-tailed weasel	*Mustela frenata*
Short-tailed weasel	*Mustela erminea*
Spotted skunk	*Spilogale putorius*
Striped skunk	*Mephitis mephitis*
Cats	
Bobcat	*Lynx rufus*
Mountain lion	*Felis concolor*
EVEN-TOED UNGULATES	
Deer	
Black-tailed deer	*Odocoileus hemionus*
North American elk	*Cervus elaphus*

BIRDS CHECKLIST

Common name	Scientific name	Spring	Summer	Fall	Winter	Nests in park
HERONS						
Great Blue Heron	*Ardea Herodias*	R	R	R	R	
SWANS, GEESE, DUCKS						
Canada Goose	*Branta canadensis*	U	R	U	U	
Mallard	*Anas platyrhynchos*	U	U	U	U	✓
Tundra Swan	*Cygnus columbianus*	R	—	R	R	
Wood Duck	*Aix sponsa*	U	U	—	—	✓
VULTURES, HAWKS, EAGLES, FALCONS						
American Kestrel	*Falco sparverius*	U	U	U	U	✓
Cooper's Hawk	*Accipiter cooperii*	U	U	U	U	✓
Merlin	*Falco columbarius*	R	—	R	R	
Peregrine Falcon	*Falco peregrinus*	U	U	R	—	✓
Northern Goshawk	*Accipiter gentilis*	R	R	R	R	
Osprey	*Pandion haliaetus*	R	U	R	—	
Red-tailed Hawk	*Buteo jamaicensis*	U	U	U	U	✓
Sharp-shinned Hawk	*Accipiter striatus*	U	U	U	U	✓
Turkey Vulture	*Cathartes aura*	U	U	U	—	
Bald Eagle	*Haliaeetus leucocephalus*	U	U	R	R	✓
PHEASANTS, GROUSE, QUAIL						
Blue Grouse	*Dendragapus obscurus*	R	R	R	R	✓
California Quail	*Callipepla californica*	R	R	R	R	
Ring-necked Pheasant	*Phasianus colchicus*	R	R	R	R	
Ruffed Grouse	*Bonasa umbellus*	R	R	R	R	✓

Key to Relative Abundance

A: **Abundant** (species is present in large numbers in an area)

C: **Common** (species very likely to be seen most of the time in a given area but in smaller numbers than an abundant one)

U: **Uncommon** (species can have a large home range and still be seen though less frequently than a common one)

R: **Rare** (species occurs in very low numbers—there may be years with no sightings)

Birds Checklist

Common name	Scientific name	Spring	Summer	Fall	Winter	Nests in park
CRANES						
Sandhill Crane	*Grus canadensis*	R	—	R	—	
GULLS						
California Gull	*Larus californicus*	U	C	C	U	
Glaucous-winged Gull	*Larus hyperboreus*	U	U	U	C	
Herring Gull	*Larus argentatus*	R	—	—	R	
Mew Gull	*Larus canus*	R	—	R	U	
Ring-billed Gull	*Larus delawarensis*	U	U	U	U	
Thayer's Gull	*Larus thayeri*	R	—	—	U	
PIGEONS, DOVES						
Band-tailed Pigeon	*Columba fasciata*	C	C	C	R	✓
Mourning Dove	*Zenaida macroura*	C	C	C	U	✓
Rock Dove	*Columba livia*	R	R	R	R	
OWLS						
Barred Owl	*Strix varia*	C	C	C	C	✓
Great Horned Owl	*Bubo virginianus*	U	U	U	U	✓
Northern Pygmy Owl	*Glaucidium gnoma*	U	U	U	U	✓
Northern Saw-whet Owl	*Aegolius acadicus*	R	R	R	R	✓
Spotted Owl	*Strix occidentalis*	R	R	—	—	
Western Screech Owl	*Otus kennicottii*	U	U	U	U	✓
NIGHTHAWKS, SWIFTS, HUMMINGBIRDS						
Anna's Hummingbird	*Calypte anna*	U	R	U	U	✓
Common Nighthawk	*Chordeiles minor*	—	U	—	—	
Rufous Hummingbird	*Selasphorus rufus*	C	C	C	—	✓
Vaux's Swift	*Chaetura vauxi*	C	C	C	—	✓
KINGFISHERS						
Belted Kingfisher	*Ceryle alcyon*	R	R	R	R	
WOODPECKERS						
Downy Woodpecker	*Picoides pubescens*	C	C	C	C	✓
Hairy Woodpecker	*Picoides villosus*	C	C	C	C	✓
Northern Flicker	*Colaptes auratus*	C	C	C	C	✓
Pileated Woodpecker	*Dryocopus pileatus*	U	U	U	U	✓
Red-breasted Sapsucker	*Sphyrapicus ruber*	U	U	U	U	✓

Common name	Scientific name	Spring	Summer	Fall	Winter	Nests in park
FLYCATCHERS						
Hammond's Flycatcher	*Empidonax hammondii*	R	R	R	—	
Olive-sided Flycatcher	*Contopus cooperi*	U	U	U	—	✓
Pacific-slope Flycatcher	*Empidonax difficilis*	C	C	U	—	✓
Western Wood Pewee	*Contopus sordidulus*	U	C	U	—	✓
Willow Flycatcher	*Empidonax traillii*	U	U	U	—	✓
SWALLOWS						
Barn Swallow	*Hirundo rustica*	C	C	C	—	✓
Cliff Swallow	*Hirundo pyrrhonota*	U	U	U	—	
Northern Rough-winged Swallow	*Stelgidopteryx serripennis*	R	R	R	—	
Purple Martin	*Progne subis*	R	R	R	—	
Tree Swallow	*Tachycineta bicolor*	U	U	U	R	✓
Violet-green Swallow	*Tachycineta thalassina*	C	C	C	R	✓
JAYS, CROWS						
American Crow	*Corvus brachyrhynchos*	C	C	C	C	✓
Common Raven	*Corvus corax*	C	C	R	C	✓
Western Scrub Jay	*Aphelocoma californica*	C	C	C	C	✓
Steller's Jay	*Cyanocitta stelleri*	C	C	C	C	✓
Gray Jay	*Perisoreus canadensis*	U	U	U	U	✓
CHICKADEES, BUSHTITS						
Black-capped Chickadee	*Parus atricapillus*	A	A	A	A	✓
Bushtit	*Psaltriparus minimus*	C	A	A	C	✓
Chestnut-backed Chickadee	*Parus rufescens*	A	A	A	A	✓
Mountain Chickadee	*Parus gambeli*	—	—	—	R	
NUTHATCHES, CREEPERS						
Brown Creeper	*Certhia americana*	C	C	C	C	✓
Red-breasted Nuthatch	*Sitta canadensis*	C	C	C	C	✓
White-breasted Nuthatch	*Sitta carolinensis*	R	R	R	R	
WRENS						
Bewick's Wren	*Thryomanes bewickii*	C	C	C	C	✓
House Wren	*Troglodytes aedon*	R	R	R	—	
Winter Wren	*Troglodytes troglodytes*	C	C	C	C	✓

Birds Checklist

Common name	Scientific name	Spring	Summer	Fall	Winter	Nests in park
DIPPERS						
American Dipper	*Cinclus mexicanus*	R	—	R	R	
KINGLETS, THRUSHES						
American Robin	*Turdus migratorius*	C	C	C	C	✓
Golden-crowned Kinglet	*Regulus satrapa*	A	C	A	A	✓
Hermit Thrush	*Catharus guttatus*	U	—	U	U	
Ruby-crowned Kinglet	*Regulus calendula*	U	—	U	U	
Swainson's Thrush	*Catharus ustulatus*	U	C	U	—	✓
Townsend's Solitaire	*Myadestes townsendi*	R	—	R	R	
Varied Thrush	*Ixoreus naevius*	C	R	C	C	
WRENTITS, WAXWINGS						
Cedar Waxwing	*Bombycilla cedrorum*	U	C	C	R	✓
Wrentit	*Chamaea fasciata*	R	R	—	—	
STARLINGS						
European Starling	*Sturnus vulgaris*	U	U	U	U	✓
VIREOS						
Hutton's Vireo	*Vireo huttoni*	R	R	R	R	
Red-eyed Vireo	*Vireo olivaceus*	R	R	R	—	
Cassin's Vireo	*Vireo cassinii*	U	U	U	—	✓
Warbling Vireo	*Vireo gilvus*	C	C	U	—	✓
WARBLERS						
Black-throated Gray Warbler	*Dendroica nigrescens*	C	C	U	—	✓
Common Yellowthroat	*Geothylpis trichas*	R	R	R	—	
Hermit Warbler	*Dendroica occidentalis*	R	—	R	—	
MacGillivray's Warbler	*Oporornis tolmiei*	U	U	U	—	✓
Nashville Warbler	*Vermivora ruficapilla*	R	R	—	—	
Orange-crowned Warbler	*Vermivora celata*	C	C	U	—	✓
Townsend's Warbler	*Dendroica townsendi*	C	R	U	R	
Wilson's Warbler	*Wilsonia pusilla*	C	C	U	—	✓
Yellow-rumped Warbler	*Dendroica coronata*	C	U	C	U	✓
Yellow Warbler	*Dendroica petechia*	U	U	U	—	✓

Common name	Scientific name	Spring	Summer	Fall	Winter	Nests in park
TANAGERS, GROSBEAKS						
Black-headed Grosbeak	*Pheucticus melanocephalus*	C	C	U	—	✓
Evening Grosbeak	*Coccothraustes vespertinus*	C	U	U	U	✓
Western Tanager	*Piranga ludoviciana*	C	C	U	—	✓
SPARROWS, TOWHEES						
Chipping Sparrow	*Spizella passerina*	R	U	R	—	✓
Dark-eyed Junco	*Junco hyemalis*	C	C	C	A	✓
Fox Sparrow	*Passerella iliaca*	U	—	U	U	
Golden-crowned Sparrow	*Zonotrichia atricapilla*	U	—	U	U	
Spotted Towhee	*Pipilo maculatus*	C	C	C	C	✓
Savannah Sparrow	*Passerculus sandwichensis*	R	R	R	—	
Song Sparrow	*Melospiza melodia*	C	C	C	C	✓
White-crowned Sparrow	*Zonotrichia leucophrys*	U	U	U	R	✓
BLACKBIRDS, ORIOLES						
Brewer's Blackbird	*Euphagus cyanocephalus*	R	R	R	R	
Brown-headed Cowbird	*Molothrus ater*	C	C	U	R	✓
Bullock's Oriole	*Icterus bullockii*	R	R	R	—	
FINCHES						
American Goldfinch	*Carduelis tristis*	U	U	U	U	✓
House Finch	*Carpodacus mexicanus*	C	C	C	C	✓
Pine Siskin	*Carduelis pinus*	A	C	C	A	✓
Purple Finch	*Carpodacus purpureus*	C	C	U	U	✓
Red-Crossbill	*Loxia curvirostra*	R	R	R	R	✓
WEAVERS						
House Sparrow	*Passer domesticus*	R	R	R	R	✓

Birds of Forest Park

Photographs by Lois Miller

Red-tailed Hawk

Bald Eagle

Band-tailed Pigeon

Great Horned Owl

Rufous Hummingbird

Downy Woodpeckers

Hairy Woodpecker

Pileated Woodpecker

Pacific-slope Flycatcher

Willow Flycatcher

Western Wood Pewee

Violet-green Swallow

Common Raven

Steller's Jay

Black-capped Chickadee

Bushtit

Chestnut-backed Chickadee

Brown Creeper

Red-breasted Nuthatch

Winter Wren

Golden-crowned Kinglet

Swainson's Thrush

Varied Thrush

Cedar Waxwing

Warbling Vireo

Black-throated Gray Warbler

Orange-crowned Warbler

Wilson's Warbler

Black-headed Grosbeak

Yellow-rumped Warbler

Western Tanager

Dark-eyed Junco

Spotted Towhee

Song Sparrow

Pine Siskin

Purple Finch

Trails of Forest Park

*You will not find any place in America, an urban park,
so close to the heart of a city, that provides the wilderness
experience five minutes from downtown. Forest Park is
unique; it is priceless.*

—Charles Jordan, Past Director, Portland Parks and Recreation

Introduction

A trip through Forest Park is both a pleasure and a privilege. The natural beauty, vast acres of solitude, and the profusion of native plants and wildlife all contribute to an exceptional woodland experience rarely available to people inhabiting a major city. Forest Park is not overrun with asphalt, swimming pools, picnic areas, or developed sports fields. Instead, since its inception sixty years ago, it has offered a quiet kind of enjoyment, the kind most cherished by all lovers of the outdoors. The eighty miles of trails and firelanes, the old-fashioned, country feeling of eleven-mile-long Leif Erikson Drive, and the hundreds of acres of hills and canyons in between, make Forest Park a haven for hikers, bird watchers, nature photographers, runners, bicyclists, equestrians, teachers, and students—in short, anyone needing close-in inspiration and natural refreshment.

Because of all it offers, however, Forest Park runs the risk of overuse in the face of intensifying recreational demands. The 1995 Forest Park Natural Resources Management Plan—a comprehensive report drafted by Portland Parks and Recreation with the assistance of citizens and technical advisory committees—has made the protection of its natural resources a central priority as it strives to provide quality recreation use. To accomplish this goal, the Portland Park Bureau has found it necessary to restrict some trails to single uses only, especially since many trails are narrow and lack sufficient line-of-sight visibility to safely allow multiple uses.

In general, all trails, roads, and firelanes in Forest Park are open to pedestrians. At the present time, twenty-nine miles or 36 percent of all trails are open to cyclists; these numbers are expected to increase after all the projects identified in the Natural Resources Management Plan are completed. Equestrians enjoy twenty-seven miles of trails throughout the park.

Trails, roads, and firelanes currently open for cyclists include the following: Leif Erikson, Saltzman, Springville, Newton, and BPA roads; firelanes 1, 3, 5, 10, 12, and 15; and Holman Lane, which, for visibility and safety reasons, is limited to one-way—uphill only. Horses are allowed on Leif Erikson, Saltzman, Springville, Newton, and BPA roads, and firelanes 1, 7, 10, 12, and 15. Cyclists and equestrians using Forest Park should be aware that these routes may change over time if signs of overuse or user conflict become apparent.

In this new edition, twenty-nine hikes are described encompassing all of the park's trails. Taken together, these can be considered an All Trails Challenge for Forest Park. To help hikers keep track of their progress, a handy checklist of the hikes is included. In addition, there is a table that denotes every trail in Forest Park, specifying its length and current acceptable use. GPS coordinates are denoted for the beginning of each hike.

Most of the hikes are presented in this book as loop trips, with the notable exception of Wildwood Trail and Leif Erikson Drive. Because of their length and for ease in hiking, these trails have been broken into sections and described as one-way trips. In many cases, side trails can be used to make these hikes into a loop. One-way trips require a vehicle at both ends.

Trail mileages are described in decimals throughout the book, except for Wildwood and Leif Erikson, which are often referred to in fractions of a mile. This discrepancy allows agreement with the posted trail mileage markers that run the length of these two major lateral routes. At quarter-mile intervals, Wildwood Trail sports blue diamonds painted on trees, while Leif Erikson has white concrete posts planted at each quarter mile. These highly visible symbols are very helpful in locating exactly where one is in the park.

The trails in Forest Park are diverse in length, steepness, and challenge. To reap the most pleasure from a short or long outing, the hiker, cyclist, or equestrian should take several steps: Take time to read through the hike you are interested in. Explanations on the hike's difficulty, the viewpoints along the trails, significant natural history features, and interesting items relating to historical events can all be found within the hike description. A quick scanning can help answer many questions and ensure the hiker the maximum level of enjoyment and safety.

Hiking trails are rated as easy, moderate, or strenuous, based on length, elevation changes, trail condition, and impacting weather-related factors. Easy trails are generally those with more gentle grades and good trail surfaces. Sometimes, however, easy trails may have short sections that are slippery and eroded. Trails ranked moderate usually have a more steep ascent or descent, and sometimes both. They also may have sections of rough or eroded surfaces and spots that may be very slippery. Hikes rated strenuous have an elevation gradient that exceeds five hundred feet per mile and have unstable trail surfaces in sections. These routes are generally not advisable for those in poor condition or for young children. Complete descriptions of a hike's difficulty, including any extenuating factors that should be considered, can be found within the trail descriptions.

When leaving for a hike, be sure your car is locked and no valuables have been left behind. Break-ins are especially prevalent at the Upper Springville Road and Lower Saltzman Road Parking Areas. Be careful not to block any access roads when parking, as they are used for emergency and maintenance purposes.

Pay attention to the weather. Even on sunny days, the temperature deep in the forest can be noticeably cooler and damp. Rain can surprise even the most experienced traveler anytime. Be prepared. Wear or carry warm clothes and rain gear.

When walking in Forest Park, sturdy shoes with good soles are important; because of high seasonal rainfall, many trails are apt to be seasonally muddy and some can be extremely slippery. Trekking poles are a great thing to have on many of the park's trails.

To maintain Forest Park's wilderness character, be sure that anything you bring in the park you also carry out. Litter and illegal dumping of garbage are ongoing problems and ruin the aesthetics of the forest for everyone.

It is a good idea to carry water on an outing lasting more than an hour or two, for Forest Park's streams are not potable.

The harvesting or picking of plants is not allowed in the park. An important exception to this rule is the invasive plant, English ivy. Ivy is the scourge of Forest Park. In places where it invades, ivy excludes native plants and shrubs and also prevents the regeneration of native conifers, notably Douglas fir. Cutting ivy away from the base of the trees is one way to limit its menacing spread.

Off-leash dogs are a very serious problem in Forest Park and can be devastating to native wildlife. Dogs must be kept on a leash at all times. Additionally, it is important to clean up all dog waste. Many trailheads in the park have plastic bags available for this purpose. Please, remember to take any used bags home with you. The Park Bureau does not collect them.

Camping, fires, woodcutting, and fishing are prohibited in the park. Also prohibited are motorized vehicles of any kind.

Forest Park's pristine and natural features are what set it apart from all other city parks in the nation. No other urban park in the United States offers anything comparable in quantity or quality. Learn to value and appreciate it. It is our treasure and what makes Portland different.

HOW TO USE THE MAPS

Inventory of maps: For a high level view of where the hikes are within Forest Park, check the Overview map on the facing page. Each hike has its own detail map accompanying the text which may be used for planning purposes or to follow along as you walk. At the end of the book is a fold-out map showing the entire park on one side, and the watersheds of Forest Park on the reverse. For a legend that explains the symbols and line styles used in the maps throughout the book, see page 2.

GPS: If you are using a GPS device, each hike's trailhead location is listed using the UTM coordinate system, and the WGS1984/NAD83 datum. You will need to make sure your GPS uses these settings in its configuration for the coordinates to match what your GPS displays. Few GPS's will have maps which show all the trails, and heavy tree cover decreases the accuracy of many GPS units.

Using the maps: All hike maps have the same orientation with respect to north (once you rotate the page so that the primary labels can be read horizontally). The hike route is designed to stand out through the use of a yellow stripe as if the route was traced with a highlighter. The green arrows alongside the route indicate the direction of travel along the route. The hike maps include topo lines at 20 foot intervals and shaded relief to allow you to visualize the topography and get a sense of your elevation. Every fifth topo line is a thicker "index" line which represents 100 foot intervals. The fold-out map allows for planning of longer routes or getting the bigger picture.

Elevation profiles are provided to show the steepness of the hike. The color of the elevation profile line represents the type of trail the hike traverses, and the locations where you change trails are marked using the same symbol as the map (small hollow circles).

Distances were measured two ways: on the ground by Fran Koenig with a measuring wheel, and by using a GIS software application with a variety of geodata including 3 foot LIDAR.

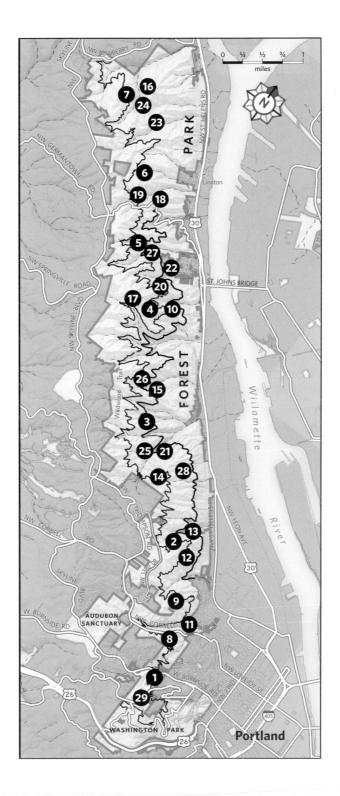

81

ALL TRAILS CHALLENGE

Distance	Global Positioning System	Difficulty Rating	Date Completed

HIKE 1. WILDWOOD TRAIL MILE 0.0 – 5.0 HOYT ARBORETUM TO MACLEAY PARK

| 4.99 miles | 45° 30' 45.35" N 122° 43' 01.13" W 522106mE 5039935mN | Moderate | ___/___/___ |

HIKE 2. WILDWOOD TRAIL MILE 5.0 – 11.2 MACLEAY PARK TO FIRELANE 1

| 6.18 miles | 45° 31' 36.54" N 122° 43' 35.97" W 521345mE 5041512mN | Moderate | ___/___/___ |

HIKE 3. WILDWOOD TRAIL MILE 11.2 – 16.0 FIRELANE 1 TO NW SALTZMAN ROAD

| 4.81 miles | 45° 33' 8.02" N 122° 44' 48.36" W 519766mE 5044330mN | Easy | ___/___/___ |

HIKE 4. WILDWOOD TRAIL MILE 16.0 – 22.5
NW SALTZMAN ROAD TO NW SPRINGVILLE ROAD

| 6.5 miles | 45° 33' 53.13" N 122° 46' 11.72" W 517955mE 5045717mN | Easy | ___/___/___ |

HIKE 5. WILDWOOD TRAIL MILE 22.5 – 24.7
NW SPRINGVILLE ROAD TO NW GERMANTOWN ROAD

| 2.17 miles | 45° 34' 43.03" N 122° 47' 7.33" W 516745mE 5047253mN | Easy | ___/___/___ |

HIKE 6. WILDWOOD TRAIL MILE 24.7 – 26.3
NW GERMANTOWN ROAD TO NW NEWTON ROAD

| 1.6 miles | 45° 35' 14.79" N 122° 47' 38.93" W 516058mE 5048232mN | Easy | ___/___/___ |

HIKE 7. WILDWOOD TRAIL MILE 26.3 – 30.12
NW NEWTON ROAD TO NW NEWBERRY ROAD

| 3.82 miles | 45° 35' 59.17" N 122° 48' 1.3" W 515570mE 5049600mN | Easy | ___/___/___ |

HIKE 8. TUNNEL TRAIL AND TRAILS SOUTH OF CORNELL ROAD

| 2.46 miles | 45° 31' 49.14" N 122° 43' 1.14" W 522099mE 5041904mN | Moderate | ___/___/___ |

HIKE 9. HOLMAN LANE—WILDWOOD TRAIL—BIRCH TRAIL LOOP

| 2.61 miles | 45° 31' 57.64" N 122° 43' 54.19" W 520943mE 5042172mN | Moderate | ___/___/___ |

HIKE 10. LOWER FIRELANE 7A (GAS LINE ROAD)—WILDWOOD TRAIL—RIDGE
TRAIL—LEIF ERIKSON DRIVE LOOP

| 3.66 miles | 45° 34' 42.27" N 122° 45' 46.93" W 518488mE 5047235mN | Strenuous | ___/___/___ |

All hikes are in UTM Zone 10 letter T, NAD83 datum

Distance	Global Positioning System	Difficulty Rating	Date Completed
HIKE 11. LOWER AND UPPER MACLEAY TRAILS LOOP			
3.26 miles	45° 32' 9.5" N 122° 42' 45.1" W 522445mE 5042533mN	Moderate	___/___/___
HIKE 12. WILD CHERRY TRAIL—LEIF ERIKSON DRIVE—DOGWOOD TRAIL— WILDWOOD TRAIL LOOP			
2.7 miles	45° 32' 18.99" N 122° 44' 2.82"W 520758mE 5042820mN	Moderate	___/___/___
HIKE 13. DOGWOOD TRAIL—LEIF ERIKSON DRIVE—ALDER TRAIL—WILDWOOD TRAIL—KEIL TRAIL LOOP			
2.92 miles	45° 32' 18.99" N 122° 44' 2.82"W 520758mE 5042820mN	Moderate	___/___/___
HIKE 14. WILDWOOD TRAIL—CHESTNUT TRAIL—NATURE TRAIL—NATURE TRAIL LOOP			
3.48 miles	45° 32' 53.19"N 122° 44' 41.94"W 519907mE 5043873mN	Moderate	___/___/___
HIKE 15. MAPLE TRAIL—WILDWOOD TRAIL LOOP			
8.35 miles	45° 33' 50.96" N 122° 45' 0.92"W 519490mE 5045654mN	Moderate	___/___/___
HIKE 16. FIRELANE 15— FIRELANE 12—BPA ROAD—WILDWOOD TRAIL LOOP, INCLUDING KIELHORN MEADOW			
6.27 miles	45° 35' 46.64" N 122° 49' 24.82"W 513761mE 5049209mN	Strenuous	___/___/___
HIKE 17. TRILLIUM TRAIL—WILDWOOD TRAIL—FIRELANE 7 LOOP			
2.8 miles	45° 34' 28.18" N 122° 47' 19.72"W 516478mE 5046794mN	Easy	___/___/___
HIKE 18. FIRELANE 9—LINNTON TRAIL—FIRELANE 10—WILDWOOD TRAIL LOOP			
3.28 miles	45° 35' 20.39" N 122° 47' 25.88"W 516340mE 5048405mN	Strenuous	___/___/___
HIKE 19. NEWTON ROAD—WILDWOOD TRAIL—FIRELANE 10—CANNON TRAIL LOOP			
3.93 miles	45° 35' 29.92" N 122° 48' 8.42"W 515418mE 5048697mN	Moderate	___/___/___
HIKE 20. RIDGE TRAIL—FIRELANE 7—HARDESTY TRAIL—LEIF ERIKSON DRIVE LOOP			
3.33 miles	45° 35' 3.74" N 122° 46' 13.48"W 517910mE 5047896mN	Strenuous	___/___/___

All hikes are in UTM Zone 10 letter T, NAD83 datum

Distance	Global Positioning System	Difficulty Rating	Date Completed
HIKE 21. LEIF ERIKSON DRIVE, PART ONE MILE 0.0 – 6.15 NW THURMAN STREET TO NW SALTZMAN ROAD			
6.15 mile	45° 32' 22.97" N 122° 43' 27.35"W 521527mE 5042946mN	Easy	___/___/___
HIKE 22. LEIF ERIKSON DRIVE, PART TWO MILE 6.15 – 11.22 NW SALTZMAN ROAD TO NW GERMANTOWN ROAD			
5.02 miles	45° 34' 9.6" N 122° 45' 46.59" W 518501mE 5046224mN	Easy	___/___/___
HIKE 23. BPA ROAD—NEWTON ROAD—WILDWOOD TRAIL LOOP			
4.88 miles	45° 35' 32.44" N 122° 48' 51.65" W 514481mE 5048773mN	Strenuous	___/___/___
HIKE 24. BPA ROAD—FIRELANES 13 AND 13A			
3.62 miles	45° 35' 32.44" N 122° 48' 51.65"W 514481mE 5048773mN	Strenuous	___/___/___
HIKE 25. FIRELANES 1, 2, AND 3—WILDWOOD TRAIL—MAPLE TRAIL—NATURE TRAIL LOOP			
6.13 miles	45° 32' 53.19" N 122° 44' 41.94" W 519907mE 5043873mN	Moderate	___/___/___
HIKE 26. FIRELANE 5—LEIF ERIKSON DRIVE—CLEATOR TRAIL—WILDWOOD TRAIL—SALTZMAN ROAD LOOP			
4.1 miles	45° 33' 43.62" N 122° 47' 0.05" W 516908mE 5045420mN	Moderate	___/___/___
HIKE 27. TOLINDA TRAIL—SPRINGVILLE ROAD—WILDWOOD TRAIL—WATERLINE TRAIL LOOP			
5.37 miles	45° 35' 17.75" N 122° 46' 43.97" W 517248mE 5048326mN	Strenuous	___/___/___
HIKE 28. LOWER FIRELANE 1—WILDWOOD TRAIL—CHESTNUT TRAIL—LEIF ERIKSON LOOP			
5.19 miles	45° 33' 15.66" N 122° 43' 59.32" W 520828mE 5044569mN	Strenuous	___/___/___
HIKE 29. HOYT ARBORETUM			
2.58 miles	45° 30' 56.52" N 122° 42' 57.42" W 522185.7mE 5040280mN	Easy	___/___/___

All hikes are in UTM Zone 10 letter T, NAD83 datum

HIKES BY DISTANCE

Distance	Hike Number and Difficulty Rating
0.0 – 3.0 Miles	5 (e), 6 (e), 8 (m), 9 (m), 12 (m), 13 (m), 17 (e), 29 (e)
3.1 – 4.0 Miles	7 (e), 10 (s), 11 (m), 14 (m), 18 (s), 19 (m), 20 (s), 24 (s)
4.1 – 6.0 Miles	1 (m), 3 (e), 22 (e), 23 (s), 26 (m), 27 (s), 28 (s)
6.1 – 8.50 Miles	2 (m), 4 (e), 15 (m), 16 (s), 21 (e), 25 (m)

e = easy; m = moderate; s = strenuous

ALL TRAILS OF FOREST PARK

MILEAGE AND ALLOWED USES

Note: p = pedestrian; c = cyclist; e = equestrian

Trail Name	Mileage	Allowed Uses
Alder Trail	0.84 mile	p
Aspen Trail	0.23 mile	p
BPA Road	1.99 miles	p, c, e
Birch Trail	0.22 mile	p
Cannon Trail	0.32 mile	p
Chestnut Trail	0.49 mile	p
Cleator Trail	0.24 mile	p
Cumberland Trail	0.41 mile	p
Dogwood Trail	1.00 mile	p
Firelane 1, Upper, to Leif Erikson Drive	0.86 mile	p, c, e
Firelane 1, Lower, Leif Erikson Drive to Highway 30	1.43 miles	p, c, e
Firelane 2	1.16 miles	p
Firelane 3	0.99 mile	p, c
Firelane 4	0.55 mile	p
Firelane 5	1.1 miles	p, c
Firelane 7 (Oil Line Road)	1.01 miles	p, e
Firelane 7A (Gas Line Road), Upper, to Leif Erikson Drive	0.57 mile	p
Firelane 7A (Gas Line Road), Lower, Leif Erikson Drive to Highway 30	0.70 mile	p
Firelane 8	0.17 mile	p
Firelane 9	0.64 mile	p
Firelane 10	1.41 miles	p, c, e
Firelane 12	1.51 miles	p, c, e
Firelane 13	0.62 mile	p
Firelane 13A	0.10 mile	p
Firelane 15	1.34 miles	p, c, e
Hardesty Trail	0.55 mile	p
Holman Lane	0.99 mile	p, c: uphill only
Keil Trail	0.17 mile	p
Keyser Trail	0.25 mile	p
Kielhorn Meadow Trail	0.18 mile	p

Trail Name	Mileage	Allowed Uses
Koenig Trail	0.27 mile	p
Leif Erikson Drive Mile 0.0 – 6.15 　NW Thurman Street to NW Saltzman Road	6.15 miles	p, c, e
Leif Erikson Drive Mile 6.15 – 11.17 　NW Saltzman Road to NW Germantown Road	5.02 miles	p, c, e
Linnton Trail	0.60 mile	p
Lower Macleay Trail	0.86 mile	p
Macleay Trail	0.28 mile	p
Maple Trail	3.59 miles	p
Morak Trail	0.08 mile	p
Nature Trail	0.93 mile	p
Newton Road	1.88 miles	p, c, e
Ridge Trail	1.38 miles	p
Saltzman Road	2.95 miles	p, c, e
Springville Road	1.04 miles	p, c, e
Tolinda Trail	0.75 mile	p
Trillium Trail	0.25 mile	p
Tunnel Trail	0.17 mile	p
Upper Macleay Trail	0.81 mile	p
Waterline Trail	0.75 mile	p
Water Tank Trail	0.20 mile	p
Wildwood Trail Mile 0.0 – 5.0 　Hoyt Arboretum to Macleay Park	5.00 miles	p
Wildwood Trail Mile 5.0 – 11.2 　Macleay Park to Firelane 1	6.20 miles	p
Wildwood Trail Mile 11.2 – 16.0 　Firelane 1 to NW Saltzman Road	4.80 miles	p
Wildwood Trail Mile 16.0 – 22.5 　NW Saltzman Road to NW Springville Road	6.50 miles	p
Wildwood Trail Mile 22.5 – 24.7 　NW Springville Road to NW Germantown Road	2.20 miles	p
Wildwood Trail Mile 24.7 – 26.3 　NW Germantown Road to NW Newton Road	1.60 miles	p
Wildwood Trail Mile 26.3 – 30.12 　NW Newton Road to NW Newberry Road	3.82 miles	p
Wild Cherry Trail	0.87 mile	p
Wiregate Trail	0.31 mile	p

MILES OF TRAILS IN FOREST PARK:　81.30　MILES

"The overall purpose of Forest Park has stayed the same—that of a reserve, a forest setting to provide Portlanders a wilderness escape from urban existence. [Its] value as a public resource and the opportunity afforded to the City of Portland [are] like no other in the United States. Forest Park is an unparalleled resource."

Bob Hostetter (1919 - 2007),
of the Oregon Chapter of the Society of American Foresters
and long-time member of the Forest Park Committee of Fifty

Wildwood Trail

INTRODUCTION

The best way to experience the full scope and grandeur of Forest Park is to explore Portland's Wildwood Trail. At 30.12 miles, this officially designated National Recreation Trail is the longest natural woodland trail winding through a city park anywhere in the United States. Stretching the entire length of the park—from downtown Portland to NW Newberry Road—Wildwood Trail offers beauty and places of solitude, and the opportunity to see scores of native plants and animals, all within close proximity to the core of a major city. In terms of naturalness and ecosystem integrity, no other trail in the nation offers such a wilderness experience in an urban setting.

Wildwood Trail is well maintained and, for most of its length, follows a gentle grade, weaving in and out of Forest Park's numerous steep ravines at a level 750 to 850-foot elevation. The trail traverses the park's eleven watersheds and intersects with many interesting perpendicular trails that can be used for making a variety of loop trips. For ease in locating where one is, mileage markers are placed along the entire trail at quarter-mile intervals, identifiable by blue diamonds painted on trees.

Forest Park is divided into three natural resource management sections; a walk along Wildwood Trail takes hikers through them all. Each segment has different attributes and challenges that guide its maintenance and care by Portland Parks and Recreation. From Washington Park to Firelane 1 is Forest Park's Southern Unit, which tends to be the most heavily used by hikers and runners, as it lies within more densely populated areas of the city. The Central Unit, from Firelane 1 to NW Germantown Road, is more moderately used, and widely displays many characteristic features of native Douglas fir forests. Finally, the remote North Unit, between NW Germantown and Newberry roads, is where recreational use is lowest and Forest Park reveals its finest ecological health. By virtue of its exceptional quality, pristine native vegetation, and sensitive wildlife habitat, the North Unit has been singled out for special consideration. The Forest

WILDWOOD TRAIL HIKES BY SECTION

	Miles	Location	Distance
Hike 1	0.0 – 5.0	Hoyt Arboretum to Macleay Park	5.0 miles
Hike 2	5.0 – 11.2	Macleay Park to Firelane 1	6.2 miles
Hike 3	11.2 – 16.0	Firelane 1 to NW Saltzman Road	4.8 miles
Hike 4	16.0 – 22.5	NW Saltzman Road to NW Springville Road	6.5 miles
Hike 5	22.5 – 24.7	NW Springville Road to NW Germantown Road	2.2 miles
Hike 6	24.7 – 26.3	NW Germantown Road to NW Newton Road	1.6 miles
Hike 7	26.3 – 30.12	NW Newton Road to NW Newberry Road	3.82 miles

Park Natural Resources Management Plan has adopted a land-use goal of reduced recreational use in the North Unit to protect and preserve the area's unique, natural resource qualities.

Beginning over sixty years ago, Wildwood Trail has been built, section by section, by dedicated hikers working in conjunction with Portland Parks and Recreation. Its construction did not occur quickly nor always come easily. In several instances along segments of trail, privately held land prevented the trail from continuing further. In these cases, concerned citizens, teaming with Friends of Forest Park and government agencies, toiled to successfully raise thousands of dollars to purchase these critical pieces. This story has been repeated throughout Forest Park's history: trail construction has been a slow but steady trajectory of labor and love by individuals who cared for Forest Park and gave a gift to future generations.

For the purposes of this book and the ease of the hiker, Wildwood Trail has been divided into seven sections, each approximately four to five miles in length. Directions to trailhead locations and specific information relating to each trail segment can be found within the separate hike descriptions. In a few cases, hikers can expect some additional walking on firelanes or roads (both closed to motorized vehicles) to access different parts of Wildwood Trail.

Wildwood Trail

HOYT ARBORETUM TO MACLEAY PARK

MILE 0.0–5.0

DISTANCE: 4.99 miles (one way)*
HIKING TIME: 2½ hours (one way)*
LOW ELEVATION: 518 feet
HIGH ELEVATION: 959 feet
CUMULATIVE ELEVATION GAIN: 515 feet
DIFFICULTY RATING: Moderate
GPS COORDINATES: 45° 30' 45.35" N   122° 43' 01.13" W
    522106mE 5039935mN
Foot traffic only.
**One way trip; requires transportation at both ends of this hike.*
NOTE: *Stay on Wildwood Trail for entire hike.*

MILEAGE AND DIRECTIONS

0.00   Begin at Wildwood Trail Trailhead at Hoyt Arboretum near the
       Vietnam Veterans Memorial.
2.48   Cross Fairview Blvd. Continue on Wildwood Trail.
2.60   Arrive at Redwood Overlook.
3.09   Intersection with W. Burnside Street. Cross Burnside and continue
       on Wildwood.
3.73   Arrive at Pittock Mansion.
4.99   End at Macleay Park Trailhead.

Wildwood Trail's first five miles can be viewed as a gradual
introduction to the native forests of the Northwest. The trail begins
in the landscaped setting of the Hoyt Arboretum—a living museum
of plants and trees collected from all around the world (see Hike

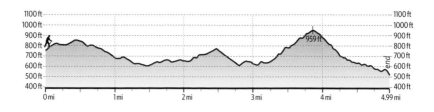

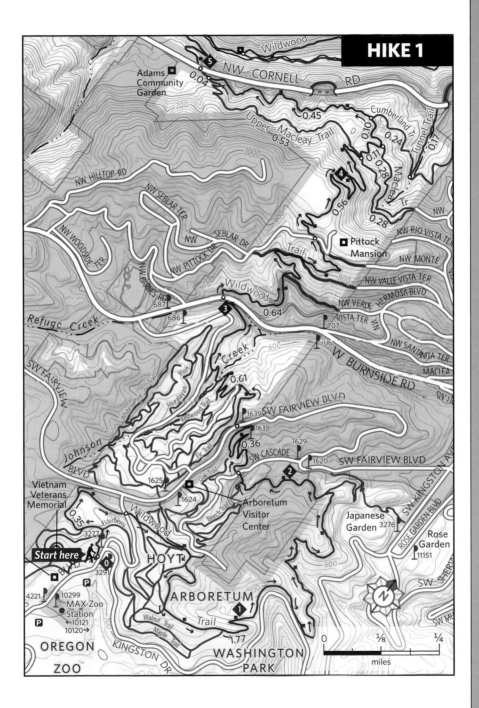

NW CORNELL RD

Wildwood

Adams
Community
Garden
0.04

5

0.45

Cumberland Tr.

Tunnel Trail

0.10
0.24

0.17

0.11

0.28

Upper Macleay Trail 0.53

Macleay Tr.

NW HILLTOP RD

0.56

0.28

NW

NW SEBLAR TER

NW

SEBLAR DR

Trail

Pittock
Mansion

NW RIO VISTA TER

NW WOODSIDE TER

NW PITTOCK DR

NW MONTE

NW BARNES RD

Wildwood

NW VALLE VISTA TER

NW VERDE

HERMOSA BLVD

687

686

3

0.64

707

VISTA TER VIN

706

NW SANTANTA TER

Refuge Creek

Creek

600

W BURNSIDE RD

MAC FA

SW FAIRVIEW

0.61

SW

Pine Trail

White Pine Trail

Hawthorn Trail

Redwood Trail

1639

SW FAIRVIEW BLVD

Johnson BLVD

Fir Trail

1638

1629

0.36

SW CASCADE

1620

SW FAIRVIEW BLVD

2

Vietnam
Veterans
Memorial

0.35

1625

Oak Trail

1624

Beech Trail

Arboretum
Visitor
Center

Japanese
Garden 3276

SW KINGSTON AV

ROSE GARDEN BLVD

Rose
Garden
11151

Elderberry

3277

Wildwood

HOYT

N

Start here

0

3291

SW SHER

4221

10299
MAX Zoo
Station
←10121
10120→

P

P

P

ARBORETUM

Walnut Trail

Maple Trail

Trail

1

1.77

600

SW M

OREGON
ZOO

KINGSTON DR

WASHINGTON
PARK

0   ⅛   ¼

miles

"Few people know and love this beautiful sample of the magnificent timber which formerly covered all the hills and ravines in the city. Aside from the luxuriance of the woodland vegetation there is the added charm of seclusion to a degree rarely found in a public park. ... The city is most fortunate in possessing this ... deep, romantic, wooded ravine called Balch Canyon."

—John Charles Olmsted and Frederick Law Olmsted, Jr., Portland, Oregon 1903

29). After crossing W. Burnside Street, Wildwood Trail becomes more natural as it enters Forest Park and begins to climb upwards to the Pittock Mansion. It then descends into beautiful Balch Creek Canyon, where fine examples characteristic of old-growth Douglas fir forests can be observed.

To reach the trailhead for Hike One, travel toward Beaverton from downtown Portland via U.S. Highway 26 and take the Washington Park Zoo exit. An alternative is to take the MAX Line to Washington Park. Continue past the World Forestry Center—an educational attraction dedicated to explaining forest resources and the forest industry—and park in the lot at the intersection of SW Knights Boulevard and Kingston Drive. The Oregon Vietnam Veterans Living Memorial is located near this intersection. This memorial, located in the serene, reflective setting of Hoyt Arboretum, was dedicated in 1987 to honor all Oregon residents who died in the Vietnam War or who are missing in action. Wildwood Trail starts across the street from the parking lot.

Wildwood Trail begins on a grassy knoll within the 185-acre Hoyt Arboretum. Almost immediately, interesting spur-trails intersect the route (Dogwood Trail, Elderberry Trail, Marquam Trail, among others). Throughout this hike, though, and for the subsequent six hikes, stay on Wildwood Trail.

After an easy quarter-mile climb, the trail crosses SW Knights Boulevard and leads uphill toward a water tank. Near this junction, an overlook allows a three-mountain view of Mts. St. Helens, Rainier, and Adams. Continue on Wildwood, passing Cherry Trail and Holly Trail and a second water tank. Wildwood then descends via several switchbacks into a forested ravine augmented with plantings of ornamental fruit trees (the arboretum's Rosaceae Collection) that give off an abundance of fragrance and color during spring flowering. At 0.85 mile, beyond a second intersection with Cherry Trail, the trail traverses an open field then reenters the forest. Immediately after Milepost 1, Wildwood drops into another level meadow paralleling Kingston Drive for approximately one hundred yards. This field is a public archery range.

After the crossing, Wildwood Trail is once again arrayed in native shrubbery; Oregon grape, sword fern, and salal grow abundantly on hillsides dominated by Douglas fir. Intermixed with the naturally occurring flora, however, is a highly destructive non-native species—English ivy—an escapee from home gardens and urban areas. Perhaps more than any other weed, ivy is the scourge of Forest Park and of all Portland parks. Once ivy takes a stronghold, it is difficult to extricate from the landscape, and threatens to dominate and eventually kill much of the native understory. The job of eradicating ivy is a constant battle fought by Portland Parks and Recreation, the Forest Park Conservancy, and scores of volunteers.

Wildwood Trail soon makes a hard left switchback and then levels off. Near Milepost 1¾, glance down the hill through the trees to observe the Portland Japanese Garden, regarded as one of the most authentic of its kind outside of Japan. At five and a half acres, this tranquil setting incorporates five separate garden styles displayed along meandering streams and waterfalls, and is well worth visiting.

Continue on Wildwood for another quarter mile. Halfway between Milepost 2 and 2¼ (after passing Magnolia Trail), the pathway intersects two paved roads, SW Cascade Drive and Upper Cascade. Cross both roads and follow a relatively steep incline to Fairview Boulevard. Cross Fairview and connect with the continuation of Wildwood Trail directly on the other side of the road.

North of Fairview, the trail meanders gently along the slopes of the Hoyt Arboretum's Conifer Collection. Past Milepost 2½, near the intersection of Spruce Trail and Bray Lane, Wildwood approaches a beautiful, newly constructed overlook. Giant sequoias and coast redwoods surround a seating area and create the feeling of a sanctuary. In this tranquil setting, new benches entice the hiker to sit a while in admiration of the superb trees where soft light filters down through their draping branches.

Beyond the overlook, Wildwood drops down into Johnson Creek Canyon, passing Redwood Trail. At Milepost 2¾, the trail crosses a rustic bridge over Johnson Creek, then briefly ascends and jogs to the right, heading towards W. Burnside Street. Along this portion, excellent examples of Columbia River basalt outcroppings are visible. Immediately after Milepost 3, the trail intersects W. Burnside Street, a three-lane, heavily trafficked highway. Cross the road with care. Plans for a much-needed pedestrian overpass are in the discussion stages, but have not yet been funded. Once on the other side, continue on Wildwood Trail, which climbs and switchbacks up an ivy-laden hill toward the Pittock Mansion.

After Milepost 3¾, Wildwood Trail crests at the Pittock Mansion Parking Area. The mansion is a Portland historic landmark originally built in 1914 by Henry L. Pittock, founder of the *Oregonian*. Considered an architectural wonder, Pittock Mansion today is fully restored, open to the public, and administered by Portland Parks and Recreation. Tours of its twenty-three rooms, decorated with historical artifacts, are available year round, except for January, when the mansion is closed.

Cross the parking lot and continue north on Wildwood Trail. For the next mile, the pathway curves back and forth down the steep and picturesque Balch Creek Canyon. In 1897, Donald Macleay gifted one hundred and five acres of virgin forest in the middle of Balch Creek Canyon to the City of Portland. Today known as Macleay Park, the land was incorporated into Forest Park when the park was created in 1948. This natural drainage still retains much of the appeal and ecological importance that the Olmsted Brothers, in their 1903 Report of the Park Board, observed over a century ago.

Beyond Milepost 4½, Wildwood Trail intersects Upper Macleay Trail. Proceed on Wildwood, following several switchbacks. Cross Macleay Trail, coming in from the right, and, 0.12 mile further, pass Cumberland Trail. Stay on Wildwood Trail and continue descending the canyon until NW Cornell Road, just before Milepost 5. Across Cornell Road is a large parking area and picnic site. Here one can decide whether to continue on or to stop, if transportation has been arranged, and save the remaining twenty-five miles of the Wildwood Trail for other enjoyable hikes.

Wildwood Trail

MACLEAY PARK TO FIRELANE 1

MILE 5.0–11.2

DISTANCE: 6.18 miles (one way)*
HIKING TIME: 3 hours (one way)*
LOW ELEVATION: 298 feet
HIGH ELEVATION: 943 feet
CUMULATIVE ELEVATION GAIN: 662 feet
DIFFICULTY RATING: Moderate
GPS COORDINATES: 45° 31' 36.54" N 122° 43' 35.97" W
    521345mE 5041512mN
Foot traffic only.
One way trip; requires transportation at both ends of this hike.
NOTE: Stay on Wildwood Trail for entire hike.

MILEAGE AND DIRECTIONS

0.00   Begin at Wildwood Trail Trailhead at Macleay Park.
0.93   Pass Holman Lane.
2.49   Intersection with Birch Trail.
2.88   Intersection with Wild Cherry Trail.
3.47   Intersection with Dogwood Trail.
4.18   Intersection with Keil Trail.
5.66   Intersection with Morak Trail.
6.18   End at Firelane 1.

The second section of Wildwood Trail, bordering the Audubon Society of Portland headquarters and winding through Macleay Park, is renowned for the giant old fir trees that line Balch Creek Canyon; it offers miles of gentle walking through mixed coniferous and deciduous forest.

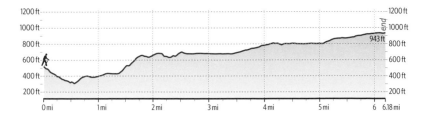

To reach the trailhead, drive west on NW Cornell Road 1.7 miles from the intersection of NW 23rd and NW Lovejoy (Lovejoy becomes Cornell Road beyond NW 25th). Look for a large stone monument honoring Donald Macleay alongside Cornell Road. Beyond the rock wall is a turnoff to the right where there is ample parking as well as picnic tables. Just north of this spot, adjoining Forest Park, are the headquarters of the Audubon Society of Portland and the Pittock, Collins, and Uhtoff bird sanctuaries, which together encompass more than one hundred and fifty acres of natural land devoted to the protection of wildlife. Four miles of interpreted trails loop through the three sanctuaries. The Audubon Society Interpretive Center is located here, as well as the Wildlife Care Center for injured birds, and an exceptionally well-stocked Nature Store with a wonderful collection of books on birds, plants, and Northwest ecology. Be sure to look at the outstanding giant sequoia tree that stands near the Wildlife Care Center. This tree was planted in the 1940s by Thornton Munger.

Begin the hike by following signs for Wildwood Trail (at Milepost 5), walking the path down a deep, heavily forested canyon known as Balch Creek Canyon. Balch Creek, which rushes through the bottom

Balch Creek Canyon is one of a few places in Forest Park where areas of old-growth habitat can still be observed. While today many people appreciate these quickly disappearing ecosystems, as recently as twenty-five years ago the term "old growth" was considered derogatory. Then, most foresters referred to ancient forests as "cellulose cemeteries." Yet, as researchers have since discovered, old growth habitats are no deserts. Rather, native, temperate Northwest forests hold a greater mass of living cell matter per acre than any other forest in the world, greater than even the lush rainforests of the tropics. Old-growth forests exhibit a tremendous diversity of trees, shrubs, and forbs, as well as age classes. Within this complex ecosystem, each part plays an important role, from the great trees themselves down to huge, fallen logs (habitat for many species) as well as standing, dead trees (which provide food and nesting sites for numerous kinds of birds).

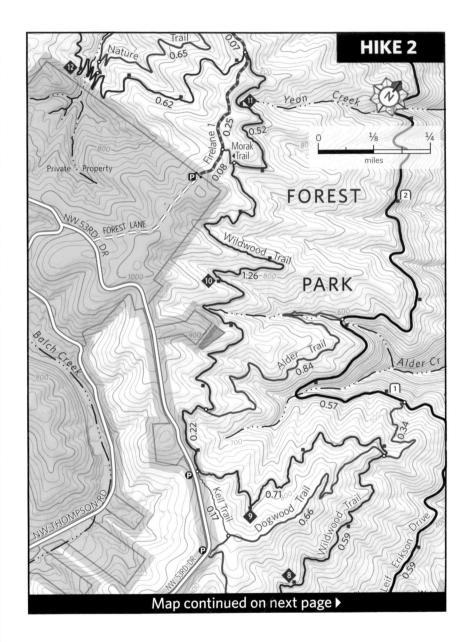

HIKE 2

Nature Trail
0.65
0.07
0.62
Yeon Creek
900
11
0.52
0.25
Morak Trail
Firelane 1
0.08
Private Property
800
P
NW 53RD DR FOREST LANE
1000
Wildwood Trail
1.26 800
FOREST
2
PARK
600
10
Balch Creek
800
900
Alder Trail
0.84
Alder Cr
1
0.57
0.34
0.22
700
P
Keil Trail
0.17
9
0.71 800
Dogwood Trail
0.66
Wildwood Trail
0.59
NW THOMPSON RD
NW 53RD DR
8
Leif Erikson Drive
0.59

0   1/8   1/4
miles

Map continued on next page ▶

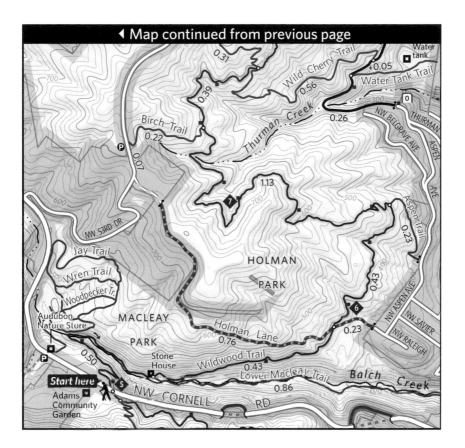

Water tank

0.31

Wild Cherry Trail

←0.05

Water Tank Trail

0.56

Thurman Creek

0.39

0.26

Birch Trail

0.22

NW BELGRAVE AVE.

THURMAN

ASPEN

AVE.

P

0.07

1.13

7

Aspen Trail

0.23

MW 53RD DR

600

HOLMAN

PARK

0.43

Jay Trail

700

Wren Trail

Woodpecker Tr.

6

NW ASPEN AVE.

NW SAVIER

Audubon
Nature Store

MACLEAY

PARK

Holman Lane

0.76

0.23

NW RALEIGH

P

0.50

Stone
House

Wildwood Trail

0.43

Balch

Creek

Start here

5

NW CORNELL

RD

Lower Macleay Trail

0.86

Adams
Community
Garden

of this steep ravine, was named after Danford Balch, an infamous early Oregon homesteader who, during a family quarrel, shot his son-in-law and was the first man to be legally hanged under Oregon law.

Balch Creek and its encompassing 1,550-acre watershed are recognized as being one of Forest Park's most valuable assets. One of only two or three year-round streams in the park, Balch Creek is a highly intact and functioning ecosystem. Scientists have documented a native population of two to four thousand cutthroat trout currently living in the creek. (Note: No fishing is allowed anywhere in Forest Park.) Follow Wildwood Trail as it meanders into the canyon, crossing Balch Creek at a bridge located at Milepost 5¼. Numerous old-growth trees, some up to eighty inches in diameter at chest height, grow along the banks of the stream.

At Milepost 5½, Wildwood intersects Lower Macleay Trail near a handsome, old stone structure built by the Works Progress Administration at the same time as Timberline Lodge. The purpose of this building, though, was more practical; for years, it was maintained as a restroom until it was heavily vandalized. At this junction, turn left on Wildwood Trail (Lower Macleay Trail heads downhill to the right) and begin a 1.2 miles climb out of the canyon.

Before Milepost 6, Wildwood nears an intersection with Holman Lane. For a short side trip, turn right on Holman Lane for 0.2 mile, ending at a large, grassy meadow with benches.

After Milepost 6¾, Wildwood Trail levels off. From Milepost 7 to 11, the vegetation is predominantly in a mid-successional forest state, the stage at which conifers begin to overtop the hardwoods. Eventually, if left undisturbed, most of the deciduous trees will reach their climax age (eighty to one hundred years) and will die out and be replaced by longer-lived Douglas fir, western red cedar, and western hemlock. Presently, because of the abundance of alder and maple trees, many birds are attracted to this area in spring to feast on their catkins or seedpods. Look for warblers, Evening Grosbeaks and Pine Siskins, and listen for Chestnut-backed Chickadees and Red-breasted Nuthatches, especially from April through June.

In the section between Mileposts 7¼ and 8¼, a ditch parallels the trail to the left. Now almost completely overgrown, it was dug in the early 1900s to bring water from the other side of Tualatin Mountain to hydraulically sluice out Westover Terrace, located below the park, for home sites. Along this portion of Wildwood, as well as other parts of the trail, care must be taken as many hard tree roots lie exposed on the pathway's surface, making it easy to trip, especially during the spring and summer months, when ground-level foliage drapes over the trail and in fall, when leaves obscure the path.

Birch Trail intersects Wildwood at Milepost 7½. Wild Cherry Trail crosses Wildwood after Milepost 7¾, and Dogwood Trail at Milepost 8½. Near Milepost 9¼, Wildwood Trail passes Keil Trail near NW 53rd Avenue. This well-maintained section of trail is a popular starting point for hikers and joggers. A short distance further, between Mileposts 9¼ and 9½, Alder Trail heads downhill to the right. At Milepost 10¼, look for the pocket of older coniferous trees interspersed with a variety of snags evidencing numerous woodpecker holes. The wild cry of a Pileated Woodpecker, and its two smaller cousins, Hairy and Downy Woodpeckers, can often be heard at this point.

Woodpeckers play a tremendously important role in forest ecosystems. Because they are insectivorous, they exert constant pressure on native insect populations, which helps prevent insects from reaching epidemic levels. Woodpeckers will consume 24 to 98 percent of a beetle population at moderate to high beetle densities.

Past Milepost 10½, Morak Trail, a short connector trail, intersects Wildwood Trail. Continue on Wildwood Trail until reaching the junction of Firelane 1, near Milepost 11¼. Here is another open meadow for resting, and a perfect spot to decide whether to continue on the next five-mile segment, which leads deep to the core of Forest Park. To end the hike here, walk 0.33 mile up Firelane 1 to arranged transportation at the locked park gate.

Wildwood Trail

FIRELANE 1 TO NW SALTZMAN ROAD

MILE 11.2–16.0

DISTANCE: 4.81 miles (one way)*
(If ending hike at Saltzman Road, add 1.12 miles to parking area.)
HIKING TIME: 2½ hours (one way)*
LOW ELEVATION: 656 feet
HIGH ELEVATION: 941 feet
CUMULATIVE ELEVATION GAIN: 373 feet
DIFFICULTY RATING: Easy
GPS COORDINATES: 45° 33' 8.02" N 122° 44' 48.36" W
  519766mE 5044330mN
Foot traffic only.
*One way trip; requires transportation at both ends of this hike.
NOTE: Stay on Wildwood Trail for entire hike.

MILEAGE AND DIRECTIONS

0.00 Begin at Wildwood Trail Trailhead at Firelane 1.
0.62 Intersection with Nature Trail.
0.95 Intersection with Chestnut Trail.
1.55 Intersection with Firelane 2.
1.65 Intersection with Maple Trail.
2.28 Intersection with tie trail to Maple Trail.
2.46 Intersection with Firelane 3.
3.04 Intersection with Koenig Trail.
4.28 Intersection with Cleator Trail.
4.81 End at Wildwood Trail intersection with NW Saltzman Road.

This portion of Wildwood Trail is scenic and rewarding and takes the hiker into the deep, central section of Forest Park, far from roads

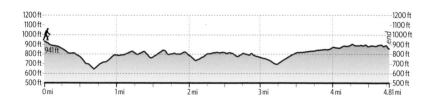

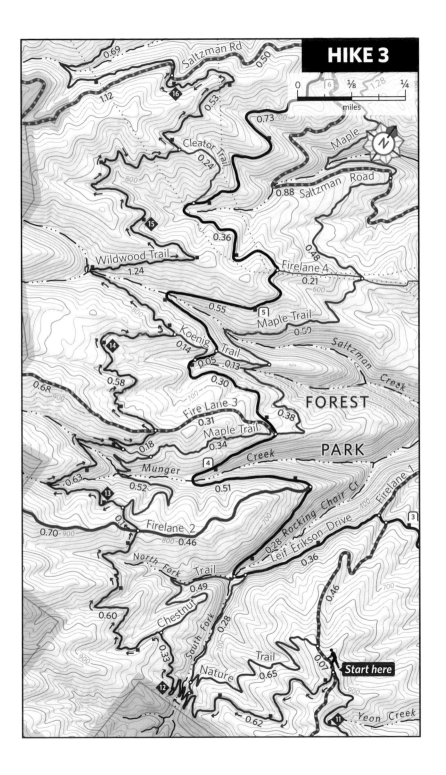

0   6   ⅛   1.28   ¼

miles

N

0.69

Saltzman Rd

0.50

1.12

16

0.53

Cleator Trail

0.24

Maple

0.73

0.88   Saltzman   Road

800

15

0.36

Wildwood Trail

0.48

Firelane 4

0.21

1.24

600

0.55

5

Maple Trail

800

Koenig

0.52

14

0.14

Trail

0.05   0.13

Saltzman

0.58

0.30

Creek

0.68

900

0.38

700

FOREST

Fire Lane 3

0.31

Maple Trail

0.18

0.34

PARK

4

Creek

Munger

0.63

0.52

0.51

700

Firelane 1

13

0.28   Rocking Chair Ct

Firelane 2

0.70

900

800

0.46

Leif   Erikson   Drive

400

3

North   Fork   Trail

0.36

0.49

0.46

700

0.60

Chestnut

0.28

South Fork

Trail

0.33

Nature

Trail

0.65

0.07

Start here

900

12

0.62

11

Yeon   Creek

or houses. It also offers the opportunity to pass through several impressive watersheds that sculpt the steep ravines of the park. The woods all along this well-maintained trail are quiet and, in places, showcase exceptionally regal stands of older, coniferous forest.

To reach the beginning of the hike, drive west 2.2 miles from the intersection of NW 23rd and NW Lovejoy along NW Cornell Road (Lovejoy becomes NW Cornell Road beyond NW 25th) until it intersects with NW 53rd Drive. Turn right on NW 53rd Drive and follow it for 1.7 miles, then turn right again on NW Forest Lane, which is marked by a sign. Follow Forest Lane (Firelane 1) until it meets a locked park gate. At this point, park your car and hike 0.33 miles to the trailhead.

The trail begins between Wildwood Mileposts 11 and 11¼, after crossing Firelane 1, which is the dividing line between two important watersheds in Forest Park. To the south is Willbridge Watershed; traveling north, Wildwood Trail enters the Saltzman Creek Watershed, at 964 acres, the third largest in Forest Park. Because of its size and good condition, Saltzman Creek Watershed plays an important role in improving the health of the Willamette River by contributing clean, nutrient-rich, aerated water to the river, far below.

Continue hiking north on Wildwood, which takes the hiker into a mid-aged conifer stand, laden with a characteristic understory of sword fern and Oregon grape. Two species of Oregon grape grow in Oregon. Cascade Oregon grape (*Berberis nervosa,* photo page 55) is a low-growing shrub that thrives in deep or partial shade, and is recognizable by its compound leaves with eleven to twenty-one leaflets. This species occurs from lowlands to mid-elevations and is often a dominant associate of Douglas fir. It is abundant throughout Forest Park. Tall Oregon grape (*Berberis aquifolium*) is a larger plant that grows up to six feet high and occurs in more open forests and forest margins of the lowlands. It displays five to eleven leaflets per leaf and is the state flower of Oregon. This variety is rare in the park.

After Milepost 11¾, Wildwood Trail crosses South Fork Rocking Chair Creek and for the next half mile gently climbs out of the canyon. Just beyond the intersection with Chestnut Trail, the trail passes through an especially scenic stand of older coniferous trees where numerous western hemlock and western red cedar trees can be seen growing beneath towering Douglas firs. This section of Saltzman Creek Watershed has been classified by Portland Parks and Recreation as displaying good and healthy conditions.

In 2003 and 2004, Portland Parks conducted surveys of its natural area parkland throughout the city to identify the native ecological functioning and health of these areas. Two significant findings resulted from this study: 1) More than 50 percent of Forest Park displays "good" and "healthy" conditions, exhibiting high levels of biological function, and 2) An overwhelming 87 percent of all "healthy" ratings in Portland's city parks are located in Forest Park.

Wildwood Trail crosses Firelane 2 near Milepost 12¾ then drops down again, curving along a series of switchbacks into Rocking Chair Creek Canyon. Along this section, large Douglas fir trees have fallen adjacent to the trail. Violent windstorms downed these trees, for Douglas firs have shallow, small root systems, making them especially vulnerable during high winds and dependent upon other nearby trees for support and protection. Near Milepost 13¼, the trail passes over Munger Creek, another major tributary to Rocking Chair Creek. Here, stately old Douglas firs create the effect of a hushed cathedral and deer and coyote tracks can often be seen.

Munger Creek was named after Thornton Munger, Yale forestry graduate and first director of the Pacific Northwest Research Station. Munger was a driving force for the creation of Forest Park. Throughout his life, he rebelled against greed, short-sightedness, and unmindfulness in entrenched bureaucracy, and he was often referred to by others as a model demonstration of how to get things done:

A crusading nature lover and conservationist, [Munger] has worked, led, pushed, cajoled, lobbied, inspired and contributed generously of his own funds. The results of his efforts have been monumental gains for this city and state in nature preservation and beautification.
—*The Oregon Journal*, 1968

Before Milepost 13½, Wildwood Trail passes a second tie trail to Maple Trail, and after that intersects with Firelane 3. Stay on Wildwood. After Milepost 14, conifers dwindle off and the trees are mostly red alder. This is a good example of vegetative succession having been set back as a result of logging, erosion, slides, and fire. Koenig Trail intersects Wildwood at Milepost 14¼, and at Milepost 14½ Wildwood crosses Saltzman Creek over a rustic footbridge.

Along this section of trail, try looking for trail plant (*Adenocaulon bicolor*, photo page 52). This is a fun plant for kids to try to identify. The low-growing plant's leaf is a nondescript triangle, green above but nearly white underneath. When travelers pass through a patch and knock against the plant, the leaf often flips over and shows its underside, which looks like a white marker. In this way, trackers historically could determine where a person had passed through an area, thereby explaining the plant's other common name, pathfinder.

Wildwood Trail crosses a large bridge over Maple Creek just past Milepost 15, and, a quarter-mile further, passes under a powerline. At Milepost 15½, near the intersection with Cleator Trail, Wildwood enters a stand of younger, even-aged Douglas fir trees that were planted by volunteers to reforest scorched hillsides after a disastrous fire ravaged the area in 1951.

Immediately after Milepost 16, Wildwood Trail comes out at NW Saltzman Road. To end the hike here, turn left on NW Saltzman Road and walk for 1.12 miles to reach the upper Saltzman Road Parking Area, which is just beyond the locked park gate. Plenty of parking is available here.

Wildwood Trail

NW SALTZMAN ROAD TO NW SPRINGVILLE ROAD
MILE 16.0–22.5

DISTANCE: 6.5 miles (one way)*

HIKING TIME: 4 hours (one way*) *(includes time for accessing the trail at both ends, an additional 1.5 miles)*

LOW ELEVATION: 786 feet

HIGH ELEVATION: 908 feet

CUMULATIVE ELEVATION GAIN: 121 feet

DIFFICULTY RATING: Easy

GPS COORDINATES: 45° 33' 53.13" N 122° 46' 11.72" W
517955mE 5045717mN

Foot traffic only.

One way trip; requires transportation at both ends of this hike.

NOTE: Stay on Wildwood Trail for entire hike.

MILEAGE AND DIRECTIONS

0.00   Begin at Wildwood Trail Trailhead at intersection with NW Saltzman Road.

0.69   Intersection with Firelane 5.

2.21   Intersection with Wiregate Trail.

2.57   Intersection with Trillium Trail.

3.42   Intersection with Firelane 7.

3.96   Intersection with Firelane 7A.

4.89   Intersection with Ridge Trail.

5.67   Intersection with Hardesty Trail.

6.50   End of hike at Wildwood Trail intersection with NW Springville Road.

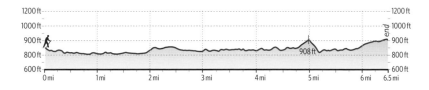

This particular section of Wildwood Trail, between NW Saltzman (Milepost 16) and Springville roads (Milepost 22½), wanders through some of the more remote areas of Forest Park and is enjoyable for its solitude. In the summer this trail is cooling on a hot day, meandering beneath overarching canopies of fir and maple trees. In spring, because of its abundance of red alder, it allows good bird-watching opportunities as migrating and breeding birds, including many varieties of warblers, flock together to feed on the abundant alder and maple catkins and seed pods.

Access to this part of Wildwood Trail is slightly more difficult than some other trails in Forest Park. Within the park boundaries, both NW Saltzman and NW Springville roads are closed to motorized vehicles, which means the hiker must plan on walking additional mileage at each end of these graveled roads.

To begin this hike at the Saltzman Road Trailhead, drive west from NW 23rd Avenue and NW Lovejoy (Lovejoy turns into NW Cornell Road after NW 25th) and travel 3.3 miles to the junction with NW Skyline Boulevard. Turn right onto Skyline and travel 2.9 miles to NW Saltzman Road. Turn right and continue 0.1 mile further to reach the Saltzman Parking Area. To park a second car at the end of this hike, drive an additional 0.9 mile on Skyline to NW Springville Road, which is to the right just beyond Skyline Milepost 7. Turn right (east) on Springville and drive 0.1 mile to a large parking area.

From the parking area at Saltzman Road, proceed on foot for 1.12 miles, where Saltzman Road intersects with Wildwood Trail. Turn left (north) onto Wildwood and begin descending into rugged Doane Creek Canyon. Near Milepost 16¼, the trail crosses the south fork of Doane Creek. A quarter mile further, near Milepost 16½, it traverses a picturesque pocket of mid-age conifer, then enters an area dominated by the robust growth of young alder and maple trees. Fire-scarred stumps and snags of old Douglas fir trees are sprinkled through here, silent remnants of past history. Just before Milepost 16¾, Wildwood crosses Firelane 5, a popular route for mountain bikers and runners. Beyond this junction for the next two miles, the footpath twists in

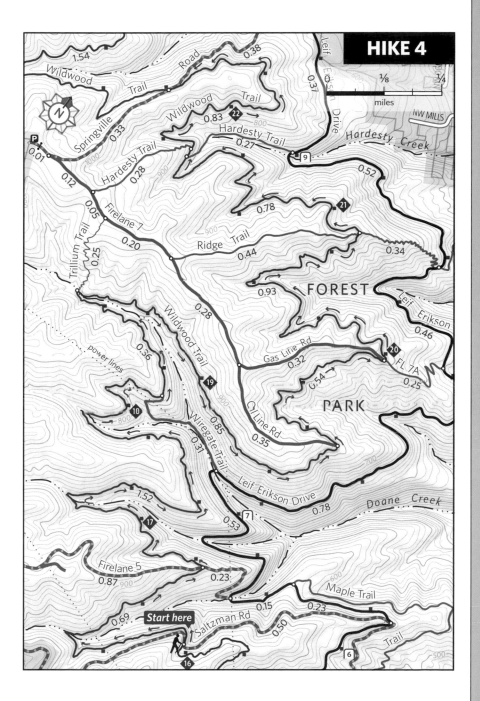

HIKE 4

1.54
Wildwood Trail
Road
0.38

0.31

Leif Erikson Drive

NW MILLS

⅛   ¼
miles

Wildwood   Trail
Springville 0.33
0.83 22 800

Hardesty Creek

Hardesty Trail
0.27
9
0.52

P
0.01

Hardesty Trail
0.28
0.12
1000
900

0.78
21

Firelane 7
0.05
0.20

Ridge   Trail
900
0.44
0.34

Trillium Trail
0.25

0.93
FOREST

0.28

Leif Erikson
0.46

Wildwood Trail
0.36

Gas Line Rd
0.32
20
FL 7A
0.25

power lines
800
10

19
900

0.54

PARK

Wiregate Trail
0.85
0.31

Oil Line Rd
0.35

700

1.52

Leif Erikson Drive
0.78

Doane   Creek

17
7
0.53

Firelane 5
0.87 900
0.23

600

Maple Trail

0.15
0.23

Start here
0.69
Saltzman Rd
0.50
Trail

500

6

16

Hike Four

111

Woods scene, eight miles northwest of Portland, 1896. OrHi neg. 26265

and out of several ravines that make up the Doane Creek Watershed. Throughout this section, numerous side creeks can be observed trickling down through the canyons in winter and spring. All are heading to the major ravine, steep Doane Creek Canyon, far below. Just beyond Milepost 18, Wildwood Trail passes by WiregateTrail, a connector to Leif Erikson Drive. This interesting trail that wends beneath powerlines was named long ago by a park employee. While clearing the trail after a storm, he found amidst the grass and shrubs an old wire gate, miles from any fence, lying in the middle of the path.

Past Milepost 18½, Wildwood crosses North Fork Doane Creek and intersects with Trillium Trail. Just beyond here, near 18¾, be sure to look for signs of logging practices from long ago.

In this area on some of the largest Douglas fir stumps, one can still see notches cut into the trunks. These notches were chopped by loggers nearly a century ago, as they worked to harvest the timber. The indentations were cut to a specific size so that springboards, usually eight inches wide by five feet long, could be fitted into them. Springboards supported the loggers, who stood on them while they cut the tree down.

Wildwood Trail intersects Firelane 7, on some maps called "Oil Line Road," near Milepost 19½, and Firelane 7A, also known as "Gas Line Road," at Milepost 20. These colloquial names refer to public utility easements for gas and oil pipelines that were put in place in 1956. Firelane 7A is the dividing ridgeline between Doane Creek and Springville Creek watersheds. Near this spot, berry-producing native shrubs grow vigorously. Fine examples of red-elderberry, red huckleberry, salmonberry, thimbleberry, and Indian plum (osoberry) plants can be observed lining the trail. Their fruits provide food for many species of native birds.

Just beyond Milepost 20¾, Ridge Trail intersects Wildwood. At Milepost 21¼, Wildwood Trail crosses a tributary to Hardesty Creek. This cool, wet section of trail, overhung by lovely assemblages of older conifers, is bordered by scores of native plants. At different times of the year, a hiker can observe trilliums, Oregon oxalis, waterleaf, sword fern, maidenhair fern, twisted stalk, and fairy bells all growing abundantly.

NW Springville Road intersects Wildwood Trail near Milepost 22½. If ending the hike here, leave Wildwood at this point and turn left onto Springville Road. Hike up the wide, quiet roadway, shaded by large fir trees and maples growing on either side, for 0.35 mile to the park gate.

Wildwood Trail

NW SPRINGVILLE ROAD TO
NW GERMANTOWN ROAD
MILE 22.5–24.7

DISTANCE: 2.17 miles (one way)*
(Add an additional 0.35 mile to access the trail from NW Springville Road)
HIKING TIME: 1 to 1½ hours (one way)*
LOW ELEVATION: 771 feet
HIGH ELEVATION: 928 feet
CUMULATIVE ELEVATION GAIN: 123 feet
DIFFICULTY RATING: Easy
GPS COORDINATES: 45° 34' 43.03" N 122° 47' 7.33" W
    516745mE 5047253mN
Foot traffic only
*One way trip; requires transportation at both ends of this hike.
NOTE: *Stay on Wildwood Trail for entire hike.*

MILEAGE AND DIRECTIONS
0.00   Begin at Wildwood Trail Trailhead, at intersection with NW
       Springville Road.
1.54   Intersection with Waterline Trail.
2.17   End at NW Germantown Road.

This section of Wildwood Trail between NW Springville (Mile 22.45) and Germantown roads (Mile 24.75) is exceptionally rewarding for its access, easy grade, beautiful stands of old fir trees, and its deep seclusion within the park. It also takes the hiker through one of the most intact and natural watersheds in Forest Park—the Springville

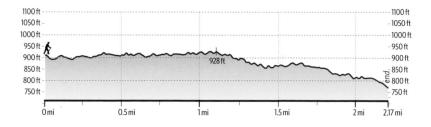

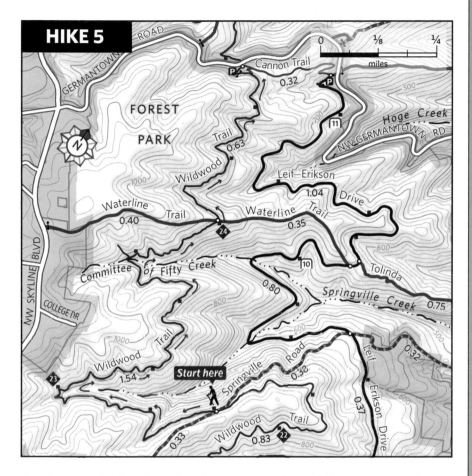

Creek Watershed—whose headwaters stretch to Skyline Boulevard and are nearly completely protected within the park boundaries.

To reach this trailhead, drive west from NW 23rd Avenue and NW Lovejoy, which will become NW Cornell Road, and travel 3.3 miles to the junction with NW Skyline Boulevard. Turn right onto Skyline and travel 3.8 miles to NW Springville Road (watch for the microwave tower looming over the trees). Turn right (east) on Springville and drive 0.1 mile to a large parking area.

Begin the hike by walking down the graveled Springville Road 0.35 mile to its intersection with Wildwood Trail. Turn left (north) on Wildwood. Milepost 22½ soon becomes visible. For most of this portion of Wildwood, the trail maintains a slight downgrade. Almost immediately, large Douglas firs create a backdrop along the trail and, in winter, rushing creeks deep in the canyon can be heard. These streams are all tributaries to Springville Creek.

Between NW Springville and NW Germantown roads, Wildwood Trail curves in and out of ravines that extend through the Springville Creek Watershed, which, in its upper reaches, is overwhelmingly dominated by native vegetation. Tall Douglas firs etch the skyline, while grand fir, western hemlock, and western red cedar grow in the Douglas firs' shade.

The flowing water within a watershed joins numerous natural attributes together. Much more than just a collection of mere creeks between two banks, a watershed is a far greater unifier: it integrates into one whole the upstream lands it drains, the aquifers it recharges, and the lands below that it inundates. The waters in its creeks are reflections of all the surfaces through which their waters have flowed before ever reaching their banks. For this reason, a well-functioning watershed—such as the Springville Creek drainage basin—is one that encompasses the rich biodiversity maintained within a native, intact ecosystem.

> "Because of the extensive protection provided by Forest Park, [its] watersheds are probably among the least altered watersheds within Portland when compared with their historical conditions."
>
> —2005 Portland Watershed Management Plan

Wildwood Trail crosses Springville Creek at Milepost 23 and Committee of Fifty Creek just past 23¾. Between the two streams, the trail passes through some exceptionally lovely stands of older firs. The large trees, though, are hardly old compared to the oldest members of their species. Douglas fir can live an enormously long time. The oldest known Douglas fir lived to be over thirteen hundred years old! Yet western hemlock and western red cedars are known to survive even longer, and in climax conditions will eventually replace the firs.

On occasion, pygmy owls can be heard along this stretch of trail. These small, secretive owls are unusual as they are active during the day rather than night. Their call is a repetitive single or double coo-like hoot. Pygmy owls prefer to nest in older, large coniferous trees growing close to streams. Scientist John Deshler, who has studied these owls intensively in Forest Park, has found an exceptional number of pygmy owls nesting in the park. Between 2007 and 2009, Deshler recorded one hundred and twenty baby pygmy owls fledging in Forest Park.

Young pygmy owl. Photo by John Deshler

At Milepost 24, Wildwood Trail crosses Waterline Trail. Three-quarters of a mile further, Wildwood intersects with NW Germantown Road; just before reaching Germantown Road, however, Cannon Trail intersects Wildwood Trail on the right. Stay to the left on Wildwood and follow the trail downhill to the Germantown Road Parking Area and the end of the hike.

Wildwood Trail

NW GERMANTOWN ROAD TO NW NEWTON ROAD
MILE 24.7–26.3

DISTANCE: 1.6 miles (one way)*
HIKING TIME: 1 hour (one way)*
LOW ELEVATION: 721 feet
HIGH ELEVATION: 836 feet
CUMULATIVE ELEVATION GAIN: 122 feet
DIFFICULTY RATING: Easy
GPS COORDINATES: 45° 35' 14.79" N 122° 47' 38.93" W
    516058mE 5048232mN
Foot traffic only
*One way trip; requires transportation at both ends of this hike.
NOTE: *Stay on Wildwood Trail for entire hike.*

MILEAGE AND DIRECTIONS
0.00   Begin at Wildwood Trail Trailhead at NW Germantown Road.
0.31   Intersection with Firelane 8.
0.73   Intersection with Firelane 10.
0.88   Intersection with tie trail to Newton Parking Area.
1.21   Tie trail to Newton Road Parking Area.
1.60   End at junction with Newton Road.

The section of Wildwood Trail between NW Germantown and NW Newton roads indeed captures the peace, solitude, and tranquility that symbolize Forest Park. It is more easily accessible than some sections of Wildwood Trail, and the Germantown Road Parking Area, where the hike begins, has plenty of room for cars. This hike is a wonderful one to do with children; it is not difficult and gives a good introduction to the wonders of a western Oregon coniferous forest.

To access the trailhead from downtown Portland, drive northwest on U.S. Highway 30 (St. Helen's Road) for 7.2 miles from its intersection with Interstate 405. Continue past the St. John's Bridge and turn left at the traffic light immediately after the bridge. This is NW Bridge Avenue and the northern ramp to the bridge. Take the first right onto NW Germantown Road and follow it for 1.6 miles, passing the first

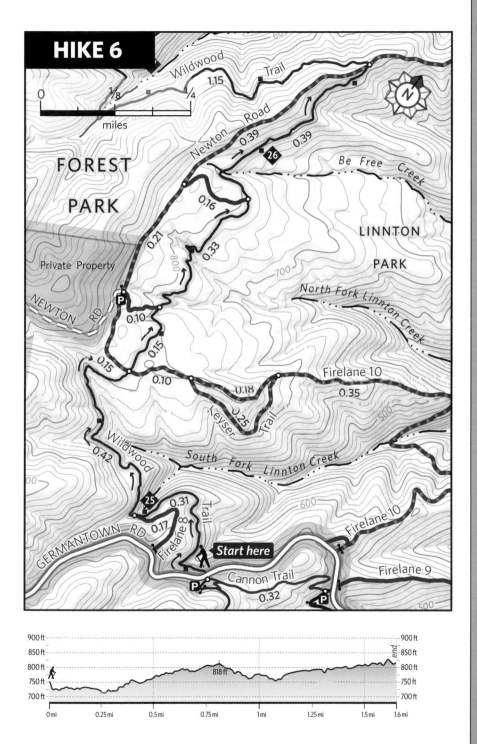

HIKE 6

0   ⅛   ¼
miles

FOREST

PARK

Wildwood   Trail
1.15

Newton   Road
0.39   0.39

N

26

Be Free   Creek

LINNTON

PARK

0.16

Private Property

0.21   0.33

800

700

North Fork Linnton Creek

NEWTON   RD

P

0.10

0.15

0.15
0.10

Firelane 10
0.35

500

Keyser   Trail
0.18
0.25

Wildwood
0.42

South   Fork   Linnton Creek

600

25
0.31

Firelane 10

600

Firelane 8
0.17

Trail

Start here

Firelane 9

GERMANTOWN   RD

P

Cannon   Trail
0.32

P

500

Hike Six

900 ft ──────────────────────────── 900 ft
850 ft ──────────────────────── end ── 850 ft
800 ft ────────────818 ft──────────── 800 ft
750 ft ──────────────────────────── 750 ft
700 ft ──────────────────────────── 700 ft

0 mi   0.25 mi   0.5 mi   0.75 mi   1 mi   1.25 mi   1.5 mi   1.6 mi

sizeable parking area, which is the outlet for Leif Erikson Drive. The Wildwood Trail Parking Area is the second pullout on Germantown Road. Here is a smaller but still sizeable pullout area for parking on the left. The trail entrance for the continuation of Wildwood is across NW Germantown Road, to the right and downhill approximately 58 yards from the parking lot.

At the beginning of this hike, Wildwood Trail gently winds through forest habitat indicative of the Western Hemlock Vegetation Zone of western Oregon and Washington. While walking along, listen closely for the characteristic bird species of this ecosystem, all of which are prevalent: Golden-crowned Kinglets, Song Sparrows, Brown Creepers, Chestnut-backed Chickadees, Steller's Jays, Red-breasted Nuthatches, and Winter Wrens (photo page 72). All of these native forest birds have easily identifiable songs that are not difficult to learn. The small, brown Winter Wren exhibits perhaps the most amazing song of all. It is high, melodic, and clear, and seems to continue on indefinitely, with the tiny bird never pausing for breath. In winter and early spring, the Winter Wren's cheery song may be the only bird heard in the forest.

At Wildwood Milepost 25, Firelane 8—a short (0.17 mile) pathway that extends back to Germantown Road—comes in from above and to the left. Stay on Wildwood Trail, which at this point crosses Linnton Creek. This seasonally intermittent stream is part of the Linnton Creek Watershed that stretches from the Waterline Trail ridgeline (Milepost 24) north to Newton Road (Milepost 26¼). The streams from this drainage exit the park near the community of Linnton, eight hundred feet below, along Highway 30, and enter the Willamette River.

Continue heading north on Wildwood Trail. Just before Milepost 25¼, a park bench honoring Bruno Kolkowsky is situated next to the trail. Beyond Milepost 25¼, the character of the forest changes intermittently. Douglas fir trees give way to a landscape more heavily dominated with red alder. In spring, red alder trees transform the woods with a blush of rosy pink. Alder is beneficial to the soil because of its ability to "fix" atmospheric nitrogen, which increases the nitrogen content and availability in the soil. In this way, it can help restore areas where soil nutrients have been depleted as a result

Bruno Kolkowsky, a long-time volunteer and steward of the park, gave hundreds of hours of his time to build and maintain its trails. The section of Wildwood Trail between NW Springville Road and NW Newton Road was in a large measure built by volunteers, and predominantly by Kolkowsky, who worked closely with Fred Nilsen, Forest Park arborculturist, and another dedicated volunteer, Bill Sauerwein. This bench tells of Kolkowsky's enduring commitment to the Park with the inscription, *This Trail is His Legacy.*

of logging or fire. Additionally, red alder leaves break down quickly after they have fallen and provide food for invertebrates that live in the creeks. In turn, these invertebrates provide a food base for fish.

Firelane 10 intersects Wildwood Trail just before Milepost 25½. Cross Firelane 10 and proceed on Wildwood, ignoring all side trails. Along this level section of trail, thick carpets of Oregon grape, red huckleberry, Indian plum, and other native shrubs grow robustly. Another common plant indicative of the Douglas fir forest is also found here: wild ginger (photo page 52). This highly fragrant plant with a spicy smell of ginger grows low to the ground and is easy to identify. Its leathery leaves are shaped like a heart and are especially visible in mid-February—making it a fitting symbol for Valentine's Day—when other shrubs and forbs have not yet leafed out.

Past Milepost 25¾, Wildwood Trail crosses a major creek in the 855-acre Linnton Creek Watershed system. Be Free Creek can be recognized by a trailside rock monument with the inscription, "Be Free Where You Are." This tribute is in the memory of Gaelle Snell, who loved Forest Park.

At Milepost 26¼, a few spectacular old-growth Douglas firs can be observed growing next to the trail in a grove of tall western hemlock trees. At Wildwood 26.3, Newton Road intersects with Wildwood Trail. At this juncture, one can decide whether to backtrack 1.7 miles to return to the parking area on NW Germantown Road, or turn left (uphill) on Newton Road for 0.6 mile to a large parking area on Newton Road. If desiring only a one-way trip, a second car can be left here.

Wildwood Trail

NW NEWTON ROAD TO NW NEWBERRY ROAD
MILE 26.3–30.12

DISTANCE: 3.82 miles (one way)*
HIKING TIME: 2 hours (one way)*
LOW ELEVATION: 599 feet
HIGH ELEVATION: 928 feet
CUMULATIVE ELEVATION GAIN: 291 feet
DIFFICULTY RATING: Easy
GPS COORDINATES: 45° 35' 59.17" N 122° 48' 1.3" W
     515570mE 5049600mN
Foot traffic only
**One way trip; requires transportation at both ends of this hike.*
NOTE: Stay on Wildwood Trail for entire hike.

MILEAGE AND DIRECTIONS
0.00   Begin at Wildwood Trail Trailhead at intersection with Newton
        Road.
1.15   Intersection with BPA Road.
1.98   Intersection with Firelane 15.
3.82   End of Wildwood Trail at Newberry Road.

This final section of Wildwood Trail continues taking the hiker into the less-travelled North Unit of Forest Park, where people are fewer and the chance to see native wildlife is enhanced. This part of the park features fine interior forest habitat—native landscape that is whole, contiguous, and unfragmented by roadways, clear cuts, or development. As such, it provides important wildlife habitat for many indigenous species. This habitat is extremely rare in the Portland area. As one travels through these natural areas among the tall trees and healthy streams, the full majesty of Forest Park becomes clear. Here it is easy to see why Forest Park is considered to be the "crown jewel" of Portland's park system.

To access the trailhead, drive northwest along NW Skyline Boulevard. After crossing the intersection of Skyline Boulevard and

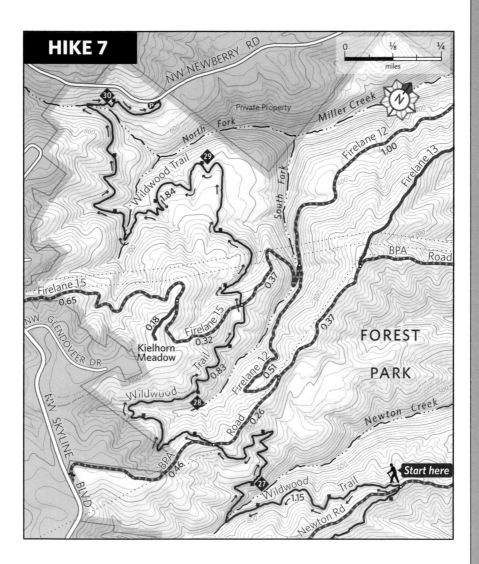

HIKE 7

NW NEWBERRY RD

Private Property

Miller Creek

Firelane 12
1.00

Firelane 13

North Fork

Wildwood Trail

1.84

South Fork

30

29

P

BPA Road

0.37

Firelane 15
0.65

0.18

Firelane 15
0.32

0.37

FOREST

NW GLENDOVER DR

Kielhorn
Meadow

Trail 0.83

PARK

Wildwood

Firelane 12
0.51

28

Newton Creek

NW SKYLINE BLVD

Road
0.26

BPA
0.46

27

Wildwood Trail
1.15

Newton Rd

Start here

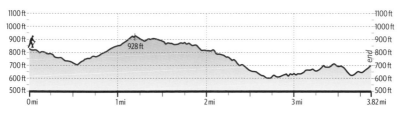

1100 ft · 1100 ft
1000 ft · 1000 ft
900 ft · 900 ft
800 ft · · · · · · · · · · · 928 ft · · · · · · · · · · · 800 ft
700 ft · 700 ft
600 ft · 600 ft
500 ft · 500 ft

0mi   1mi   2mi   3mi   3.82mi

NW Cornell Road, continue 5.1 miles further on Skyline to reach NW Newton Road. Turn right on Newton Road and continue for 0.3 mile where the road ends at a parking lot. From this point, motorized vehicles are not permitted.

There are two park gates at the Newton Road Parking Area. The northern gate is the continuation of Newton Road. (The gate to the south leads to Firelane 10.) To access Wildwood Trail, hike down Newton Road for 0.6 mile. After 0.24 mile, there is a tie trail to the right that leads to Wildwood Trail. For the purposes of this hike, however, stay on Newton Road until its juncture with Wildwood, 0.36 mile further. From this intersection, turn left on Wildwood and begin heading northwest.

Almost immediately, Wildwood Trail enters quiet, deep woods that are characteristic of Douglas fir forests of the Western Hemlock Zone. From Milepost 26½ to 27¼, the path traverses Newton Creek Canyon, where an outstanding variety of native trees, shrubs, and plants can be observed. Along the way, see if you can find multiple examples of the beautiful lily family, which bloom during many months of the year (photos pages 48-52): Solomon's plume, Hooker's fairy bells, star-flowered Solomon's seal, clasping twisted stalk, fairy lantern, false lily-of-the-valley, and western trillium.

Near Milepost 27¼, Wildwood climbs slightly. It switchbacks along an alder ridge and vistas open up as the path approaches BPA Road, where Red-tailed Hawks are frequently seen flying or perching on one of the tall power poles. Just before Milepost 27½, the trail comes out at the powerline access road. Turn left on BPA Road and walk uphill for 100 feet to access the continuation of Wildwood Trail.

After crossing over the roadway, Wildwood leaves Newton Creek Canyon and enters the Miller Creek Watershed. At nine hundred acres, this drainage is the third largest in the park. Unlike the other waterways in the park, which drain into the Willamette River, Miller Creek and its tributaries empty into Multnomah Channel.

Wildwood Trail crosses the south fork of Miller Creek after Milepost 27¾. Just before Milepost 28½ it intersects Firelane 15.

At Milepost 28¾, the trail winds along a ridge that opens up into a beautiful, level glade. For the next half mile, widely spaced, tall cedar and hemlock trees grow among stately maple and red alder while fields of native sword ferns cover the ground. Throughout this stretch, native woodpeckers are frequently heard drumming.

The Miller Creek Watershed exhibits some of the best health in all of Forest Park. Its vitality is the result of the pristine quality of much of its native vegetation and the fact that its headwaters are predominantly intact; only a few small pockets of private development occur in its upper basins. Miller Creek is one of only two streams in Forest Park (the other being Balch Creek) that is known to support fish. It contains small but essential populations of sea-run cutthroat trout, steelhead, and Coho salmon. The creek is one of the last remaining free-flowing streams in the city of Portland that still provides spawning habitat for anadromous fish.

Near Milepost 29, the trail crosses the North Fork of Miller Creek. Near this bridge, look for springboard notches, cut by loggers long ago, on some of the large stumps. Listen also for Ravens, which can sometimes be heard calling high above the canyon.

After Milepost 29, Wildwood Trail crosses seven more bridges while twisting in and out of numerous small ravines. It enters a beautiful cedar canyon after Milepost 29½, where a careful observer might spy a rare Varied Thrush (photo page 72). At Milepost 30, the pathway makes a quick ascent uphill, then reaches NW Newberry Road.

This intersection marks the present end of Wildwood Trail, at 30.2 miles. To access this trailhead from downtown Portland, drive U.S. Highway 30 approximately ten miles from its intersection with Interstate 405. Turn left onto Newberry Road and travel 1.5 miles. (Skyline Boulevard will be 0.5 mile further up the road.) Wildwood Trail, marked by a small trail sign, is on the left side of the road. Limited space is available for parking alongside Newberry Road.

Tunnel Trail and Trails South of Cornell Road

DISTANCE: 2.46-mile loop

HIKING TIME: 1 to 1½ hours

LOW ELEVATION: 395 feet

HIGH ELEVATION: 717 feet

CUMULATIVE ELEVATION GAIN: 348 feet

DIFFICULTY RATING: Moderate

GPS COORDINATES: 45° 31' 49.14" N 122° 43' 1.14" W
    522099mE 5041904mN

Foot traffic only.

MILEAGE AND DIRECTIONS

0.00   Begin at Tunnel Trail Trailhead on Cornell Road. Hike Tunnel Trail.

0.17   Turn right on Cumberland Trail.

0.41   Turn right on Wildwood Trail.

0.86   Turn left on Upper Macleay Trail.

1.39   Cross Wildwood Trail. Stay on Upper Macleay.

1.67   Make sharp left onto (lower) Macleay Trail.

1.95   Turn right on Wildwood Trail.

2.05   Turn right on Cumberland Trail.

2.29   Turn left on Tunnel Trail.

2.46   End at Tunnel Trail Trailhead.

This medley of interlinking trails offers an excellent short hike very close to the city, with all the beauty most often associated with deep, secluded forests. This walk is perfect for an afternoon ramble, relaxing yet invigorating, and gives the hiker a chance to experience the subtle changes and seasonal moods of this great, wilderness park. As a cautionary note, Tunnel Trail, being short but relatively steep and in some places worn down to bedrock, can be slippery after a rain. A trekking pole can be helpful here.

To reach the trailhead, drive through Northwest Portland, traveling west from NW 23rd on Lovejoy Street (Lovejoy changes to Cornell Road after NW 25th) until just past the first tunnel (1.1 miles). At this point, there is a pullout on the left and a trail marker, sometimes

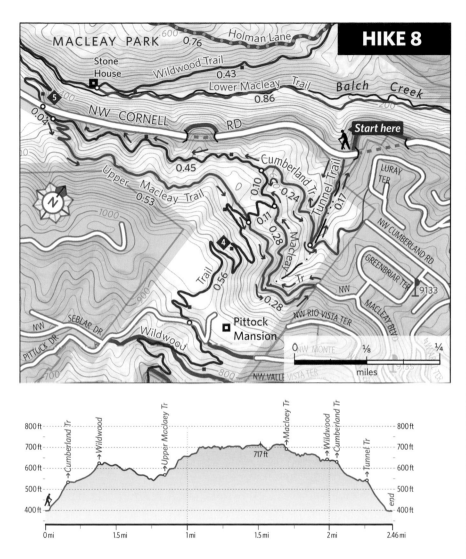

hard to see, denoting Tunnel Trail. Park here, and hike south (left) on Tunnel Trail.

For most of its short length, Tunnel Trail climbs uphill following a narrow ravine where Douglas firs grow alongside Pittock Creek, a tributary to Balch Creek. The path soon ends at an intersection with Cumberland Trail. Turn right onto Cumberland Trail and follow its gentle grade, bending in and out of ravines among stands of mid-aged conifer. Cumberland Trail is wide, well maintained, and lined

129

with luxuriant ferns, predominantly graceful lady ferns and sword ferns.

English ivy can choke out and kill low-growing native plants but can destroy trees as well. A dense cover of ivy can prevent conifers, notably Douglas fir, from ever reestablishing a site. As a result, much food and cover is eliminated for many birds, small mammals, and amphibians, wreaking havoc for native wildlife populations. Constant vigilance and eradication of invasive species is required throughout Forest Park to keep these detrimental invaders from smothering the diverse and healthy Northwest native vegetation. The Forest Park Natural Resources Management Plan has deemed the removal of ivy the park's highest natural resource management priority.

Unfortunately, non-native, troublesome species such as English ivy and English holly are also widespread along the trails and in the ravines of the southern portions of Forest Park. Ivy and holly can easily escape from nearby yards and soon gain a foothold at the expense of naturally occurring plants. This is the general rule of Forest Park: the closer one is to the city and human habitation, as well as places where the native landscape has been fragmented by roads, the greater the percentage of non-native species of vegetation and wildlife. Farther away, at the park's more rural, northwest end, these introduced specimens are rare.

After a quarter mile, Cumberland Trail reaches a junction with Wildwood Trail. Turn right on Wildwood and follow it for almost a half mile as it parallels high above Cornell Road. The trail slowly descends and allows some exquisite views of the forested hillsides rising up from Balch Creek Canyon, across Cornell Road. In fall, these hills are a patchwork of color.

Continue on Wildwood Trail as it curves along the sides of ravines, pausing to look at the old snags dotted with woodpecker holes. Pileated Woodpeckers, large, shy birds native to Oregon forests, often frequent these woods. These great, black woodpeckers (photo page

70), with their distinctive white wings (undersides) and bright red crests, are considered by many ornithologists as the true symbol of Northwest forest wilderness.

As Wildwood Trail nears Cornell Road, Upper Macleay Trail comes in from the left. Turn left onto this trail and continue uphill. The trail, which parallels Wildwood from above, is sporadically vegetated with immense Douglas fir trees, many two to four hundred years old. Also interspersed are giant old maple trees with green licorice ferns growing thickly out of their gnarly trunks.

At slightly over a half mile, Upper Macleay Trail again intersects Wildwood Trail. Stay straight and continue on Upper Macleay for a quarter mile further until it ends at a parking area on NW Macleay Boulevard in Westover Heights. At this junction, make a sharp left turn onto Macleay Trail.

This short but very peaceful trail slopes gently downhill. After 0.25 mile, Macleay Trail ends, intersecting with Wildwood Trail. Stay to the right, traveling downhill on Wildwood Trail. In spring, listen for the lively bird calls of singing Bushtits, Golden-crowned Kinglets, Brown Creepers, Black-capped Chickadees, Winter Wrens, and robins. All are species native to the Northwest and their songs emanate from the tall trees growing within these deep canyons.

Several hundred yards farther, Wildwood Trail approaches Cumberland Trail. Turn right on Cumberland. At Cumberland's junction with Tunnel Trail, turn left and descend the steep Tunnel Trail. Tunnel Trail ends at Cornell Road, concluding the hike.

Holman Lane, Wildwood Trail, and Birch Trail Loop

DISTANCE: 2.61 miles

HIKING TIME: 1 to 1½ hours

LOW ELEVATION: 334 feet

HIGH ELEVATION: 808 feet

CUMULATIVE ELEVATION GAIN: 462 feet

DIFFICULTY RATING: Moderate

GPS COORDINATES: 45° 31' 57.64" N 122° 43' 54.19" W
520943mE 5042172mN

Foot traffic only on Wildwood Trail and Birch Trail. Holman Lane allows bicycles traveling uphill only.

MILEAGE AND DIRECTIONS

0.00 Begin hiking Holman Lane at its intersection with NW 53rd Drive.

0.76 Turn left at the junction with Wildwood Trail.

1.19 Intersection with Aspen Trail. Continue on Wildwood Trail.

2.32 Turn left on Birch Trail.

2.54 Intersection with NW 53rd Drive Trailhead.

2.61 End at the NW 53rd Drive Trailhead.

This short, easy loop offers a taste of wild Northwest areas and examples of native plants and animals, all within a ten-minute drive from the city.

To reach the trailhead, drive from NW 23rd Avenue along NW Lovejoy Street, which becomes NW Cornell Road after NW 25th, and travel for 2.2 miles. At the intersection of Cornell with NW 53rd Drive, turn right on 53rd and continue for 0.5 mile. On the right is a wide shoulder for parking. At the end of this area is a sign on the right denoting Birch Trail. Park here. To reach Holman Lane and the beginning of the trail, walk down 53rd Drive 200 yards to an unmarked gravel road. (Mailboxes are located here, with addresses beginning at 422.) Turn left onto the road, which is a public right of way, and hike 0.06 mile to a locked park gate that demarcates Holman Lane.

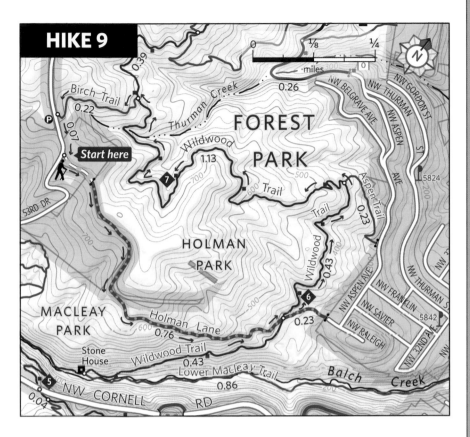

HIKE 9

Birch Trail 0.22 0.39

0.07

Start here

53RD DR

Thurman Creek 0.26

Wildwood 1.13

7

700

500

FOREST

PARK

Trail

600

NW BELGRAVE AVE

NW THURMAN

NW ASPEN

NW GORDON ST

AVE

ST

5824

500

Aspen Trail

0.23

Wildwood

0.43

Trail

400

500

HOLMAN

PARK

MACLEAY

PARK

Holman Lane

0.76

600

500

6

0.23

200

NW ASPEN AVE

NW FRANKLIN

NW SAVIER

NW RALEIGH

NW THURMAN ST

5842

NW 32ND AVE

Stone
House

Wildwood Trail

0.43

5

0.04

Lower Macleay Trail

0.86

NW CORNELL RD

Balch Creek

200

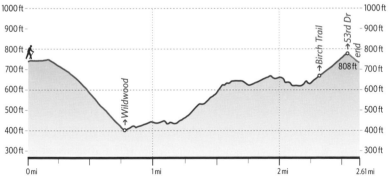

1000 ft	1000 ft
900 ft	900 ft
800 ft	800 ft
700 ft	700 ft
600 ft	600 ft
500 ft	500 ft
400 ft	400 ft
300 ft	300 ft

→Wildwood

→Birch Trail

→53rd Dr
end

808 ft

0 mi   1 mi   2 mi   2.61 mi

Once past the gate, Holman Lane soon becomes a grassy, wide pathway with a peaceful ambiance. The gentle trail is part of the 1,550-acre Balch Creek Watershed. For three-quarters of a mile, it gradually descends into the Balch Creek Canyon. When the leaves are off the trees, views of Macleay Park, the Balch Creek ravine, NW Cornell Road (across the canyon), and even the Willamette River can be seen.

Holman Lane was named for Frederick, Mary, and George Holman, children of a pioneering family, who donated fifty-two acres to the city for a park in 1939. The Holmans' wish was for their property to connect to Portland's Macleay Park. At the end of Holman Lane, close to Forest Park's Raleigh Street entrance, is a picturesque open meadow. At one time, this pleasing spot was the showpiece of what used to be known as Holman Park. Frederick Holman, a prominent lawyer and avid rose exhibitor, remains distinguished in Portland's history as the person who gave Portland the name "City of Roses."

Holman Lane intersects Wildwood Trail just before Wildwood Milepost 6. Turn left (north) on Wildwood and hike for 1.5 miles. Throughout this portion of trail, native plants characteristic of Western Oregon can be seen. Try to identify these signature plant and shrub species of the Douglas fir ecosystem: Indian plum, also known as osoberry (the first shrub to bloom in spring), sword fern, red huckleberry, Oregon grape, and waterleaf. Invasive species are also observable here and are in some places prominent—primarily English ivy.

Since 1993, volunteer groups such as the No Ivy League and the Forest Park Conservancy have cooperatively worked with Portland Parks and Recreation in a tenacious, ongoing battle to eliminate and stop the spread of ivy and other destructive invasive species. Championed by the late Sandra Diedrich, who made ivy removal her life's work and helped found the No Ivy League, thousands of people have joined the cause. Their progress can be observed all along this part of the trail, where ivy has been pulled out by its roots and girdled at the base of tall trees. Cutting ivy vines off at a tree's trunk level is an effective way to curtail the plant's rapid growth and free the conifers and maples from future strangulation.

After Milepost 6¼, Aspen Trail joins Wildwood to the right. This quarter-mile trail leads to another park trailhead, Aspen Avenue. For purposes of this hike, however, continue on Wildwood and follow several switchbacks that gradually rise several hundred feet as the trail climbs up the ravine. Between Mileposts 6½ and 7, Wildwood Trail winds through a beautiful stand of straight, tall firs. Here, impressive views deep into the canyon and up the ridge emit a sense of the splendor of the Pacific Northwest.

Just before Milepost 7½, Birch Trail intersects Wildwood. Turn left onto Birch Trail and ascend 0.22 mile through stands of red alder and bigleaf maple. Birch Trail comes out at NW 53rd Drive, concluding the loop. Across the street is another open meadow—a perfect spot for a picnic or for just relaxing in the sun after an enjoyable hike.

Lower Firelane 7A (Gas Line Road), Wildwood Trail, Ridge Trail, and Leif Erikson Drive Loop

DISTANCE: 3.66 miles

HIKING TIME: 2 hours

LOW ELEVATION: 73 feet

HIGH ELEVATION: 878 feet

CUMULATIVE ELEVATION GAIN: 802 feet

DIFFICULTY RATING: Strenuous

GPS COORDINATES: 45° 34' 42.27" N 122° 45' 46.93" W
    518488mE 5047235mN

Foot traffic only on Firelane 7A, Wildwood Trail, and Ridge Trail. Leif Erikson Drive also allows bicycles and horses.

NOTE: *Bridge Avenue on U.S. Highway 30 is a busy highway heavily used by trucks. Although there are sidewalks on either side, parents with young children are advised not to use this entrance to Lower Firelane 7A.*

MILEAGE AND DIRECTIONS

0.00   Begin at Lower Firelane 7A Trailhead on the southern ramp of the St. John's Bridge at U.S. Highway 30.

0.70   Turn right on Leif Erikson Drive (near Milepost 8).

0.84   Turn left on Upper Firelane 7A.

1.09   Turn right onto Wildwood Trail.

2.02   Turn right on Ridge Trail.

2.36   Turn right on Leif Erikson Drive.

2.82   Intersection with Upper Firelane 7A. Continue on Leif Erikson Drive.

2.96   Turn left on Lower Firelane 7A.

3.66   End at Lower Firelane 7A Trailhead.

This hike is a challenge and one that requires some exploration. Lower Firelane 7A, also referred to as Gas Line Road, is not well marked in places, and necessitates following white and orange gas line identification posts—similar to sighting cairns for directional purposes on lightly used trails in the wilderness. The gas line posts are spaced in close proximity, however, and easy to spot. While the

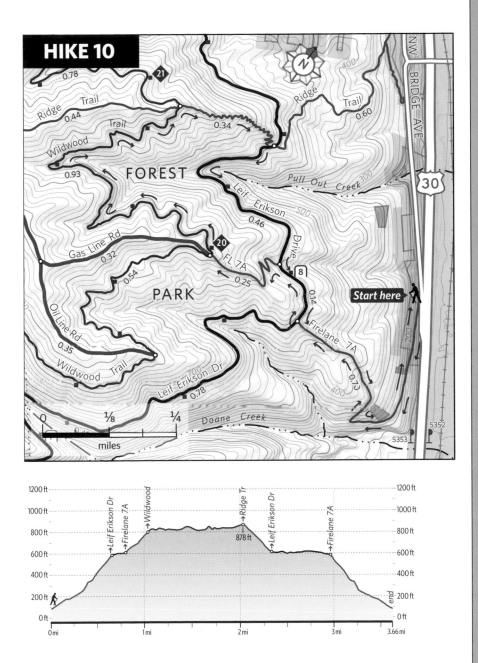

HIKE 10

21

0.78

Ridge Trail

0.44

Wildwood Trail

0.93

FOREST

0.34

Ridge Trail

0.60

Pull Out Creek 300

Leif Erikson 0.46

Drive 500

400

NW

BRIDGE AVE

30

Gas Line Rd 0.32

20

FL 7A

0.25

PARK

0.54

Oil Line Rd

0.35

Wildwood Trail

700

Leif Erikson Dr

0.78

8

Start here

0.14

Firelane 7A

0.73

400

Doane Creek

5352

5353

0   ⅛   ¼

miles

Elevation profile:

→ Leif Erikson Dr
→ Firelane 7A
→ Wildwood
→ Ridge Tr
878 ft
→ Leif Erikson Dr
→ Firelane 7A
end

1200 ft — 1200 ft
1000 ft — 1000 ft
800 ft — 800 ft
600 ft — 600 ft
400 ft — 400 ft
200 ft — 200 ft
0 ft — 0 ft

0 mi   1 mi   2 mi   3 mi   3.66 mi

beginning of the trail can be slightly jarring with sounds and sights of heavy industry, it is still a worthwhile loop and a good workout, and leads the hiker into the very center of the park, where the beauty and tranquility of the urban wilderness will soon transcend all reminders of the city.

To reach the trailhead, drive northwest on U.S. Highway 30 (St. Helen's Road) for 6 miles. Turn left at the intersection leading to the south ramp of the St. John's Bridge. Continue up the ramp for 0.3 mile to a parking area on the left, known as the Pull-Out Creek Parking Area. Park here, carefully cross the street to the pedestrian sidewalk on the other side, and walk down the ramp for 0.2 mile. A locked park gate identified as Firelane 7A is directly across the street and marks the start of the trail.

Firelane 7A begins as an ivy-strewn, rocky road-cut that parallels U.S. Highway 30. For a quarter mile, the wide, little-used trail climbs at a gradual angle among vegetation under siege by ivy (the battle for its eradication continues) as well as native poison oak. Along the stony pathway, broken concrete posts delineate the old roadway and one can see remnants of building foundations and old steps that today lead to nowhere. Proceeding uphill, a hiker's first impressions are generally not those of wildness but rather of noisy sirens, trucks, blasting train horns, and loud car radios.

Yet impressions quickly begin to change. As Firelane 7A approaches Doane Creek Canyon, there are pleasing views of the Willamette River, Burlington Northern (railroad) Bridge, and Willamette Cove. The cacophony of traffic drops off while the songs of native birds can be heard from the trees. In the spring, assemblages of migrating birds, including colorful Black-throated Gray Warblers and Orange-crowned Warblers, can be observed busily flitting among the maples and alder trees. Rufous Hummingbirds (whose calls resemble a high-pitched sneeze) are regularly seen darting among blooming shrubs.

In 0.3 mile, Lower Firelane 7A arrives at an overlook high above Doane Creek Canyon. From here, the steep basalt cliffs surrounding the drainage are fully visible and impressive. Below is the site of an old rock quarry, no longer in use. Many times during the year raptors (hawks and falcons) can be observed soaring through Doane Creek Canyon.

The Doane Creek Watershed, at 1,037 acres, is the second largest in Forest Park. From this overlook, one can begin to understand the connection between the forest, the creek, and the Willamette River.

> "In the Pacific Northwest, rivers and the lands they drain are a living link with the region's history and heritage. They have supported human life for millennia ... and nurtured species such as salmon and Douglas fir that have become icons of our unique region, people and lifestyle. This is especially true in Portland, where today—as in the past—the city is defined socially, culturally and economically by the Willamette River, its tributaries and the lands they drain."
>
> —2005 Portland Watershed Management Plan

Lower Firelane 7A splits at this overlook. The trail following a fence line hugs the canyon wall and eventually ends at a pretty spot next to Doane Creek. To continue on the firelane, though, turn right at the junction and continue uphill on a path that quickly becomes more steep.

During the wet season, trekking poles can be helpful along this stretch of trail, which heads straight up the ridge-line separating Doane Creek and Springville Creek watersheds. The slope can be slippery. Begin to look for the gray or white posts painted with one or two orange bands; these markers, identified with the words "Gas Pipeline," indicate the trail. As one climbs up the hill, the way becomes more scenic and the presence of ivy, because of intensive eradication work, much reduced. In its place, native waterleaf, trilliums, sword ferns, salal, and yellow wood violets grow abundantly.

Lower Firelane 7A makes one last steep pitch just before it exits onto Leif Erikson Drive. Once on the road, turn right and hike Leif Erikson Drive north for 0.14 mile to access the upper portion of Firelane 7A. Along this short section, pause to look to the southeast for a beautiful view deep into the Doane Creek Watershed.

Just beyond Leif Erikson Milepost 8, turn left onto the upper section of Firelane 7A. The 0.11 mile connector trail makes a few quick switchbacks, then joins with the wider section of the firelane (Gas Line Road). Continue heading uphill and, at the intersection with Wildwood Trail, turn right. Once on Wildwood, head north for almost a mile.

The section of Wildwood Trail between Mileposts 20 and 20¾ traverses Pull Out Creek Canyon. At Milepost 20½, Wildwood Trail crosses Pull Out Creek, an intermittent stream. This is the same creek that can be observed at the parking area (of the same name) on the south ramp of the St. John's Bridge. After Milepost 20¾, Ridge Trail intersects Wildwood. Turn right on Ridge Trail and head downhill for 0.35 mile. Along this narrow trail, the vegetation is more shrub-like, with red elderberry bushes growing profusely. Chestnut-backed Chickadees, Red-breasted Nuthatches, and Golden-crowned Kinglets are commonly heard calling from the red alder trees.

At the junction of Ridge Trail with Leif Erikson Drive, turn right (south) onto Leif Erikson for 0.75 mile. Be on the lookout for Lower Firelane 7A, which is approximately 250 yards past Milepost 8. The access point is easy to miss but identifiable by the gas line white post. Leave Leif Erikson Drive at this point and drop over the bank to retrace the hike down Lower Firelane 7A. As before, be watchful for the gas line posts acting as trail markers. In less than a mile the deep forest will be left behind as one reenters the city streets and finishes the loop.

Lower and Upper Macleay Trails Loop

DISTANCE: 3.26 miles

HIKING TIME: 2 hours

LOW ELEVATION: 85 feet

HIGH ELEVATION: 704 feet

CUMULATIVE ELEVATION GAIN: 605 feet

DIFFICULTY RATING: Moderate

GPS COORDINATES: 45° 32' 9.5" N 122° 42' 45.1" W
    522445mE 5042533mN

Foot traffic only.

NOTE: *This loop involves crossing NW Cornell Road and some walking on side streets. If traveling with small children, an alternative is to hike Lower Macleay Trail only and return.*

MILEAGE AND DIRECTIONS

0.00   Begin at Lower Macleay Park Trailhead at NW Upshur.

0.86   Junction with Wildwood Trail. Stay straight on Wildwood.

1.36   Junction with Cornell Road. Cross Cornell. Stay on Wildwood.

1.40   Turn right on Upper Macleay Trail.

1.93   Turn left on Wildwood Trail.

2.04   Junction with Macleay Trail on right. Go to the left, remaining on Wildwood.

2.14   Turn right on Cumberland Trail.

2.38   Turn left on Tunnel Trail, just before a bridge.

2.55   Junction with NW Cornell Road. Cross Cornell and walk behind tunnel. Stay on Cornell Road until it makes a V at a No Outlet sign.

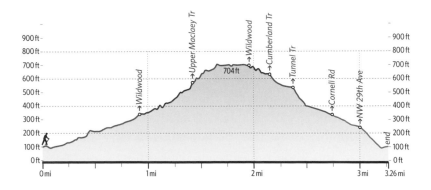

2.85 Turn left at the V, at the No Outlet sign.

2.89 Turn right on NW 30th Avenue.

2.93 Turn right on NW Quimby Street.

3.02 Turn left on NW 29th Avenue. Continue on 29th for four blocks. After passing Thurman St. the road becomes a pedestrian trail.

3.20 Turn left on NW Upshur Street.

3.26 End at Lower Macleay Park Trailhead.

One of the most scenic trails in Forest Park, Lower Macleay Trail is a magnificent introduction to all the natural beauty of the park. It boasts rushing streams and giant primordial trees, and is easily accessible to persons traveling by car or bus. The trail is a good example of the Pacific Northwest's Western Hemlock Zone, considered by scientists as unique among all temperate forests in the world. In addition, the full loop offers a chance to experience the richness of the Balch Creek Watershed. Balch Creek, with its natural qualities exceptionally intact, is considered as one of the highest valued resource areas in the city of Portland.

To reach the trailhead from downtown Portland, drive north on NW 23rd Avenue until reaching NW Thurman Street. Turn left on Thurman. After five blocks, Thurman intersects with NW 28th Avenue. Turn right on 28th Avenue, and continue for one block to NW Upshur. Turn left on Upshur, and stay on the street (crossing 29th at the stop sign) until Upshur dead ends at the Lower Macleay Park headquarters. There are several picnic tables and restrooms available at the trailhead.

Begin the hike at the entrance to Lower Macleay Trail, located in Macleay Park. Macleay Park was named for Donald Macleay, banker and civic leader, who in 1887 donated 105 acres of land to the City of Portland for a park. The land still retains the same name although it has been incorporated into Forest Park. The hike begins as a paved path that passes under the Thurman Street Bridge and follows alongside Balch Creek. At the start of the hike, the creek can be seen dropping approximately forty feet to enter a large underground storm sewer. This sewer runs through the Northwest industrial area of Portland and eventually leads to the Willamette River, where the

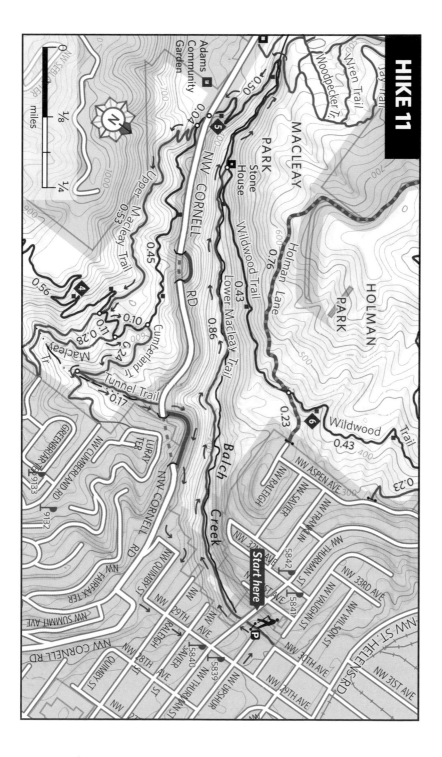

HIKE 11

Adams Community Garden

MACLEAY PARK

Stone House

HOLMAN PARK

Jay Trail

Wren Trail

Woodpecker Tr.

Holman Lane

Wildwood Trail

Lower Macleay Trail

Upper Macleay Trail

Macleay Tr.

Tunnel Trail

Cumberland Tr.

NW CORNELL RD

NW CORNELL RD

Balch Creek

Wildwood

Trail

0.50
0.04
0.53
0.45
0.56
0.10
0.28
0.11
0.24
0.17
0.76
0.43
0.86
0.23
0.43
0.23

NW SEVIER TER

700
1000
900
600
700
600
500
400
300
0

miles
0 1/8 1/4

N

5
4
6

NW SEVIER AVE
NW RALEIGH
NW FRANKLIN
NW THURMAN ST
NW 31ST AVE
NW 33RD AVE
NW VAUGHN ST
NW WILSON ST
NW ST HELENS RD
NW UPSHUR ST
NW 30TH AVE
NW 29TH AVE
NW 31ST AVE
NW ASPEN AVE
NW RALEIGH
5842
5841
Start here
P
5840
5839
NW SEVIER AVE
NW THURMAN ST
NW RALEIGH ST
NW 29TH AVE
NW QUIMBY ST
NW SUMMIT AVE
NW FAIRFAX TER
NW CUMBERLAND RD
GREENBRIAR TER
9133
9132
LURAY TER
NW CORNELL RD
NW QUIMBY ST
NW 28TH
NW 29TH

Hike Eleven

143

water is discharged. A prominent wooden structure over the water is visible at this point; it is a trash rack built to catch debris from entering the storm sewer.

Balch Creek is Forest Park's largest creek. At some times of the year, especially in winter, the creek can become a surging stream, and home to a fascinating bird known as an American Dipper.

> The American Dipper is a small, slate-gray, rapids-loving bird that is easily identified by its loud, melodic song ringing above a rushing stream and its characteristic habit of bobbing up and down on creek-side rocks. Dippers prefer fast-moving, clear, unpolluted creeks and scientists believe that their presence reflects healthy river ecosystems and good water quality. The birds also display an astonishing talent: they are acquatic. In their search for larval invertebrates and fish, dippers can be observed actually standing underwater!

Lower Macleay Trail gently winds up Balch Creek Canyon, crossing over several footbridges and passing by massive Douglas fir trees. The area manifests the three characteristic features of older coniferous forests: large snags, downed logs across the creek, and huge individual trees, including some giant old-growth specimens. At 0.86 mile, Lower Macleay Trail ends at a well-marked junction with Wildwood Trail, Milepost 5½. At this location, the remains of an unusual, significant stone structure stand prominently.

Constructed in 1936, the stone house was erected during the Works Progress Administration (WPA) era under President Franklin D. Roosevelt. Skilled artisans and craftsmen idled by the Depression were put to work designing public buildings across the country during this period. Before it fell into disrepair, the structure along Lower Macleay Trail was a beautiful example of fine stonework. The purpose of the building, while not illustrious, was yet functional. It was created to be used as a public restroom.

Continue upstream on Wildwood Trail as it follows Balch Creek. Prominent old-growth trees adorn the path and highly visible outcroppings of Columbia River basalt can be seen along the creek walls. After crossing a footbridge at Milepost 5¼, Wildwood Trail leaves the

"Timberline Lodge is not the only work of art in our vicinity to come out of the Works Progress Administration (WPA) era. The comfort station in Lower Macleay Park was constructed during the same period ... Observing the meticulous way in which the stones are fitted, no one who studies this picturesque ruin can doubt that the workmanship was of the highest caliber. ... Once upon a time, it was the handsomest comfort station in the land."

—Marvin Witt, Architect

creek and immediately begins to gain elevation as it switchbacks up to NW Cornell Road. The trail intersects Cornell Road near Milepost 5 (located at a parking area). Adjacent is a picnic area with tables, providing a place to stop for a water break. Located 300 yards west of this spot is the headquarters of the Audubon Society of Portland. A trip to its nature center, excellent bookstore, and adjoining three wildlife sanctuaries is highly recommended.

For a short hike that does not include walking along busy Cornell Road, turn around here and retrace steps to return to the Lower Macleay Trailhead. To make the full loop, however, continue hiking on Wildwood as it follows next to a wooden fence. After a short distance, cross Cornell Road at the crosswalk and continue hiking on the uphill portion of Wildwood Trail.

After 100 yards, Wildwood Trail intersects Upper Macleay Trail. Turn right onto Upper Macleay Trail and follow it as it parallels Cornell Road and Wildwood Trail from above. Along the route, keep a lookout for all four of the major native ferns that grow plentifully in Forest Park (photos page 48): sword fern, lady fern, licorice fern, and delicate maidenhair fern. Through the trees, fine views of the Balch Creek ravine can be seen across the road. Upper Macleay intersects once again with Wildwood Trail after a half mile. Leave Upper Macleay Trail at this point and turn left onto Wildwood Trail. (Upper Macleay continues for 0.28 mile to end at a residential area.) Continue downhill on Wildwood. The trail passes Macleay Trail, which takes off to the right, after 0.15 mile. The junction is a little confusing; be sure to stay left on Wildwood. Wildwood Trail intersects Cumberland Trail in 0.12 mile. Turn right on Cumberland Trail. Along this pathway is a bench honoring well-known architect Pietro Belluschi, who died in 1994 at ninety-five years of age. Belluschi loved the outdoors, as reflected by his quote on the bench's inscription, *We never could design a building as beautiful as the trees.*

Cumberland Trail intersects Tunnel Trail after 0.24 mile just before a bridge crossing. Turn left onto Tunnel Trail and walk down the short but steep and often slick path that follows Pittock Creek, a tributary to Balch Creek. Tunnel Trail ends at NW Cornell Road.

For the remainder of the loop, the hike leaves Forest Park and continues on city streets for a half mile. Carefully cross Cornell Road after exiting Tunnel Trail, and connect with an unnamed trail that goes safely behind the tunnel. The path comes out again on the other side of the tunnel along Cornell Road. Continue to walk down the shoulder of Cornell, being mindful of traffic, which can be busy at rush hour. At a V intersection past the tunnel, make a sharp left. This road is marked with a No Outlet sign. Follow the road to NW 30th Street. Turn right on 30th and walk to its intersection with NW Quimby Street, one block ahead. Turn right on Quimby then left at 29th Street. Continue on 29th for four blocks, crossing Raleigh, Savier, and Thurman streets. (29th becomes a pedestrian-only footpath after crossing Thurman.) At the intersection of 29th with Upshur Street, turn left onto Upshur. Continue walking one block more to the Upshur Parking Area in Lower Macleay Park, which completes the loop.

Wild Cherry Trail, Leif Erikson Drive, Dogwood Trail, and Wildwood Trail Loop

DISTANCE: 2.7 miles
HIKING TIME: 1 to 1½ hours
LOW ELEVATION: 386 feet
HIGH ELEVATION: 862 feet
CUMULATIVE ELEVATION GAIN: 454 feet
DIFFICULTY RATING: Moderate
GPS COORDINATES: 45° 32' 18.99" N 122° 44' 2.82" W
    520758mE 5042820mN
Foot traffic only on Wild Cherry Trail, Wildwood Trail, and Dogwood Trail. Leif Erikson Drive is also open to both bicycles and horses.

MILEAGE AND DIRECTIONS

0.00   Begin at Wild Cherry Trailhead on NW 53rd Drive. Hike Wild Cherry Trail.
0.87   Turn left onto Leif Erikson.
1.46   Turn left on Dogwood.
1.80   Turn left onto Wildwood Trail.
2.39   Turn right on Wild Cherry.
2.70   End at Wild Cherry Trailhead.

For an easily accessible, short walk, the Wild Cherry—Leif Erikson—Wildwood Trail loop is one of the nicest in Forest Park. Young children might find these trails an excellent introduction to the joys of hiking. Others will appreciate its more open woods, where native shrubs and wildflowers can be readily observed. Not far from the center of the city, these trails yet impart quiet, naturalness, and beauty. Here, the bustling urban area seems to fade away.

To reach the trailhead, follow NW Lovejoy Street from NW 23rd (Lovejoy will become NW Cornell Road), for a total of 2.2 miles, passing through two tunnels and, on the right, the Audubon Society of Portland. Turn right on NW 53rd Drive and follow the road uphill for 0.9 mile to a large parking area on the right.

Dogwood and Wild Cherry trails are joined at the start. Walk approximately fifty yards then turn right at the entrance to Wild Cherry Trail, which is marked with a sign.

Wild Cherry Trail starts off down a slight grade, which it maintains for most of its 0.87-mile length. The trees along the trail are predominantly red alder and bigleaf maple intermixed with many second-growth Douglas firs, some reaching very large and impressive proportions. Native plants grow thickly in the understory, and varieties of sparrows, wrens, nuthatches, kinglets, and other native songbirds can be heard calling from the woods as one follows the pleasing footpath.

Forest Park is unique among the nation's city parks in that it is a true natural area. In spite of its proximity to a major metropolis, it yet remains a genuine representative of a Douglas fir forest ecosystem and provides a place for people to learn about and experience indigenous plants and wildlife. This value continues to be one of Forest Park's most important features—a fact recognized in the park's management philosophy since the park's creation:

"The objectives stated in the 1947 City Club report are not so different from those of today. Our goals are still to provide passive outdoor recreation, to encourage diversity of flora and thereby the wildlife, and to continue to provide educational opportunities in this beautiful urban wilderness."

—Fred Nilsen, Forest Park Arboriculturist, from 1986 to 2008

Continue hiking Wild Cherry Trail for 0.31 mile until it intersects with Wildwood Trail. At this point, if desiring a gentler, shorter (1.56 mile) hike that omits the steeper and potentially slippery parts of the loop, turn left on Wildwood Trail. Then, after 0.6 mile, just before Milepost 8½, turn left on Dogwood Trail. Walk up the pathway a half mile more to return to the trailhead.

To make the longer loop, cross Wildwood Trail (taking a short jog to the right) and begin hiking the lower section of Wild Cherry

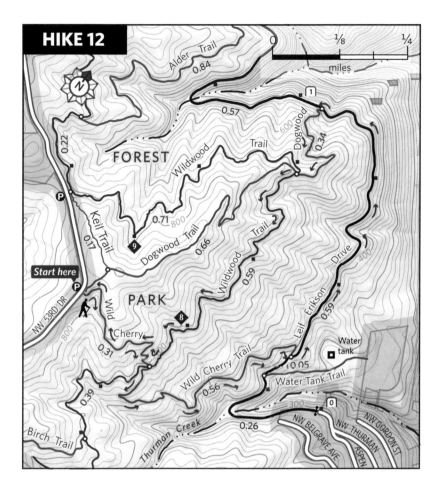

HIKE 12

Alder Trail 0.84

1/8 1/4

miles

0.57

1

Dogwood

0.34

600

0.22

FOREST

Wildwood   Trail

Keil Trail

0.17

0.71 800

9

Dogwood Trail

0.66

Wildwood   Trail

0.59

Leif Erikson   Drive

400

0.59

Start here

P

NW 53RD DR

800

PARK

Wild

8

Cherry

0.31

Wild Cherry Trail

Water
tank

0.05

Water Tank Trail

0.56

300

0

0.39

Thurmon Creek

0.26

NW BELGRAVE AVE

NW THURMAN

ASPEN

NW GORDON ST

Birch Trail

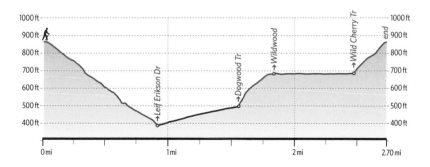

1000 ft
900 ft
800 ft
700 ft
600 ft
500 ft
400 ft

→ Leif Erikson Dr
→ Dogwood Tr
→ Wildwood
→ Wild Cherry Tr
end

1000 ft
900 ft
800 ft
700 ft
600 ft
500 ft
400 ft

0 mi   1 mi   2 mi   2.70 mi

Trail towards Leif Erikson Drive. The destructive weed, English ivy, appears on these lower reaches, and is being constantly battled by the Portland Park Bureau and by scores of volunteers. While a massive and never-ending undertaking, the hard work pays off in returning degraded parts of the park to healthier conditions.

> The key plants of Forest Park are not difficult to learn. Along the trails, try to pick out three common plants that grow abundantly and year round:
>
> SWORD FERN (photo page 48). This most common fern is plentiful on most hillsides in Forest Park. Its fern leaflets stand erect up to four feet tall and in luxuriant, showy clumps, growing almost like a bunch grass.
>
> OREGON GRAPE (photo page 55). Another widespread shrub, its leaves resemble those of holly. In spring, the plants sport clusters of bright yellow flowers. Later, its purplish-blue berries, looking like little grapes, are easily visible.
>
> SALAL (photo page 55). An attractive evergreen shrub with thick, oval, almost leathery leaves. The plant in Forest Park grows from one to three feet high, and can create a dense ground cover. The fruit is a small, purplish-black berry.

After a half mile, Wild Cherry ends at Leif Erikson Drive. At this intersection, turn left (north) on Leif Erikson and hike along the wide, level, paved road, which is closed to all motorized vehicles except those on official park business. Be aware that bicycles sometimes come speeding down Leif Erikson on the lower sections of the road near Thurman Street. For this reason, it is prudent to keep to the right when hiking north on the road.

Stay on Leif Erikson Drive for slightly over a half mile. Views of the Willamette River, the city of Portland, and snow-capped mountains are visible through the trees. At the ½ Milepost white marker on Leif Erikson, the pavement ends; the remainder of the road is a combination of gravel and dirt surface.

Leif Erikson Drive intersects Dogwood Trail coming in from the left. Turn left on Dogwood Trail, which rises, sometimes sharply, for 0.34 mile until it is intersected by Wildwood Trail. At this junction, turn left (south) on Wildwood Trail. This section of Wildwood is a level, well-maintained trail. Following a steady 700-foot elevation, it curves among numerous ravines that meander through the Thurman Creek Watershed. After a half mile, Wild Cherry Trail again intersects Wildwood Trail. Turn right onto Wild Cherry and proceed up the hill to return to the trailhead and finish the loop.

Dogwood Trail, Leif Erikson Drive, Alder Trail, Wildwood Trail, and Keil Trail Loop

DISTANCE: 2.92 miles round trip
HIKING TIME: 1½ hours
LOW ELEVATION: 494 feet
HIGH ELEVATION: 903 feet
CUMULATIVE ELEVATION GAIN: 389 feet
DIFFICULTY RATING: Moderate
GPS COORDINATES: 45° 32' 18.99" N 122° 44' 2.82" W
    520758mE 5042820mN

Foot traffic only on Dogwood Trail and Alder Trail. Leif Erikson also allows both bicycles and horses.

MILEAGE AND DIRECTIONS

0.00 Begin at Dogwood Trail Trailhead at NW 53rd Drive.
0.06 Hike Dogwood Trail.
0.72 Cross Wildwood Trail. Continue on Dogwood.
1.06 Turn left on Leif Erikson Drive.
1.63 Turn left onto Alder Trail.
2.47 Turn left on Wildwood.
2.69 Turn right on Keil Trail.
2.86 Turn right at Dogwood/Wild Cherry trail junction.
2.92 End at NW 53rd Drive.

This relatively easy loop close to town is perfect for an early morning walk on a sunny day. In fall, the trails are especially scenic, owing to the predominance of deciduous trees with their colorful, changing leaves. For most of its way, the route weaves through open groves of maple and alder, interspersed with vigorous, tall Douglas firs. The more open sections provide a chance to observe a chattering chickaree, a wild black-tailed deer, or perhaps even a rare goldback fern—ample rewards for this short, well-maintained loop trip.

To reach the trailhead, travel on NW Lovejoy Street from NW 23rd Avenue (Lovejoy becomes NW Cornell Road just after NW 25th) and drive 2.2 miles. Turn right on NW 53rd Drive and continue for 0.9 mile further, to a large parking area along the side of the road.

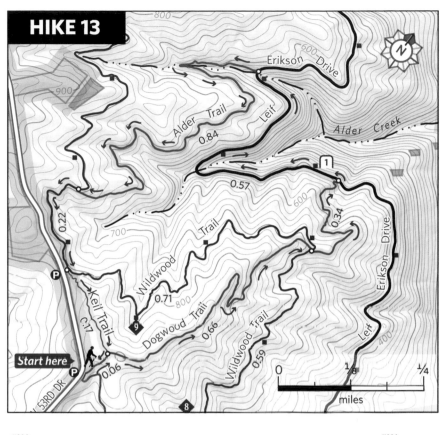

HIKE 13

Map labels:
800
900
Erikson Drive
600 Drive
Alder Trail
Leif
Alder Creek
0.84
0.57
1
0.22
600
0.34
700
Wildwood Trail
Erikson Drive
0.71
800
9
Dogwood Trail
0.66
Wildwood Trail
Leif
400
Keil Trail
0.17
0.59
Start here
P
P
0.06
NW 53RD DR
8
N
0   1/8   1/4
miles

Elevation profile labels:
1100 ft
1000 ft
900 ft
800 ft
700 ft
600 ft
500 ft
903 ft
→Leif Erikson Dr
→Alder Tr
→Wildwood
→Keil Tr
end
0 mi
1 mi
2 mi
2.92 mi

Dogwood and Wild Cherry trails are joined at the start. After 50 yards, they split. At this spot there is a plaque dedicated to the memory of Larry Mauritz, who loved this trail. Its inscription captures the sentiments of what many feel about Forest Park: *Here rest your wings when they are weary. Here lodge as in a sanctuary.*

Turn left and begin hiking on Dogwood Trail. Soon the trail turns sharply right and climbs up through the forest. For years, the viewpoint from this hill was known as "Inspiration Point" as it revealed panoramas of the Willamette River and the city of Portland. With the growth of trees through the decades, however, today the site is almost unidentifable. Dogwood Trail dips down after the rise and gradually begins a descent that it maintains for its length.

After a half mile, Dogwood Trail intersects Wildwood Trail; continue downhill on lower Dogwood, which becomes more steep after this junction. As the trail nears Leif Erikson Drive, it twists along several switchbacks that can be slippery in wet conditions and, in dry times, equally slick owing to a layer of small gravel atop the hard dirt surface. At the intersection of Dogwood Trail with Leif Erikson Drive, turn left and begin hiking north.

At many locations along Leif Erikson Drive look for well-defined outcroppings of Columbia River basalt. Several species of plants thrive in the cracks of the rock, notably licorice fern, sword fern, and, more rarely, goldback fern—a delicate plant that can be identified by

Dogwood Trail was originally named for a patch of wild, native Pacific dogwood trees that was discovered growing along a portion of the pathway. Many of those trees are gone, but others occur sporadically throughout Forest Park. In spring, dogwood's showy white blossoms are unmistakable. How the tree came by its name, however, is more debatable. One theory is that its bright red fruit was considered so disagreeable in taste that it was deemed unfit for even a dog to eat. Another explanation is that the name is derived from the Spanish word *daga*, meaning dagger. Historically, the wood of the dogwood tree was used to make pointed instruments including skewers for butchers.

its small triangular fronds, green above but with spores resembling flecks of gold underneath.

At Leif Erikson Milepost 1½, Alder Trail intersects the road, coming in from above and to the left. Turn left on Alder Trail and follow it as it ascends the canyon, sometimes at a moderate pitch. Alder Trail is aptly named—red alder trees are abundant throughout and grow interspersed with bigleaf maples. These two deciduous trees are easy to differentiate. The leaves of alder (photo page 53) resemble those of an aspen, while the shape of maple leaves (photo page 53) resembles a spreading hand. The bark of red alder is smooth and gray, with light horizontal markings and usually is covered with lichens. Trunks of bigleaf maple are not smooth; they have long, vertical furrows in their bark and often have noticeable growths of green licorice fern sprouting from them. A whiff of the root of a licorice fern can make one easily understand where the fern's name comes from; it has a decided smell of anise.

The last hundred yards of Alder Trail are steep. After 0.84 mile, Alder Trail intersects Wildwood Trail. Turn left on Wildwood Trail and continue 0.22 mile to an intersection with Keil Trail, entering on the right.

Keil Trail is named for William "Bill" Keil, who was Forest Park Forester from 1952 to 1956. Keil was instrumental in developing a fire protection plan for the forest and helped create all the firelanes that run throughout the park. He also coordinated numerous tree plantings in areas devastated by the 1951 Bonny Slope burn. Next to the old Inspiration Point are some fine examples of large Port Orford cedars that Keil planted nearly sixty years ago. One of the original members of the Forest Park Committee of Fifty, he remained an integral member of that Board of Directors for decades. Today, Keil still works to advocate for Forest Park.

Continue on Keil Trail for 0.17 mile and merge right onto Dogwood Trail for 0.07 mile to return to the parking area and complete the loop.

Wildwood Trail, Chestnut Trail, and Nature Trail Loop

DISTANCE: 3.48 miles round trip

HIKING TIME: 1½ hours

LOW ELEVATION: 550 feet

HIGH ELEVATION: 984 feet

CUMULATIVE ELEVATION GAIN: 502 feet

DIFFICULTY RATING: Moderate

GPS COORDINATES: 45° 32' 53.19" N 122° 44' 41.94" W
    519907mE 5043873mN

Foot traffic only.

MILEAGE AND DIRECTIONS

0.00   Begin at the Firelane 1 Trailhead at the gated parking area off Forest Lane.

0.33   Wildwood Trail intersects Firelane 1. Turn left on Wildwood Trail.

0.95   Intersect Nature Trail. Stay on Wildwood.

1.28   Turn right onto Chestnut Trail.

1.77   Turn right on Leif Erikson Drive.

1.80   Turn right on Nature Trail.

2.73   Intersection with Firelane 1. Turn right.

2.80   Turn left on Wildwood Trail.

3.32   Turn right on Morak Trail.

3.40   Turn left on Firelane 1.

3.48   End at Firelane 1 Parking Area.

This peaceful medley of well-maintained trails offers beauty, solitude, and natural features of educational value in a relatively gentle terrain. All the trails lie north of Firelane 1 within picturesque Rocking Chair Creek Canyon, named for a lone rocking chair discovered long ago sitting in the middle of the stream at the bottom of the ravine.

To reach the trailhead, drive from NW 23rd Avenue along NW Lovejoy Street, which becomes NW Cornell Road after NW 25th. Continue for 2.2 miles on NW Cornell Road, then turn right onto NW 53rd Drive for 1.7 miles. Turn right again on NW Forest Lane

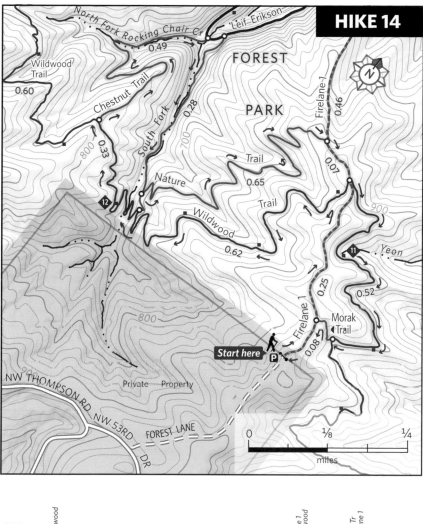

HIKE 14

FOREST

PARK

North Fork Rocking Chair Cr   'Leif Erikson
0.49

Wildwood
Trail
0.60

Chestnut Trail

South Fork

0.28

700

800

0.33

12

Firelane 1

0.46

0.07

900

Trail
0.65

Nature

Wildwood

Trail

0.62

11   Yeon

0.25

0.52

800

Morak
Trail

Firelane 1

Start here   P

0.08

NW THOMPSON RD
NW 53RD
DR   FOREST LANE

Private   Property

0   ⅛   ¼

miles

1200 ft — Wildwood — Chestnut Tr — Leif Erikson Dr — Nature Tr — Firelane 1 — Wildwood — Morak Tr — Firelane 1 end — 1200 ft
1000 ft   1000 ft
900 ft   984 ft   900 ft
800 ft   800 ft
700 ft   700 ft
600 ft   600 ft
500 ft   500 ft
0 mi   1 mi   2 mi   3 mi   3.43 mi

(Firelane 1), which is marked by a sign; continue until the road ends at a park gate.

To begin the loop, hike Firelane 1 for 0.33 mile to reach the Wildwood trailhead. At this junction, turn left (north) onto Wildwood Trail (Milepost 11¼). The trail gently descends into a forested canyon. Notice the pistol-butted Douglas firs along the way. The lower part of the trunks of these trees is curved like the grip of a pistol. This phenomenon is the result of earth slides that occurred when the trees were young, forcing them to angle downhill. In an effort to reach out for sunlight, the trees compensated by growing upward. Pistol-butted trees are commonly observed in Forest Park and in most Douglas fir forests of western Oregon wherever there are steep, moist ravines.

Beyond Milepost 11¾, a side trail coming in from the right adjoins Wildwood. This is a tie trail leading to Nature Trail. For a shorter hike, leave Wildwood at this point and proceed right on the tie trail, then right again on Nature Trail, which loops back 1 mile to the parking area. For the main loop, however, continue on Wildwood Trail. At the bottom of the ravine, cross South Fork Rocking Chair Creek, where many young hemlock trees are thriving—growing out of the remnants of old Douglas fir stumps.

Throughout the length of Wildwood Trail, many fallen logs or remnants of Douglas fir trees can be observed. Many of these old stumps act as "nurses" for new trees. Western hemlock trees, in particular, have difficulty seeding themselves directly on the matted forest floor. The bare top of a fallen log or tree stump in its early stages of decay, however, teeming with nutrients and decomposing humus made from the decay of twigs and needles falling from above, create a perfect bed on which tree seedlings can begin to grow.

After passing over the creek, continue uphill on Wildwood Trail for 0.5 mile. Beyond Milepost 12, Chestnut Trail joins Wildwood from the right. Turn right onto Chestnut Trail and descend a narrowing canyon along several switchbacks. Part way down the ravine, the path parallels North Fork Rocking Chair Creek, an exceptionally pretty stream. Pronounced exposures of Columbia River basalt are visible along the walls of the stream.

In 0.34 mile, Chestnut Trail ends at Leif Erikson Drive. A large American chestnut tree grows at the junction and generously drapes over a new park bench. This tree was planted in the early 1950s by conservationist and forester Fred Cleator and is the namesake of Chestnut Trail.

> Forest Park is fortunate to have a mature representative of this splendid tree that once dominated the hardwood forests of the eastern United States. Historically, American chestnuts were believed to total over three billion in number, and made up 25 percent of the trees in the Appalachian Mountains. Valued for their superb straight-grain and hard wood, highly resistant to decay, they were a premier timber tree. They were also very important to wildlife: their delicious nuts were a primary food source for white-tailed deer, wild turkeys, and the now extinct passenger pigeon. Today, however, because of a devastating blight accidentally introduced into North America in 1904, these trees have been wiped out of the eastern US. Within their former range, less than a hundred are thought to remain. Some surviving large specimens, like this one at the end of Chestnut Trail, can be found in western North America—a region still free from the chestnut blight.

At this intersection of Chestnut Trail with Leif Erikson, turn right. Walk on the road for a few hundred feet then turn right again onto Nature Trail. Proceed uphill on Nature Trail and notice almost immediately Rocking Chair Dam, a small drainage retention structure at the bottom of Rocking Chair Creek. In late fall and winter, the often muddy, grass-covered sediment behind the dam is an excellent place to look for tracks, especially those of raccoon, black-tailed deer, coyote, and perhaps even bobcat.

Continue on Nature Trail, which follows South Fork Rocking Chair Creek and passes over several footbridges. While hiking uphill, notice the native shrubs that commonly line the Forest Park trails. Thimbleberry, salmonberry, and osoberry (Indian plum) are native denizens of western Oregon coniferous forests and can often be found where the ground is moist. Nature Trail ends at a grassy meadow next to Firelane 1 after 1 mile. New park benches and several inviting picnic tables make this open area a welcome spot to relax and perhaps enjoy a picnic.

At this junction, turn left (south) onto Wildwood Trail. Here, Wildwood enters the Willbridge Watershed. The woods are open and overwhelmingly dominated by alder trees interspersed with young conifers. At Milepost 11, Wildwood crosses Yeon Creek, an intermittent stream within a steep canyon. A quarter-mile further, the trail enters the Alder Creek Watershed, where fine views stretch out to the southeast.

Past Milepost 10¾, Wildwood Trail is intersected by Morak Trail. This short, winding path connects to upper Firelane 1.

Morak Trail is named after volunteer Robert Morak, who almost single-handedly built this trail and has given to Forest Park in many other ways as well. Morak's most visible contribution is the wooden signage denoting all the trails within Forest Park. For years, he has painted and continues to paint all the signs that help guide visitors traveling through the forest. Morak is one of the many dedicated volunteers who has donated his time and talent to protect, augment, and improve Forest Park. Quietly behind the scenes, these devoted men and women have worked in countless ways for the park's benefit—making signs, building and maintaining trails, eradicating ivy, and giving money to purchase threatened inholdings. Without their tireless advocacy, the park would not be what it is today.

Turn right onto Morak Trail. At the junction with Firelane 1, turn left for 0.08 mile to return to the parking area, completing the loop.

Maple Trail and Wildwood Trail Loop

DISTANCE: 8.35 miles round trip. (Can be broken up into smaller trips.)

HIKING TIME: 4 to 4 ½ hours

LOW ELEVATION: 213 feet

HIGH ELEVATION: 897 feet

CUMULATIVE ELEVATION GAIN: 882 feet

DIFFICULTY RATING: Moderate

GPS COORDINATES: 45° 33' 50.96" N 122° 45' 0.92" W
    519490mE 5045654mN

Foot traffic only on Maple and Wildwood trails. Saltzman and Leif Erikson roads are also open to bicycles and horses.

MILEAGE AND DIRECTIONS

0.00   Begin at Lower Saltzman Road Trailhead off Highway 30. Hike Saltzman Road.

0.45   At intersection with Maple Trail, turn left on Maple Trail.

0.93   Cross Firelane 4. Stay on Maple.

1.52   Cross Koenig Trail. Stay on Maple.

1.90   Cross Leif Erikson Drive. Continue on Maple.

2.26   Tie trail to Wildwood. Stay on Maple Trail.

2.76   Maple intersects Wildwood Trail. Turn right on Wildwood.

3.57   Firelane 3 intersection. Stay on Wildwood.

4.15   Koenig Trail intersection.

5.39   Intersection with Cleator Trail.

5.89   Wildwood intersects Saltzman Road. Turn right on Saltzman Road.

6.39   Turn left on Leif Erikson.

6.62   Turn right on Maple Trail.

7.90   Turn left on Saltzman Road.

8.35   Hike ends at Lower Saltzman Road Trailhead.

Maple Trail is one of the most scenic and, in parts, serene of all pathways in Forest Park. Its glory is especially apparent in fall when its abundance of bigleaf maples shimmers with colorful, sunny highlights against the dark green of the tall, straight firs and hemlocks. A quiet hike deep within the park, Maple Trail imparts a peaceful remoteness exceedingly rare in any major city. This combination loop of Maple and Wildwood trails offers some of the finest woodland hiking experiences in all of Forest Park.

To reach the trailhead, drive west on U.S. Highway 30 (St. Helens Road) 5.3 miles from the intersection with Interstate 405. Look for NW Saltzman Road on the left. Turn left onto Saltzman and drive the paved, winding road 0.7 mile to a locked park gate. Parking is available along the road.

Begin the hike by walking approximately a half mile up Saltzman Road. From the gate on, the road is closed to all motorized traffic except park and emergency vehicles. To the right (north) notice steep Maple Creek Canyon, which is part of Doane Creek watershed. Maple Creek, far below, drains eventually into Doane Lake, east of Highway 30. At the intersection of Saltzman Road with Maple Trail, turn left onto the southern portion of Maple Trail.

At first, Maple Trail heads gradually uphill. Soon it begins to level out and wanders among spacious, open groves of red alder and bigleaf maples with an understory dominated by low-growing sword ferns. In spots, one hundred-year-old Douglas firs can be seen towering above the maples and alder. Growing in the shade beneath the canopy are vigorous grand fir, western red cedar, and western hemlock trees. If left undisturbed, these native conifers will replace the shorter-lived maples within the next one hundred years.

Maple Trail crosses Firelane 4 after a half mile and passes underneath transmission lines. This is the dividing line between Doane Creek and Saltzman Creek watersheds. Presently, Firelane 4 is a little-used, primitive path. To the right, the firelane climbs for 0.21 mile to Leif Erikson Drive. To the left, it leads to the Saltzman Road Parking Area, a quarter of a mile below.

For an exploratory side trip, turn left and follow Firelane 4 up a relatively steep hill for 0.08 mile. At the top, when the leaves are off the trees, there is a broad view of the Willamette and Columbia rivers, mountain peaks, bridges, the city, and the industrial area. Beyond the overlook, Firelane 4 drops down precipitously, following under two sets of powerlines on a wide ridge separating two major canyons— Maple Creek Canyon to the north and Saltzman Creek Canyon to the

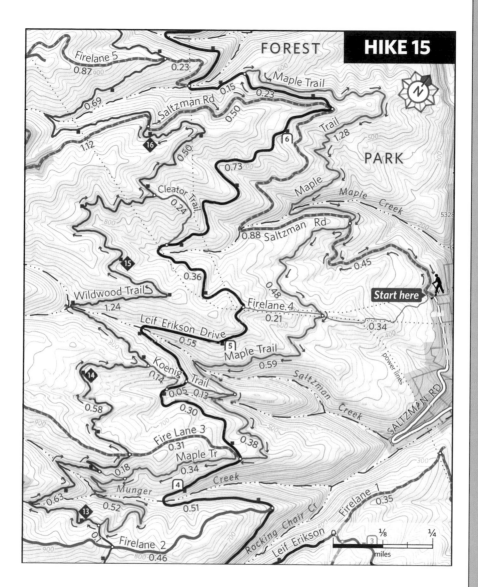

FOREST

PARK

Firelane 5
0.87
0.23
0.69
Maple Trail
0.15
0.23
Saltzman Rd
0.50
1.12
16
0.50
Trail
1.28
0.73
Maple
Maple Creek
5328
Cleator Trail
0.24
0.88 Saltzman Rd
0.45
15
0.36
Wildwood Trail
1.24
Leif Erikson Drive
0.55
0.48
Firelane 4
0.21
Start here
0.34
5
Maple Trail
0.59
Koenig Trail
0.74
Saltzman
14
0.05 0.13
0.58
0.30
Creek
SALTZMAN RD
power lines
0.38
Fire Lane 3
0.31
Maple Tr
0.34
0.18
4
Creek
Munger
0.63
0.52
0.51
Firelane 1
0.35
13
Rocking Chair Ct
Leif Erikson
Firelane 2
0.46
3
⅛
¼
miles

1200 ft
1000 ft
800 ft
600 ft
400 ft
200 ft
0 ft

Maple Tr
Wildwood
Saltzman Rd
897 ft
Leif Erikson Dr
Maple Tr
Saltzman Rd
end

1200 ft
1000 ft
800 ft
600 ft
400 ft
200 ft
0 ft

0 mi   1 mi   2 mi   3 mi   4 mi   5 mi   6 mi   7 mi   8   8.35 mi

south. Keep an eye out for deer tracks in the mud. Look too for native Anna's and Rufous Hummingbirds that in spring seek the bright blooms of red-flowering currant bushes. In late fall, over-wintering Sandhill Cranes can often be heard calling plaintively in the distance.

Continue the loop by crossing Firelane 4 and heading south on Maple Trail. Soon the trail enters one of the loveliest sections of central Forest Park, and introduces the hiker to the rugged Saltzman Creek Watershed. The narrow woodland path drops down into a pristine canyon of cedar and hemlock and crosses Saltzman Creek on a footbridge. Verdant moss drapes from the trees and sprightly Oregon oxalis plants cover the forest floor like green shamrocks. As the trail proceeds up the slopes of the ravine, Maple Trail intersects with Koenig Trail. Stay on Maple Trail, which soon leads to a second rustic bridge, crossing another tributary to Saltzman Creek.

Eventually, groves of cedars and hemlocks blend into maples, and the footpath becomes more open, with thick understories of sword fern, Oregon grape, salal, thimbleberry, and red-elderberry shrubs. At the intersection of Maple Trail and Leif Erikson Drive, cross Leif Erikson and continue on Maple Trail. Firelane 3 also intersects Leif Erikson at this point—immediately to the right (north) of Maple Trail. Continue on Maple Trail as it crosses Leif Erikson Drive and Firelane 3.

This continuation of Maple Trail ascends gently but steadily, while following the hillsides of Saltzman Creek Watershed. At 2¼ miles, a tie trail to Wildwood intersects Maple Trail. Unless desiring a shorter route, disregard the tie trail and stay on Maple Trail for a half mile more. The trail begins a descent, via several switchbacks, into the canyon, and crosses Munger Creek. It then climbs back out of the ravine to join Wildwood Trail, just before Wildwood Milepost 13.

At this junction, turn right (north) on Wildwood Trail. For the next 3 miles, the trail continues its serpentine path as it winds along hillsides and ravines and crosses several creeks. Along the way, numerous native birds can often be spotted at different times of the year, including Western Tanagers, Red-breasted Nuthatches, Winter

Wrens, Chestnut-backed Chickadees, Golden-crowned Kinglets, and Ravens.

Immediately before Milepost 14¼, Koenig Trail intersects Wildwood on the right.

Koenig Trail was named for a volunteer who in the history of Forest Park had no equal. Fran Koenig (1912–2008) devoted over sixty years and immeasurable hours to his beloved park. He first discovered the area in 1942 and since that time contributed to the park in countless ways. For over twenty years he led weekly hikes throughout the park, sponsored by the Park Bureau. His greatest legacy, however, is the signage of the trails in Forest Park, in particular, Wildwood Trail. Koenig devised an ingenious measuring wheel outfitted with a tire to navigate rough terrain to compute trail lengths. The precision of this device was unprecedented. Koenig marked his wheel with red lines to indicate 1/1,000 mile! From his excellent calculations, he helped create and later display the blue diamond signage found at every quarter mile along Wildwood Trail. Until his death at age ninety-six, Koenig could be found almost daily hiking the park and helping others to understand how precious this resource was to him and to all who explore its trails.

At Milepost 14½, Wildwood Trail crosses over Saltzman Creek on a rustic footbridge and, at Milepost 15, crosses Maple Creek on a second bridge. Just before Milepost 15½, Wildwood intersects Cleator Trail. At Milepost 16, the trail drops down to intersect NW Saltzman Road.

Leave Wildwood Trail at this point and turn right onto Saltzman Road. Stay on the road for a half mile until its intersection with Leif Erikson Drive, where there is a viewpoint overlooking the historic St. John's Bridge, Rivergate Industrial Area, and the confluence of the Willamette and Columbia rivers.

At the junction, turn left sharply onto Leif Erikson Drive, and head downhill. Around the first corner of Leif Erikson Drive is a white concrete milepost marker denoting 6¼ miles. Continue north on Leif

Erikson for a quarter-mile until a sign, located in a clearing to the right, demarcates Maple Trail.

Turn right on Maple Trail. This mile-long, northernmost section of trail is highly picturesque. Overhung by draping western hemlock trees, the footpath contours through numerous damp ravines and crosses footbridges surrounded by lush waterleaf plants and many varieties of native ferns. After passing over Maple Creek, the trail rises out of the canyon and again intersects Saltzman Road. Turn left on Saltzman and head downhill for a half mile to reach the trailhead, completing the loop.

Firelane 15, Firelane 12, BPA Road, and Wildwood Trail Loop
INCLUDING KIELHORN MEADOW

DISTANCE: 6.27 miles

HIKING TIME: 3 to 3½ hours

LOW ELEVATION: 246 feet

HIGH ELEVATION: 1023 feet

CUMULATIVE ELEVATION GAIN: 1042 feet

DIFFICULTY RATING: Strenuous

GPS COORDINATES: 45° 35' 46.64" N 122° 49' 24.82" W
   513761mE 5049209mN

Foot traffic only on Wildwood Trail and Kielhorn Meadow Trail. Firelane 15, Firelane 12, and BPA Road also allow bicycles and horses.

MILEAGE AND DIRECTIONS
0.00   Begin at Firelane 15 Trailhead on Skyline Blvd. Hike Firelane 15.

0.97   Cross Wildwood Trail. Stay on Firelane 15.

1.34   Turn left on Firelane 12.

2.34   Firelane 12 intersects with NW Creston Drive (near Highway 30).

3.34   Return up Firelane 12 to intersection with Firelane 15. Continue on Firelane 12.

3.85   Turn right on BPA Road.

4.11   Turn right onto Wildwood Trail.

4.94   Turn left on Firelane 15.

5.26   Turn left onto Kielhorn Trail.

5.44   Arrive Kielhorn Meadow.

5.62   Return to Firelane 15. Turn left.

6.27   End at Firelane 15 Trailhead.

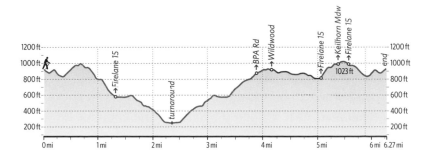

These little-traveled, northernmost trails in Forest Park provide the best chance to see wildlife rarely observed near a major city. Their distance from the city and from population concentrations allows native animals—black-tailed deer, elk, coyote, Red-tailed Hawks, bobcat, Pileated Woodpeckers, Pygmy Owls, and even an occasional Bald Eagle—the opportunity to move more freely and openly, and greatly rewards the quiet, patient observer who spies them.

Along this hike, it is easy to observe the corridor of forest that connects Portland's great urban park with the Coast Range (see image on page 57). This corridor, presently free from urbanization, is a primary reason for Forest Park's wildlife diversity. It allows easy access of native birds and mammals from other species pools into Forest Park. In fact, the future capacity of Forest Park to support wildlife will largely be determined by the park's boundary conditions. If this corridor of natural habitat is cut off from Forest Park, making the park an island surrounded on all sides by urban growth, the capability of the park to sustain a diversity of wildlife and plant species will be dramatically reduced.

To reach the trailhead, drive northwest along NW Skyline Boulevard 6.3 miles from the intersection of Skyline Boulevard and NW Cornell Road. Parking is alongside Skyline Boulevard and limited. The entrance to Firelane 15 is identifiable by a park gate on the east side of Skyline Boulevard beneath two major transmission lines that pass over the road at this point.

The firelanes and trails of this loop all lie within the beautiful Miller Creek Watershed. Begin hiking Firelane 15 as it descends, levels off, drops again, then climbs through a variety of second- and third-growth fir trees. At several spots, Firelane 15 reveals scenic views of the Columbia River, Sauvie Island, Mt. Rainier, Mt. St. Helens, and the corridor of forestland connecting Forest Park's northwestern boundary with the rural habitat of the Coast Range.

Stay on Firelane 15 until it ends at an intersection with Firelane 12. For the full hike, turn left onto Firelane 12 and continue downhill.

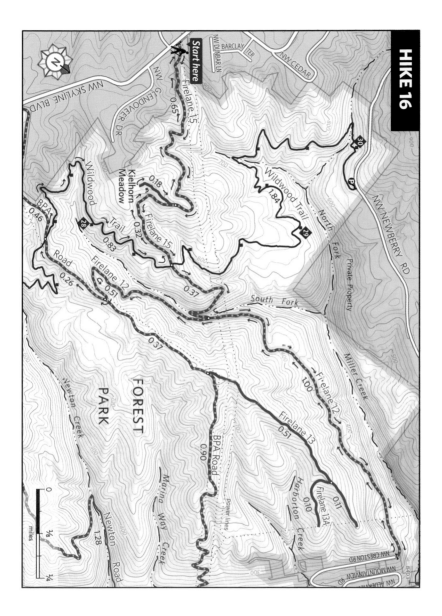

Start here

NW DUNBAR LN

NW BARCLAY TER

NW CEDAR

Firelane 15

0.65

NW GLENDOVEER DR

NW SKYLINE BLVD

0.18

Kielhorn
Meadow

Wildwood

30

P

Wildwood Trail
1.84

North Fork

NW NEWBERRY RD

Trail

28

0.32

Firelane 15

Private Property

BPA
0.46

0.83

0.37

Road

Firelane 12

0.26

0.51

29

South   Fork

Miller Creek

0.37

Newton   Creek

FOREST
PARK

1.00

Firelane 12

Firelane 13

0.51

BPA Road

Marina Way Creek

0.90

Power lines

Harborton Creek

0.10

Firelane 13A

0.11

NW CRESTON RD

NW MOUNTAINVIEW RD

NW ALDER...

Newton
Road

1.28

0

⅛

¼

miles

If desiring a shorter, less strenuous outing, omit the lower portion of Firelane 12 and turn right, heading uphill on Firelane 12, which connects in a half mile to BPA Road. Lower Firelane 12 narrows down to become a beautiful trail for most of its 1-mile length. In wet winter months, however, some parts of the trail are rocky and muddy, and may be slippery. As with other slick sections of Forest Park, trekking poles can be useful here. Many species of graceful ferns, including the delicate maidenhair fern, can be observed along the trail, which is lined with mature red alder trees and large old Douglas firs. For most of the year, small, exuberant Winter Wrens can be heard singing their sprightly call. In summer, Black-headed Grosbeaks (photo page 73) are almost constant companions on the trail. Firelane 12 ends at Creston Avenue at an orange park gate adjacent to Highway 30. No parking is available here. At this junction, turn around and head back uphill on the firelane for 1 mile, to its intersection with Firelane 15.

At the intersection of Firelanes 15 and 12, stay left, and continue uphill on the upper portion of Firelane 12. Climb out of the canyon along Firelane 12's relatively steep incline. After a half mile, Firelane 12 ends and joins BPA Road.

At this confluence, three rock monuments tell an important story that has been often repeated in Forest Park's history. The property surrounding this intersection of Firelane 12 and BPA Road was a vital part of the park but for years was held in private ownership. Then, in the late 1990s, investors unveiled plans to develop these seventy-three acres located in the park's core. Deeply alarmed, dozens of concerned citizens, in cooperation with the Friends of Forest Park, Metro, and Portland Parks and Recreation, worked fervently to raise money to purchase the property. In 1999, the "Hole in the Park" was at last acquired and donated to the city. The engraved rocks situated here list the donors who contributed their time and money to save this critical area.

Continue hiking uphill on BPA Road for a quarter-mile. At the road's intersection with Wildwood Trail, turn right. Hike north for 1 mile on Wildwood Trail through groves of western red cedar. This section of Wildwood offers glimpses into beautiful, deep Miller Creek canyon. After Mile 28¼, Wildwood Trail comes out at Firelane 15. Turn left on Firelane 15.

After 0.32 mile, Firelane 15 intersects with Kielhorn Meadow Trail. To visit the meadow, a tranquil forest clearing, turn left for 0.20 mile. As there is no exit to Skyline from here, conclude the hike by returning to Firelane 15. Turn left and hike up the firelane to return to the trailhead.

Trillium Trail, Wildwood Trail, and Firelane 7 Loop

DISTANCE: 2.80 miles round trip
HIKING TIME: 1½ to 2 hours
LOW ELEVATION: 809 feet
HIGH ELEVATION: 1078 feet
CUMULATIVE ELEVATION GAIN: 217 feet
DIFFICULTY RATING: Easy
GPS COORDINATES: 45° 34' 28.18" N 122° 47' 19.72" W
    516478mE 5046794mN

Foot traffic only on Trillium Trail and Wildwood Trail. Firelane 7 is also open for horses, but no bicycles are permitted.

MILEAGE AND DIRECTIONS

0.00 Begin at Firelane 7 Trailhead at Springville Road Parking Area. Hike Firelane 7.
0.18 Turn right onto Trillium Trail.
0.43 Turn left on Wildwood Trail.
1.28 Intersection with Firelane 7 (Oil Lane Road). Stay on Wildwood Trail.
1.82 Turn left onto Firelane 7A (Gas Line Road).
2.14 Turn right onto Firelane 7.
2.80 End at Springville Road Parking Area.

This short, pleasant hike is aptly named: in spring these trails abound with showy trilliums—the beautiful native flower that, under natural conditions, grows luxuriantly throughout the forest, creating in places carpets of white. But the loop is interesting in other seasons as well. Wildwood Trail offers impressive views into deep canyons of Douglas

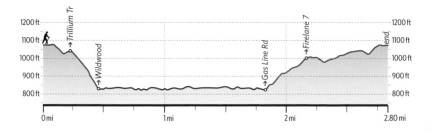

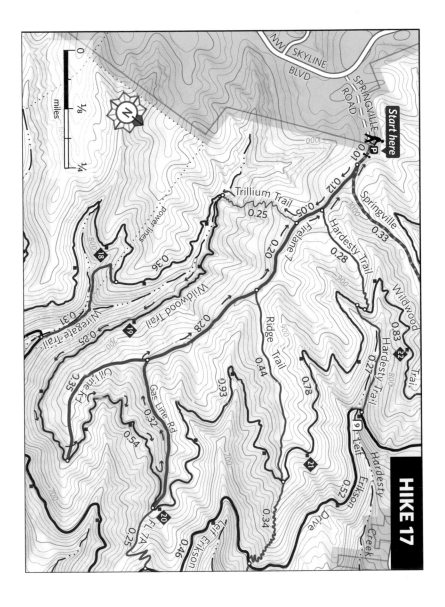

Start here

NW SKYLINE BLVD

SPRINGVILLE ROAD

0.01

0.12

Trillium Trail

0.25

0.05

0.20

Fireline 1

Springville

0.33

Hardesty Trail

0.28

Wildwood Trail

0.36

power lines

18

0.31

Wiregate Trail

0.35

19

0.28

Oil Line Rd

0.35

Ridge Trail

0.44

0.93

Gas Line Rd

0.32

0.54

900

0.78

Wildwood Trail

0.83

22

Hardesty Trail

0.27

21

Hardesty

9. Left

Erikson Creek

0.52

Erikson Drive

0.34

20

FL 7A

0.25

0.46

Leif Erikson

miles

0 ⅛ ¼

N

HIKE 17

fir, hemlock, and cedar trees in the Doane Creek Watershed. Firelanes 7 and 7A follow the dividing ridgeline between Doane Creek (1,037 acres) and Springville Creek (695 acres) watersheds.

From downtown Portland, drive northwest on U.S. Highway 30 (St. Helens Road) for 7.2 miles from its intersection with Interstate 405. Continue past the St. John's Bridge and turn left at the traffic light immediately after the bridge. This is NW Bridge Avenue and the northern ramp to the bridge. Take the first right onto NW Germantown Road and follow it for 2.1 miles until its intersection with NW Skyline Boulevard. Turn left on Skyline Blvd. and go 0.8 mile to NW Springville Road. Turn left and continue for 0.1 mile to reach the parking area. Remember to take all valuables with you and leave nothing in the car.

Begin the hike by walking around a locked park gate and veer to the right onto Firelane 7. The path narrows down and passes several white posts with orange bands. These denote a NW Natural gas line—an eight-inch buried line under pressure—and continue at intervals down the entire length of Firelane 7. To the north, at 0.13 mile past the park gate, runs the Hardesty Trail. Do not follow this trail, but continue on Firelane 7 about 100 yards further, to reach Trillium Trail. At this junction, turn right (south) and begin walking down the narrow and, in spots, fairly steep and oftentimes muddy trail. In places, exposed tree roots extend across the path, making it important to watch footing, especially in autumn when fallen leaves obscure the trail surface.

Later in the spring and early summer, many native birds seem to congregate along Trillium Trail. During this time, a lucky observer can hope to see Wilson's Warblers, Warbling Vireos, Orange-crowned Warblers, Pacific-slope Flycatchers, Spotted Towhees, Song Sparrows, Dark-eyed Juncos, and Brown Creepers flitting energetically among the trees and shrubs.

After 0.25 mile, Trillium Trail ends at its intersection with Wildwood Trail and North Fork Doane Creek. Turn left (north) onto Wildwood Trail, and continue for approximately 1.5 miles.

Notice that along this section of trail are many tall, dead snags interspersed among the vigorously growing red alder and bigleaf maple trees. These silent, blackened remnants tell the story of a devastating forest fire, known historically as the Bonny Slope Burn, that swept through Forest Park and the other side of the ridge sixty years ago. In 1951, over twelve hundred acres of the park were burned in three days. Since that time, stringent plans for fire suppression have been enacted and no serious fires have occurred in the park.

In late February and early March be on the watch for the first trilliums of spring along Trillium Trail. The name trillium means triple, and refers to the fact that all parts of the plant are in threes—three leaves, three sepals, and three petals. Preferring deep shade, these lightly scented flowers sometimes form large patches of closely growing plants that seem to turn the ground nearly white. As the flower ages, the petals change in color from snowy white, to pink, and then to purple.

Firelane 7, sometimes referred to as Oil Line Road, intersects Wildwood Trail approximately 300 yards past Wildwood Milepost 19¼. For a shorter trip, take this trail to return to the Springville Parking Area after a gentle but steady uphill climb for 1 mile. To continue the full loop, however, stay on Wildwood Trail for a half mile further until the intersection with Firelane 7A (Gas Line Road), immediately before Milepost 20.

Turn left on Firelane 7A. While walking the wide path, look for beautiful orange, native tiger lilies, which in early summer grow from one to eight feet tall and are abundant in Forest Park. As with all native plants, they should never be picked but should be left to regenerate year after year for everyone's enjoyment.

Continue climbing uphill on Firelane 7A for 0.33 mile. At this point, the trail ends at an intersection with Firelane 7. Turn right and proceed up Firelane 7 until the trail's conclusion at the Springville Road Parking Area, which completes the loop.

Firelane 9, Linnton Trail, Firelane 10, and Wildwood Trail Loop

DISTANCE: 3.28 miles

HIKING TIME: 2 to 2½ hours

LOW ELEVATION: 74 feet

HIGH ELEVATION: 814 feet

CUMULATIVE ELEVATION GAIN: 758 feet

DIFFICULTY RATING: Strenuous

GPS COORDINATES: 45° 35' 20.39" N 122° 47' 25.88" W
    516340mE 5048405mN

Foot traffic only on Firelane 9, Linnton Trail, Keyser Trail, Wildwood Trail, and Cannon Trail. Firelane 10 is also open to both bicycles and horses.

MILEAGE AND DIRECTIONS

0.00   Begin at Firelane 9 Trailhead adjacent to NW Germantown Road/ Leif Erikson Parking Area. Hike Firelane 9.

0.64   Arrive MacKay Avenue in the town of Linnton. Follow road instructions in text to access Linnton Trailhead.

0.93   Arrive Linnton Trailhead. Hike Linnton Trail.

1.53   At junction with Firelane 10, continue straight on Firelane 10.

1.88   Turn left on Keyser Trail.

2.13   At intersection with Firelane 10, turn left onto Firelane 10.

2.23   Turn left on Wildwood.

2.96   Arrive at NW Germantown Road. Cross Germantown and intersect with Cannon Trail. Hike Cannon Trail.

3.28   End at NW Germantown Road/Leif Erikson Parking Area.

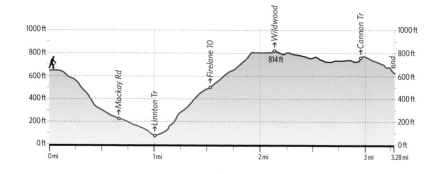

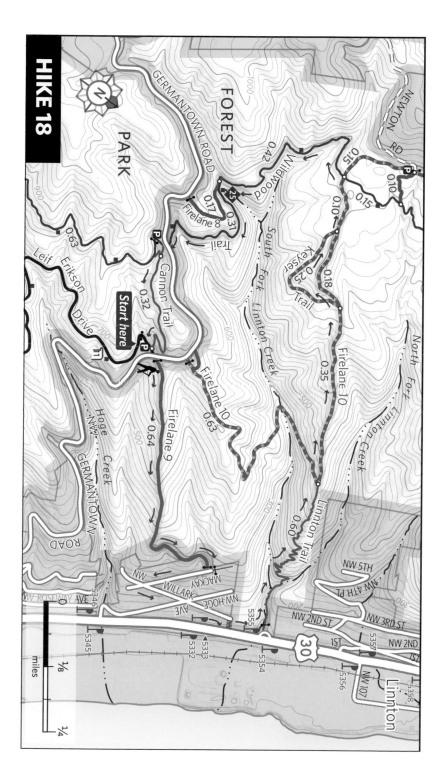

HIKE 18

FOREST

PARK

GERMANTOWN ROAD

0.63

Leif Erikson Drive

Hoge Creek

GERMANTOWN ROAD

900

700

500

600

P 0.32

Cannon Trail

Start here

P

Firelane 10 0.64

Firelane 9

Firelane 10 0.63

0.17

Firelane 8

0.31

0.42

South Fork Linnton Creek

0.25

Keyser Trail

0.18

0.10

Firelane 10 0.35

Linnton Trail 0.60

Wildwood Trail

0.10

0.15

P

0.10

NEWTON RD

North Fork Linnton Creek

1000

500

300

NW MACKAY

NW WILLARK AVE

NW HOGE AVE

NW ROSEWAY AVE

5346

5345

5332

5333

5354

5355

NW 5TH

NW 4TH PL

NW 2ND ST

NW 3RD ST

1ST

30

NW 2ND

5357

5356

NW 107

5358

Linnton

miles

1/8

1/4

This mosaic of forest trails and firelanes provides a good workout for the hiker wishing more strenuous exercise. But while the loop indeed affords a challenge, being steep and in places quite slippery when wet, it also offers excellent opportunities for close-up bird watching, especially in spring with the return of throngs of colorful migrating songbirds. Additionally, Linnton Trail, beginning at the small town of Linnton, takes the walker through beautiful mature groves of oak, cedar, yew, and fir trees along picturesque Linnton Creek. Linnton Trail is one of only a few pathways that currently can be accessed from Highway 30, the park's eastern boundary. Little public parking is available here, however.

To reach the trailhead from downtown Portland, drive northwest on U.S. Highway 30 (also called St. Helens Road) for 7.2 miles from its intersection with Interstate 405. Continue past the St. John's Bridge and turn left at the traffic light immediately after the bridge. This is NW Bridge Avenue and the northern ramp to the bridge. Take the first right onto NW Germantown Road, and follow it for 1.3 miles to a large parking area on the left, which marks the end of Leif Erikson Drive.

To begin the loop, carefully cross Germantown Road and look for a locked park gate marked Firelane 9, which is located directly across from the parking lot. Walk around the gate and proceed down the steep firelane. During parts of the year when the leaves are off the trees, views of the Willamette River are visible for much of Firelane 9's 0.64 mile. Native red alder and bigleaf maple are the predominant trees along the trail. In spring, when both of these varieties are bearing seeds and catkins, exuberant songbirds often flock together to feast upon them. On occasion, a fortunate bird watcher will spy colorful Western Tanagers, Warbling Vireos, Orange-crowned Warblers, Black-throated Gray Warblers, and Evening Grosbeaks all feeding together in one cluster of trees and creating a raucous harmony.

As Firelane 9 nears St. Helen's Road, the trail levels out and zigzags towards the town of Linnton. An intermittent creek is observable here, as well as several debris catchers built at intervals along the

creek to catch trash and forest debris before it can enter a large culvert that goes underneath the road. Also visible is the remains of an old abandoned concrete reservoir that in the past was used to store water for the town of Linnton.

At its terminus, Firelane 9 intersects with MacKay Avenue. Continue walking along MacKay Avenue, while noticing a rock monument that tells of the history of Clark and Wilson Park. At this location, eighteen acres were donated to the City of Portland in 1927 by O. M. Clark of Clark and Wilson Lumber Company. Clark's wish was that a sample of native western Oregon forest be preserved in perpetuity for "public enjoyment." When Forest Park was created in 1948, this small park became a park within a park. In 2005, Friends of Forest Park, Metro, and Portland Parks and Recreation spearheaded the purchase of additional acreage to the Clark and Wilson Park, funded by descendants of O. M. Clark and other generous donors.

Follow MacKay Avenue until it joins NW Wilark Avenue. At this point, a hiker leaves the park for 0.3 mile. Turn left on Wilark, cross Hoge Avenue, and continue walking on Wilark until its very end. To the right is a public staircase, a little hard to see, that leads to St. Helens Road. Descend the steps and turn left at the bottom onto a walkway that parallels and is separated from the road. The walkway comes out at the Linnton bus turnout. Continue walking halfway around the turnout until Linnton Trail becomes visible on the left, just northwest of Linnton Creek.

Begin heading up the trail, leaving St. Helen's Road behind. For most of its length, Linnton Trail follows along the banks of Linnton Creek. Numerous small switchbacks wend back and forth as the trail climbs steadily upward in the throat of Linnton Canyon through an assortment of different tree species. In sections, old Oregon white oak trees predominate. In other places, large western red cedar grow alongside the trail, as well as giant Douglas firs, some approaching five feet in diameter at breast height. An alert observer may also catch sight of Pacific yew trees growing intermixed with the firs and western hemlock. Pacific yew, a native evergreen tree known for its cancer-fighting chemical taxol, is uncommon in Forest Park but identifiable by its soft, reddish-purple bark.

After 0.6 mile, Linnton Trail intersects with Firelane 10. Continue straight on Firelane 10 and ascend the pathway, which is arduous in parts. Sometimes in summer Bald Eagles and Osprey can be seen flying above the forested canyons. Listen, too, for the wild, plaintive call of the Pileated Woodpecker that frequents this area. This bird, the largest of all woodpeckers found in North America, is considered a hallmark species of mature Douglas fir forests of the Northwest.

Pygmy Owls are also sometimes heard along Firelane 10. These small, highly secretive owls prefer to breed in sloped, forested habitat, far from the forest edge.

After 0.4 mile, turn left at the junction with Keyser Trail. This side route omits the steepest section of Firelane 10 and provides a gentle alternative as a hiker ascends the slope.

Keyser Trail is a peaceful pathway, with tall bowers of maple trees and western red cedar and thickly carpeted with sword fern and Oregon grape. It is often used by wildlife and deer tracks can regularly be seen. The trail is named after C. Paul Keyser, who was superintendent of the Portland Bureau of Parks for thirty-two years, from 1917 through 1949. Keyser embraced the idea of a wilderness park along Portland's Tualatin Mountain, and worked closely with ardent supporters Thornton Munger, Fred Cleator, and Ding Cannon to move the vision to fruition.

After 0.35 mile, Keyser Trail again rejoins Firelane 10. Turn left on the firelane. Just to the north of this junction is a small forested wetland and pond—an ecosystem extremely rare in Forest Park. Continue up Firelane 10 until its intersection with Wildwood Trail. Turn left and hike for 0.82 mile on Wildwood, heading south. At Milepost 25, near the intersection of Firelane 8, observe the stream coursing down the canyon. This is the upper portion of Linnton Creek, the same creek that was seen at the start of Linnton Trail.

Continue on Wildwood until its junction with Germantown Road. Cross Germantown once again, being careful to watch for cars, and head to the right to reach the upper Germantown Road Parking Area. Be on the lookout for Cannon Trail, the entrance of which is located at the left side, lower portion of the parking area. Cannon Trail acts as a connector between Wildwood and Leif Erikson parking lots, and provides a safe passage, away from the busy road. Hike Cannon Trail for 0.32 mile until its end at the trailhead, completing the loop.

Newton Road, Wildwood Trail, Firelane 10, and Cannon Trail Loop

DISTANCE: 3.93 miles

HIKING TIME: 2½ hours

LOW ELEVATION: 369 feet

HIGH ELEVATION: 892 feet

CUMULATIVE ELEVATION GAIN: 542 feet

DIFFICULTY RATING: Moderate

GPS COORDINATES: 45° 35' 29.92" N 122° 48' 8.42" W
   515418mE 5048697mN

Foot traffic only on Wildwood Trail. Newton Road and Firelane 10 allow both horses and bicycles.

MILEAGE AND DIRECTIONS

0.00   Begin at Newton Road Trailhead off NW Skyline Blvd. Hike Newton Road.

0.60   Turn right on Wildwood Trail.

1.47   Turn left on Firelane 10. Hike all of Firelane 10.

2.73   Arrive at NW Germantown Road. Cross Germantown to the Leif Erikson parking lot and Cannon Trail Trailhead. Hike Cannon Trail.

3.05   Arrive Upper Germantown Parking Area. Cross Germantown and continue north on Wildwood Trail.

3.78   Intersection with Firelane 10. Turn left on Firelane 10.

3.93   End at Newton Road Trailhead.

This hike offers rigor and variety. From the rolling terrain of Newton Road, the very steep but scenic downgrade and upgrade of Firelane 10, and the tranquil beauty of Wildwood Trail, the loop is both a

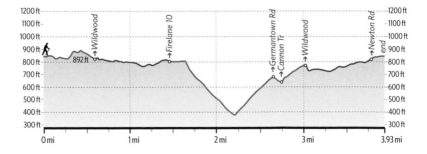

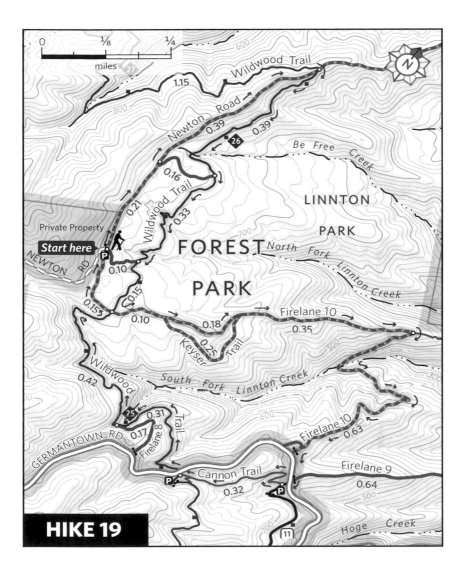

0 ⅛ ¼
miles

Wildwood Trail

1.15

Newton Road

0.39 0.39

26

Be Free Creek

LINNTON

0.16

Wildwood Trail

0.21

0.33

PARK

Private Property

Start here

NEWTON RD

P

0.10

0.15

0.155

0.10

FOREST

North Fork

700

PARK

Linnton Creek

500

Firelane 10

0.18

0.35

0.25

Keyser Trail

300

Wildwood

0.42

South Fork Linnton Creek

600

25

0.31

Trail

0.17

Firelane 8

GERMANTOWN RD

Firelane 10

0.63

Firelane 9

0.64

500

Cannon Trail

P

0.32

P

11

Hoge Creek

HIKE 19

workout and a forest respite combined. It is also easily accessible from NW Skyline Boulevard and has plenty of parking available.

The trail begins at the large parking area on Newton Road. To reach the trailhead, drive northwest along NW Skyline Boulevard. After crossing the intersection of Skyline Boulevard and NW Cornell Road, continue 5.1 miles further on Skyline to reach NW Newton Road. Turn right on Newton Road and continue for 0.3 mile where the road ends at the parking lot. From this point, motorized vehicles are not permitted.

There are two gates at the Newton Road Parking Area. Begin the loop by walking around the northern gate on the continuation of Newton Road. (The gate to the south leads to Firelane 10.) Initially, the grade of Newton Road is gentle, but soon climbs uphill sharply. After this rise, however, the trail levels out again for easy walking. Along this section, notice the deep coniferous forest that stretches to the north. This is the border of the beautiful Newton Creek Watershed. Here, in isolated pockets, majestic old-growth trees, giant downed logs, and large snags can be found. All of these features are remnants of the old-growth forest that historically covered much of Forest Park.

After slightly more than a half mile, Newton Road intersects with Wildwood Trail. Turn right on Wildwood and begin walking on the level, pleasurable trail. After 0.4 mile, Wildwood Trail crosses Be Free Creek, a significant stream in the Linnton Creek Watershed. Located near Milepost 25¾, Be Free Creek courses through a relatively steep canyon until it ends at the community of Linnton, where it is routed under U.S. Highway 30 and eventually discharged into the Willamette River.

Continue on Wildwood until its intersection with Firelane 10. Turn left on Firelane 10, a dirt and gravel road that widens and narrows at intervals. Initially, it heads steeply downhill. For a more moderate descent, take the side path, Keyser Trail, which connects with Firelane 10, coming in on the right. Keyser Trail is an easier hiking option with a gentler grade that omits the steepest part of

Firelane 10. After 0.26 mile, Keyser Trail rejoins Firelane 10. Turn right onto the firelane and continue descending the roadway. In wet conditions, footing can be difficult and trekking poles are helpful. Despite its strenuous nature, the trail has a beauty all its own. Dense displays of native Douglas fir and western hemlock array the canyons adjoining this remote firelane. The full canopy produced by these large trees is highly beneficial for several reasons. The overstory helps to filter out pollutants created by automobile and industrial emissions. In addition, the canopy moderates the effects of storms and wind and slows the runoff of precipitation, thereby protecting downstream neighborhoods from flooding and landslides.

After 0.64 mile, Firelane 10 intersects with Linnton Trail. Turn right and continue on Firelane 10. For approximately 0.15 mile, the firelane goes downhill to a crossing at Linnton Creek. A look along the north-facing slopes reveals many regal Grand fir trees, some approaching two hundred feet tall. After crossing the stream, Firelane 10 proceeds uphill, sometimes at a very sharp angle. A half mile further, it comes out at NW Germantown Road. Turn left and walk for approximately 100 yards along this busy road to reach the Leif Erikson parking lot. With caution, cross Germantown Road and be watchful for Cannon Trail, which takes off to the right from the parking area.

Built in 2006 thanks to a generous donation from the Oregon Parks Foundation, Cannon Trail provides a safe 0.32-mile connector passage to Wildwood Trail and avoids the necessity of walking on hazardous Germantown Road. The trail is named after Garnett "Ding" Cannon, a well-respected Portland businessman and past president of Standard Insurance Company.

At the intersection of Cannon Trail with the Upper Germantown Road Parking Area, turn right, carefully cross Germantown Road again, and look for the entrance to Wildwood Trail, heading north. Continue on Wildwood, which leads down into a ravine. At Wildwood Milepost 25, the trail crosses over the upper reaches of Linnton Creek and provides an overlook into Linnton Creek Canyon. This creek, which is often dry during the summer months, exemplifies

Of all the people involved in its creation, Ding Cannon (1906–1988) would be rightfully considered the "Father of Forest Park." For nearly fifty years, Cannon was unwavering in his advocacy and without his tenacious involvement the park may never have been established. An active member of the City Club of Portland, in 1945 Cannon chaired a study of Forest Park's feasibility. In 1946, he founded the Forest Park Committee of Fifty, the organization credited with the formation of Forest Park in 1948. For the next forty years, Cannon served on the board of directors of the Committee of Fifty and worked tirelessly to protect the integrity of the park. Through all that time, his strongest belief remained the same: that all the properties within the boundaries of Forest Park needed to be preserved. Until his death at age eighty-two, Cannon never swerved from this goal and many crucial inholdings were attained through his leadership. One of Cannon's lasting legacies, benefiting all who use Forest Park, was his persistence in acquiring properties in the park's North Unit that allowed for the continuation of Wildwood Trail. The critically important job of land acquisition within the park's boundaries continues today.

the "intermittent creeks" that so frequently occur in Forest Park's watersheds. Characteristically, streams within the park have well-defined, steeply graded channels. In the wet seasons of the year, they can be charged with runoff. In summer, they can dry up. Erosion and flood damage resulting from "flashy flows" that can occur during the rainy months are mitigated in Forest Park, however, because of the luxuriant vegetative growth that borders these streams.

If desiring a respite on the return trip, a nice place to stop is just before Milepost 25¼ where there is a bench honoring long-time Forest Park volunteer Bruno Kolkowsky. The construction of Wildwood Trail, from Springville Road to Newton Road, was one of his major projects, and was completed before he died at age eighty.

A quarter-mile further, Firelane 10 intersects Wildwood Trail. Turn left on Firelane 10. Proceed 0.15 mile to reach the Newton Road Parking Area, which completes the loop.

Ridge Trail, Firelane 7, Hardesty Trail, and Leif Erikson Drive Loop

DISTANCE: 3.33 miles

HIKING TIME: 2 hours

LOW ELEVATION: 194 feet

HIGH ELEVATION: 1045 feet

CUMULATIVE ELEVATION GAIN: 898 feet

DIFFICULTY RATING: Strenuous

GPS COORDINATES: 45° 35' 3.74" N 122° 46' 13.48" W
    517910mE 5047896mN

Foot traffic only on Ridge Trail, Hardesty Trail, and Wildwood Trail. Firelane 7 is also open to horses. Leif Erikson Drive is open to cyclists, equestrians, and pedestrians.

NOTE: *The St. John's Bridge on-ramp is definitely not a safe place for children to walk; semi-trucks barrel down this road. Families with small children should use an alternate route.*

MILEAGE AND DIRECTIONS

0.00 Begin at Ridge Trail Trailhead entrance on the South Ramp of the St. John's Bridge. Hike Ridge Trail.

0.60 Ridge Trail intersects Leif Erikson Drive. Turn left 40 yards then right on the continuation of Ridge Trail.

0.94 Continue straight ahead at the junction of Wildwood Trail.

1.38 Turn right at the junction with Firelane 7.

1.63 Turn right at junction with Hardesty Trail.

1.91 Intersect Wildwood Trail. Turn right on Wildwood Trail for 76 yards, then left on the continuation of Hardesty Trail.

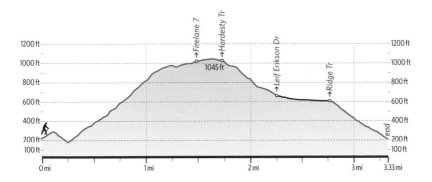

2.21   Turn right at the intersection with Leif Erikson, Milepost 9.

2.73   Turn left at the junction with Ridge Trail.

3.33   End at Ridge Trail entrance at the St. John's Bridge.

Of almost all the hiking trails in the forest, this loop most dramatically reveals the dynamic interface of the many components that combine to give Forest Park its unique vitality. Views of bridges, highways, and industry mingle with vistas of mountains, rivers, quiet woods, and native canyons. Together they create an unusual expression of wildness, naturalness, and beauty framed, in part, in a robust industrial setting. This is a popular trail for runners and is easily accessible from the St. John's Bridge.

To reach the trailhead, drive northwest on U.S. Highway 30 (St. Helens Road) for 6 miles. Turn left at the intersection leading to the south ramp of the St. John's Bridge. Continue up the ramp for 0.3 mile to a parking area on the left, known as the Pull Out Creek Parking Area. From here, walk 0.1 mile up the ramp on a narrow sidewalk that runs alongside the highway. On the left, near the top of the ramp, there is a steep staircase of forty-eight steps. Climb the stairs, which lead to the trailhead of Ridge Trail. A second access point to Ridge Trail takes off from the north ramp of the bridge. The two trails soon combine into one, however.

Ridge Trail begins with a blasting of noise from nearby industry, cars, and semi-trucks. Underfoot, dense growths of ivy, clematis, and other invasive plants threaten to crowd out native vegetation—a common condition anywhere Forest Park comes into contact with Highway 30 and the industrial area. But the initial path is not unpleasant: after a few hundred yards a small wooden bridge crosses the ravine, and from here there is a spectacular close-up view of the historic St. John's Bridge, with a backdrop of Mt. St. Helens and the Willamette River.

After the crossing, the trail climbs steadily upward as it rises through Pull Out Creek Canyon. Before long, it begins to leave the city behind. Ivy declines, more natural vegetation prevails, and the jostling sounds of urban activities drop off. Climbing higher,

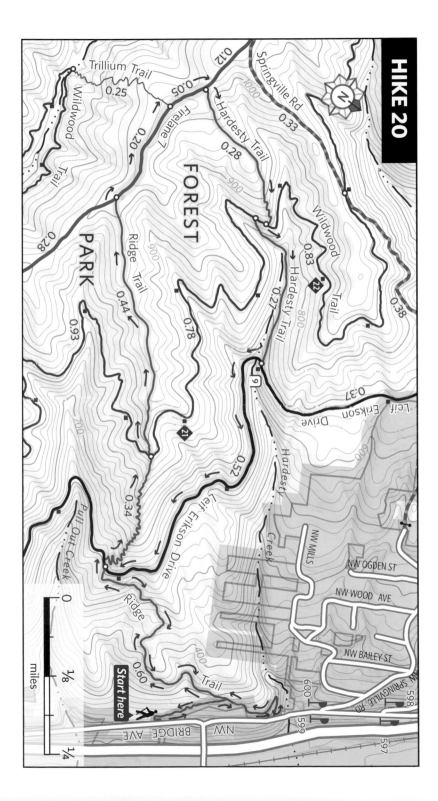

FOREST

PARK

Trillium Trail

0.25

Wildwood Trail

0.05

0.12

Fireline 7

0.20

Hardesty Trail

0.28

Springville Rd

0.33

1000

900

Ridge Trail

0.28

900

0.44

0.93

0.78

Hardesty Trail

0.27

800

Wildwood Trail

0.83

22

0.38

700

21

0.34

Pull Out Creek

0.52

Left Erikson Drive

Hardesty

6

Leif Erikson Drive

0.37

600

Creek

600

NW MILLS

NW OGDEN ST

NW WOOD AVE

Ridge

400

Trail

0.60

Start here

NW BRIDGE AVE

NW BAILEY ST

NW SPRINGVILLE RD

600

599

598

597

0   1/8   1/4

miles

cathedral-like firs come into view. After a half mile, off to one side is a small, roughhewn bench provides an enticing spot to stop and reflect.

At 0.6 mile, Ridge Trail intersects Leif Erikson Drive. Turn left on Leif Erikson for approximately 40 yards to access the upper portion of Ridge Trail. Turn right and continue on Ridge Trail, which climbs up the middle of two adjoining canyons. To the left (south) is Pull Out Creek Canyon; to the right (north) is Hardesty Creek Canyon. After 0.35 mile, Ridge Trail intersects Wildwood Trail; stay straight on Ridge Trail as it begins to level out while passing among graceful archways made up of draping branches of native vine maple.

Firelane 7 intersects Ridge Trail in a half mile. Here, turn right and continue climbing uphill. Along this section of Firelane 7, be sure to keep an eye open for deer tracks, which are especially noticeable in muddy spots.

After 0.2 mile, Firelane 7 intersects Hardesty Trail. Turn right onto Hardesty Trail and carefully descend the narrow pathway. When the trail is wet in winter and spring, footing can be precarious. As a result of its dampness, however, this trail abounds with interesting varieties of luxuriant mosses and unusually shaped lichens.

Wildwood Trail intersects Hardesty Trail after a quarter-mile. To access the lower portion of Hardesty Trail, turn right on Wildwood Trail and walk approximately 76 yards around a bend. The continuation of lower Hardesty Trail takes off to the left. While this lower section is even steeper in places, it is a pretty trail, following

Hardesty Trail is named after William B. Hardesty, an early member and benefactor of the Mazamas, a non-profit mountaineering organization. For years, Hardesty dedicated his time following the ideals of the group's constitution, written in 1896, working for the "preservation of the forests and other features of mountain scenery as far as possible in their natural beauty." In 1944, the Portland chapter of the Mazamas, led by Fred Cleator of the U.S. Forest Service, participated in building this trail in Forest Park and dedicated it in Hardesty's honor.

Hardesty Creek. Numerous young western hemlock trees grow in the canyon, many from huge stumps acting as nurse logs. Several of the largest stumps show evidence of springboard notches, remnants of logging activities from long ago.

Hardesty Trail emerges at Leif Erikson Drive at Leif Erikson Milepost 9. Turn right (south) onto Leif Erikson next to a large road cut. On this outcropping, a sheer wall of delicate maidenhair ferns can be seen clinging to the Columbia River Basalt. After Milepost 8½, lower Ridge Trail comes in on the left. Turn here, continue downhill, and head back towards the St. John's Bridge. The forest loop ends in 0.6 mile where the city, once again, begins.

Leif Erikson Drive

PART ONE

NW THURMAN STREET TO NW SALTZMAN ROAD

MILE 0 – 6.15

DISTANCE: 6.15 miles (one way)* *(Parking is not available at the Leif Erikson/Saltzman Road intersection; the closest parking to the end of the trail is an additional 1.3 miles down Saltzman Road.)*

HIKING TIME: 3 hours (one way)*

LOW ELEVATION: 320 feet

HIGH ELEVATION: 724 feet

CUMULATIVE ELEVATION GAIN: 405 feet

DIFFICULTY RATING: Easy

GPS COORDINATES: 45° 32' 22.97" N 122° 43' 27.35" W
521527mE 5042946mN

Leif Erikson Drive is open to pedestrians, bicycles, and horses. Walkers are to yield to horses. Bicycles are to yield to walkers and horses.

*One way trip; requires transportation at both ends of this hike.

NOTE: *Because this is a multi-use trail, be sure to exercise caution and awareness on corners where visibility between cyclists and pedestrians may be limited.*

MILEAGE AND DIRECTIONS

0.00   Begin at Thurman Road Trailhead.

0.26   Intersection of Water Tank Trail.

0.31   Intersection of Wild Cherry Trail.

0.90   Intersection of Dogwood Trail.

1.47   Intersection of Alder Trail.

3.01   Intersection of Firelane 1.

3.37   Intersection of Nature Trail.

3.65   Intersection of Firelane 2.

4.16   Intersection of Maple Trail and Firelane 3.

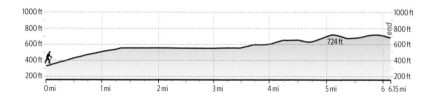

4.46   Intersection of Koenig Trail.
5.06   Intersection of Firelane 4.
5.42   Intersection of Cleator Trail.
6.15   End at intersection with NW Saltzman Road. Lower Saltzman Road
       Parking Area is 1.3 miles down Saltzman Road.

If land developer Richard Shepard had not had great expectations, Leif Erikson Drive may well have never come to be. And, if Leif Erikson Drive had never been built, there may never have been a "Forest Park." In 1914, Shepard's dream began a string of events that eventually led to the creation of Forest Park thirty-four years later. A park was never Shepard's intent; rather, his vision was one of thousands of home sites platted along a scenic country road.

In 1914, Shepard spearheaded the construction of Hillside Drive (as Leif Erikson was originally called). The road ran through the center of the planned development—six hundred feet above the Willamette River through the forest, from NW Germantown to downtown Portland. But the construction of the road brought with it serious problems. The price tag was double what was anticipated. Then, during the first winter, the instability of the soil upon which it was built became unfortunately apparent. In just a few months time, Leif Erikson Drive was pummeled by mudslides and closed.

Bills for the road's construction and subsequent repairs were attached as assessments to all adjacent land owners. Incensed, the great majority refused to pay, preferring to forfeit their property. Shepard's plan was viewed as a total failure. Over time, however, in a fortuitous turn of events, the twin accidents of speculation and geology merged to a result that Shepard could never have foreseen. Rather than homesites, the vacated lots became the building blocks of Forest Park. Three decades after his development catastrophe, "Shepard's Folly" rose up to become Portland's most splendid natural asset, and Leif Erikson Drive, later reopened, a showcase to access it.

Today, Leif Erikson Drive is a popular road used by hikers, equestrians, and cyclists. Its 11.2 level miles, closed to all motorized vehicles except those on official business, adjoin dozens of side trails

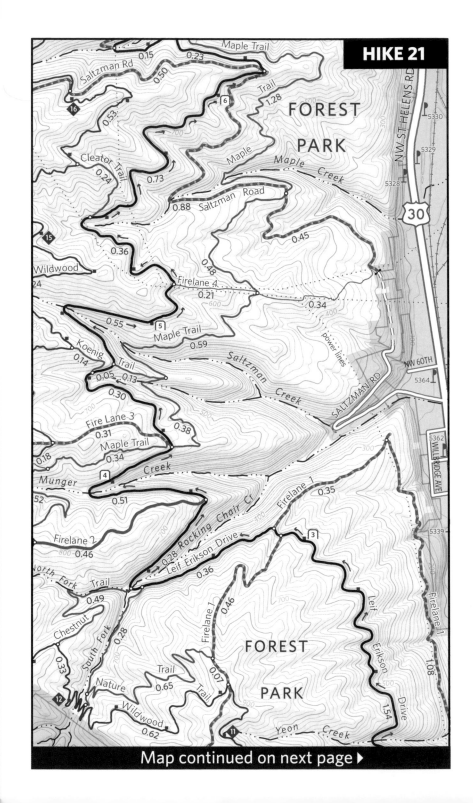

HIKE 21

Maple Trail

Saltzman Rd   0.15   0.23

0.50

16   Trail   6   1.28

0.53   FOREST

Cleator Trail   Maple   PARK

0.24   0.73   Maple   Creek

0.88 Saltzman Road

15   0.45

0.36

Wildwood   0.48

24   Firelane 4

0.21   0.34

0.55   600

Koenig   5   Maple Trail   400

0.14   0.59

0.05   0.13   Saltzman

0.30   Creek

Fire Lane 3   0.38

0.31   500

Maple Trail

0.18   0.34   300

Munger   Creek

52   4   0.51   Firelane 1   0.35

400

Firelane 2   Rocking Chair Ct   3   5339

800   0.46   0.28   Firelane 1

North Fork   Leif Erikson Drive   0.36

Trail   700

0.49   Firelane 1   0.46   Leif

Chestnut   South fork   0.28   Erikson   1.08

0.33   FOREST   Drive

Nature   Trail   0.07   1.54

12   0.65   PARK   500

Wildwood   Trail   900

0.62   11   Yeon   Creek

Map continued on next page ▶

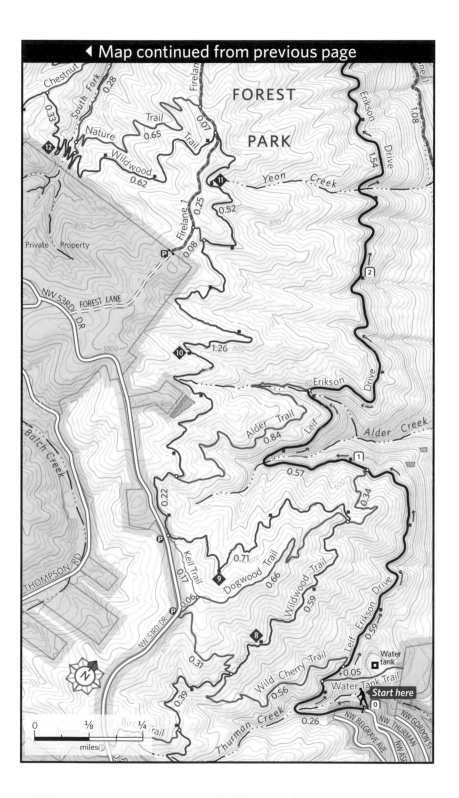

FOREST

PARK

Chestnut

South Fork 0.28

0.33

Nature Trail 0.65

Firelane 1

0.07

Trail

Wildwood 0.62

Erikson Drive 1.54

1.08

11

Yeon Creek

0.25

0.52

Firelane 1

0.08

Private Property

NW 53RD DR

FOREST LANE

1000

800

2

10

1.26

800

Erikson

Alder Trail 0.84

Leif

Drive

Alder Creek

1

Batch Creek

0.22

0.57

0.34

700

P

Keil Trail 0.17

0.71

Dogwood Trail

0.66

Wildwood Trail

Leif Erikson Drive

THOMPSON RD

9

P 0.06

0.59

NW 53RD DR

8

0.59

0.31

Water tank

Wild Cherry Trail

0.05

Water Tank Trail

Start here

0

0.39

Birch Trail

0.56

0.26

Thurman Creek

NW BELGRAVE AVE

NW THURMAN

NW GORDON ST

N

0   ⅛   ¼

miles

useful to create loop trips and pass over numerous streams. A trip along Leif Erikson is an opportunity to step across the names of Forest Park history, as many of the pathways and creeks it crosses are named after people who helped create the park, who built and maintained its trails, and who tenaciously held to the vision of a "wilderness within a city"—a unique vision that still lives on today.

To reach the trailhead for Leif Erikson Drive, travel through Northwest Portland, going north on NW 23rd Avenue to NW Thurman Street. Turn left on Thurman Street and continue until the road ends at a locked park gate. This is the entrance to Leif Erikson Drive, which is closed to all motorized vehicles.

Leif Erikson Drive begins as a wide roadway, paved in small sections for the first half mile. For the most part, though, the surface is primarily rock and dirt. White concrete posts mark the mileage at quarter-mile intervals along the entire road, beginning at the Thurman Street gate. The first mile of Leif Erikson is the most heavily used and is often busy with an assortment of active recreationalists. Beyond this, however, the heavy use begins to slowly drop off as people spread out and the playground ambiance begins to meld with the solitude of the forest.

Just past the first white post at a quarter mile, Water Tank Trail intersects Leif Erikson on the right and takes off downhill. This little used pathway ends in 0.20 mile at a large water tank adjacent to Alexandra Street. A nice, daisy-strewn meadow is located here that

Traveling along Leif Erikson, one can see some of the best examples of geologic outcroppings in all of Forest Park. The road has been cut through hillsides made up of Columbia River Basalt. This formation, which originally was fluid lava spewed from fissures in southeastern Washington and northeastern Oregon sixteen million years ago, covers tens of thousands of square miles and underlies much of Tualatin Mountain. The basalt exposures are usually covered with green ferns—predominately licorice ferns—that take root in the worn crevices of rock.

is perfect for picnicking on sunny days. Continue on Leif Erikson, however, where Wild Cherry Trail intersects on the left 0.05 mile further. This is one of only two spots on the entire drive where there are Porta-Potties, available for use all year. The next rest stop is at the end of Leif Erikson Drive near Germantown Road, eleven miles away.

After Milepost 1, Leif Erikson enters the steep Alder Creek Watershed. Take a moment to look down into the nearly vertical canyon and, for scale, scope out tall Douglas fir trees, whose crowns are beneath you. Many of these straight-trunked trees are over one hundred feet tall, revealing the precipitous slope of this ravine.

For the next mile, when leaves are off the trees in fall and winter, there are widespread views of the mountains, rivers, and the industrial area. At Mile 2¼, Leif Erikson crosses over Yeon Creek, named for John Baptiste Yeon, an early Oregon pioneer and conservationist, and his son, John Yeon II, internationally acclaimed architect famous for creating the Pacific Northwest regional style, along with his contemporary Pietro Belluschi.

John Yeon (1910–1994) was an ardent conservationist and for six decades worked to preserve the landscape of the Northwest. He inspired the creation of the Columbia River Gorge Scenic Area and was involved in protecting many important natural areas in Oregon and Washington, including Olympic National Park. Yeon was an integral member of the Forest Park Committee of Fifty, on which he served for several decades.

Continue on Leif Erikson to Milepost 3, where Firelane 1 soon intersects. After crossing the firelane, the drive enters Saltzman Creek Watershed, arguably the most beautiful watershed along the entire road. Past Mile 3¼, Nature Trail intersects Leif Erikson. Here the road crosses the southernmost tributary to Rocking Chair Creek. About fifty feet up Nature Trail is evidence of an old dam on the creek, and a sluice gate for stream impoundment. This is a good place to stop and look for animal tracks in the wet mud. Take a moment, too, to admire the beautiful American chestnut tree just past Nature

Trail at the intersection of Leif Erikson Drive with Chestnut Trail. Planted by Fred Cleator in the 1950s, this tree is a surviving, western representative of a species that has been wiped out from its original range in eastern North America, falling prey to a deadly blight introduced into the US in 1904.

Just before Milepost 3¾, Firelane 2 intersects with Leif Erikson. Along this portion of the road—an exceptionally quiet part of the forest—wonderful escarpments of Columbia River Basalt can be viewed. At Mile 4, the drive crosses Munger Creek, named for Thornton Munger, pioneering research scientist, who was instrumental in the founding of Forest Park.

From Milepost 4¼ and for the next 2 miles, Leif Erikson winds in and out of the steep and picturesque Saltzman Creek canyon made up predominantly of conifers with understories of vine maples that, in fall, turn brilliant yellow.

At Mile 4½, Koenig Trail crosses Leif Erikson. This short connector pathway between Maple Trail and Wildwood was named for the late Fran Koenig, who for sixty years spent countless hours caring for and

mapping the trails in Forest Park and was responsible for all the blue diamonds seen at quarter-mile intervals on Wildwood Trail.

After Mile 5, Firelane 4—an undeveloped path—intersects Leif Erikson at a powerline crossing overhead. This is the ridgeline that divides Saltzman Creek and Doane Creek watersheds. Just prior to Mile 5½, the road crosses Maple Creek. This quiet spot is a good place to listen for the native birds that inhabit Forest Park. Red-breasted Nuthatches, Winter Wrens, Golden-crowned Kinglets, Chestnut-backed Chickadees, and Spotted Towhees can often be heard along this stretch of road calling from the woods of hemlock, cedar, and maple.

Cleator Trail, named after Fred Cleator, intersects Leif Erikson at Milepost 5½. Cleator worked for the U.S. Forest Service in the early part of the twentieth century and was an early proponent of preserving wilderness areas in the Northwest. Along with Thornton Munger and Ding Cannon, Cleator was instrumental in the creation of Forest Park.

Saltzman Road intersects Leif Erikson Drive after Milepost 6. If ending here, turn right onto Saltzman Road and continue for 1.3 miles to the Lower Saltzman Road Parking Area, which completes the hike.

Leif Erikson Drive

PART TWO

NW SALTZMAN ROAD TO NW GERMANTOWN ROAD

MILE 6.15 – 11.22

DISTANCE: 5.02 miles (one way)* *(Add an additional 1.3 miles if beginning from the lower Saltzman Road Parking Area, the nearest to the trailhead.)*
HIKING TIME: 2½ - 3 hours (one way)*
LOW ELEVATION: 575 feet
HIGH ELEVATION: 703 feet
CUMULATIVE ELEVATION GAIN: 198 feet
DIFFICULTY RATING: Easy
GPS COORDINATES: 45° 34' 9.6" N 122° 45' 46.59" W
    518501mE 5046224mN
Leif Erikson Drive is open to foot traffic, bicycles, and horses. Walkers need to yield to horses. Bicyclists yield to walkers and horses.
One way trip; requires transportation at both ends of this hike.
NOTE: *Because this is a multi-use trail, be sure to exercise caution and awareness on corners where visibility between cyclists and pedestrians may be limited.*

MILEAGE AND DIRECTIONS

0.00   Begin at NW Saltzman Road intersection with Leif Erikson Drive.
0.23   Intersection with Maple Trail.
0.38   Intersection with Firelane 5.
0.91   Intersection with Wiregate Trail.
1.69   Intersection with Lower Firelane 7A (Gas Line Road).
1.83   Intersection with Upper Firelane 7A (Gas Line Road).
2.29   Intersection with Ridge Trail.
2.81   Intersection with Hardesty Trail.
3.18   Intersection with Springville Road.
3.98   Intersection with Waterline Trail.
5.02   End at NW Germantown Road.

This second section of Leif Erikson Drive is a tour through the center of Forest Park. Lying midway between the ridge top of NW Skyline

Boulevard and the Willamette River, framed between the boundaries of NW Saltzman and NW Germantown roads, this section of Leif Erikson Drive allows the chance to explore a shoulder of Forest Park that traverses three distinct watersheds. Along the way, the opportunity to see large game crossing Leif Erikson is a real possibility for a lucky observer.

To reach the trailhead from the Lower Saltzman Road Parking Area, drive west on U.S. Highway 30 (NW St. Helens Road) 5.3 miles from the intersection with Interstate 405. Look for NW Saltzman Road on the left. Turn left and drive the paved, winding road 0.7 mile to a locked park gate. From here, walk approximately 1.3 miles to reach the intersection of NW Saltzman with Leif Erikson Drive and the start of the hike.

Turn right and begin heading downhill on Leif Erikson Drive after taking a moment to scan the view. The Willamette and Columbia rivers, the St. John's Bridge, Vancouver Lake, Pier Park, and Terminal 6 are all visible from this overlook. Once on Leif Erikson Drive, the character of the trail soon changes. At Milepost 6¼, the road winds along a shady, north-facing slope heavily vegetated with middle aged Douglas fir, western red cedar, and western hemlock trees. This is the beginning of the scenic Doane Creek Watershed, whose four major ravines snake in and out along the eastern slope of Tualatin Mountain for the next two miles.

Leif Erikson passes the north entrance to Maple Trail slightly before Milepost 6½. It intersects Firelane 5 shortly after, at the site of a large green water-holding tank, long abandoned. This lower section of Firelane 5 has recently been renovated into a single-track trail open to mountain biking—a joint effort between Portland Parks and Recreation and volunteers from Northwest cycling groups and the Forest Park Conservancy.

Just past Milepost 7, Wiregate Trail intersects Leif Erikson. This connector trail is actually a powerline access route that leads to Wildwood Trail. Also along the road at this site is a culvert that routinely fails and needs replacement. Washouts of Leif Erikson Drive

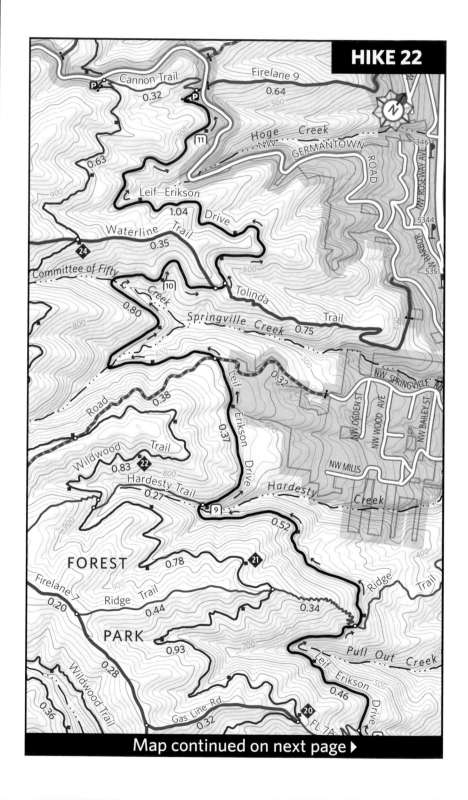

HIKE 22

Cannon Trail
0.32
P
P
Firelane 9
0.64
500
11
Hoge Creek
NW GERMANTOWN ROAD
NW HARBOR
5346
5344
5351
0.63
Leif Erikson
1.04 Drive
900
Waterline Trail
0.35
24
Committee of Fifty
10
Creek
0.80
Tolinda
Springville Creek 0.75 Trail
600
800
600
500
0.32
Road
0.38
Leif
Erikson
0.37
Drive
600
NW SPRINGVILLE RD
NW OGDEN ST
NW WOOD AVE
NW BAILEY ST
Wildwood Trail
0.83 22
Hardesty Trail
0.27
9
Hardesty
NW MILLS
Creek
0.52
400
FOREST
0.78
21
Ridge Trail
0.34
Firelane 7
0.20
Ridge Trail
0.44
900
PARK
0.93
700
Pull Out Creek
0.28
Wildwood Trail
Leif Erikson
0.46
Drive
500
0.36
Gas Line Rd
0.32
20
FL 7A

Map continued on next page ▸

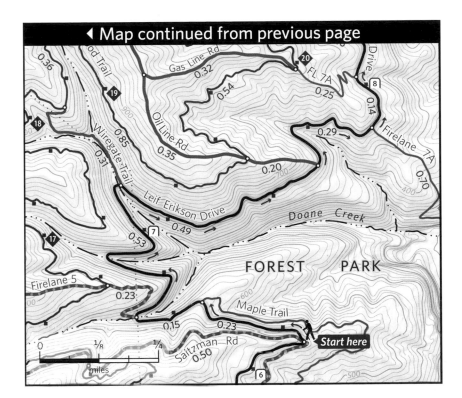

0.36
od Trail
Gas Line Rd
0.32
[20]
FL 7A
Drive
[19]
0.54
0.25
[8]
900
0.14
[18]
Oil Line Rd
0.29
Firelane 7A
Wiregate Trail
0.85
0.35
0.20
700
0.70
0.31
400
Leif Erikson Drive
0.49
Doane Creek
[17]
[7]
0.53
FOREST PARK
Firelane 5
0.23
600
Maple Trail
0.15
0.23
Start here
0
1/8
1/4
Saltzman Rd
0.50
miles
[6]
500

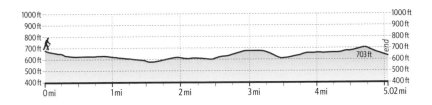

1000 ft — 1000 ft
900 ft — 900 ft
800 ft — 800 ft
700 ft — 700 ft
600 ft — 600 ft
500 ft — 703 ft — 500 ft
400 ft — 400 ft
0 mi   1 mi   2 mi   3 mi   4 mi   5.02 mi

are a common malady that require continual maintenance and verify the difficulty of constructing a road on highly erodable surfaces.

Just before Milepost 8½ on Leif Erikson, Ridge Trail intersects the road. This trail is the dividing edge between the Doane Creek Watershed to the south, and Springville Creek Watershed to the north. Once entering the Springville drainage, much of the vegetation is of the mid-aged conifer type. These more mature woods allow for the possibility of hearing birds that prefer these conditions, such as Ravens and Pygmy Owls. Mammals such as black-tailed deer—sometimes larger bucks—are occasionally observed fleeting across the road.

Throughout Leif Erikson, one sees repeated evidence of geologic instability. Localized landslides are a common occurrence. In many places, trees on the road's upper hillsides have curving trunks, indicating tenacious roots clinging to a ground that moves and erodes beneath them. The primary reason for all the construction headaches in Forest Park is due to a layer of poor foundation material—known as Portland Hills Silt—that lies atop the base rock of Columbia River Basalt.

Portland Hills Silt is the final capping foundation in most of the West Hills in Portland, with its greatest thicknesses occurring in Forest Park. This formation was laid down during the last million years of Pleistocene time, the result of two forces working together—the river and the wind—as the Columbia River's floodplain was being created. As the river carved its channels, large quantities of fine-textured, yellowish-brown, clay silt was transported by the wind to lands south and west.

Portland Hills Silt is highly unstable when wet and in areas of high seasonal rainfall, such as Portland, makes for a poor foundation material. It can be seen at many of the cut banks of Leif Erikson Drive resting on top of the thicker basalt layer.

At Milepost 9, Leif Erikson crosses Hardesty Creek and immediately afterward intersects Hardesty Trail coming in from the left. This creek and trail were named for W. P. Hardesty, a founding member of the Mazamas. Hardesty is recognized as being the father of the modern-day urban walk, which he began in 1912. Today, almost a century later, urban walks are still being offered by Mazama leaders who regularly meet for different hikes that are open to the public.

After Milepost 9¼, Leif Erikson intersects Springville Road. A half mile further, it crosses Committee of Fifty Creek. This clear stream follows Waterline and Tolinda trails and runs year round, beginning at a water tower at the crest of Skyline Boulevard and flowing to lower Germantown Road. By virtue of being almost being completely within the boundaries of Forest Park and not developed, the headwaters of this stream are in excellent condition, benefiting the entire drainage system. Committee of Fifty Creek was named after the Forest Park Committee of Fifty—the organization founded in 1946 that ardently undertook the decades-old task to preserve a "6,000-acre, forest-park" for Portland, at last meeting with triumphant success.

For its final mile, Leif Erikson Drive narrows slightly. After Milepost 11, where a Porta-Potty is located, the pathway drops down to approach NW Germantown Road. At 11.2 miles, Germantown Road marks the end of the hike. Fittingly, also at this intersection is the new Cannon Trail, named in honor of Garnett "Ding" Cannon, who is recognized as being the founder of Forest Park, and its most loyal supporter throughout his lifetime. This is the boundary between the Central and North Units of Forest Park. Plenty of parking is available here.

BPA Road, Newton Road, and Wildwood Trail Loop

DISTANCE: 4.88 miles

HIKING TIME: 3 hours

LOW ELEVATION: 83 feet

HIGH ELEVATION: 1065 feet

CUMULATIVE ELEVATION GAIN: 1024 feet

DIFFICULTY RATING: Strenuous

GPS COORDINATES: 45° 35' 32.44" N 122° 48' 51.65" W
    514481mE 5048773mN

Foot traffic only on Wildwood Trail. BPA Road and Newton Road also allow both bicycles and horses.

MILEAGE AND DIRECTIONS

0.00 Begin hike at BPA Road Trailhead on Skyline Blvd.

0.46 Intersection with Wildwood Trail. Stay on BPA Road.

0.72 Intersection with Firelane 12. Stay on BPA Road.

1.09 Intersection with Firelane 13. Stay on BPA Road.

1.99 Junction with Highway 30. Turn right onto Newton Road.

3.27 Newton Road intersects Wildwood Trail. Turn right on Wildwood.

4.42 Turn left on BPA Road.

4.88 End at BPA Road Trailhead.

Of all the hiking trails in Forest Park, this loop is one of the most diverse, as it ranges from one of the highest points of the park along Skyline Boulevard to descend to eighty-three feet at Highway 30 (NW St. Helens Road), a drop of nearly a thousand feet. While difficult in places, this hike rewards the walker with outstanding views of

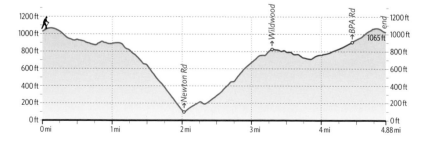

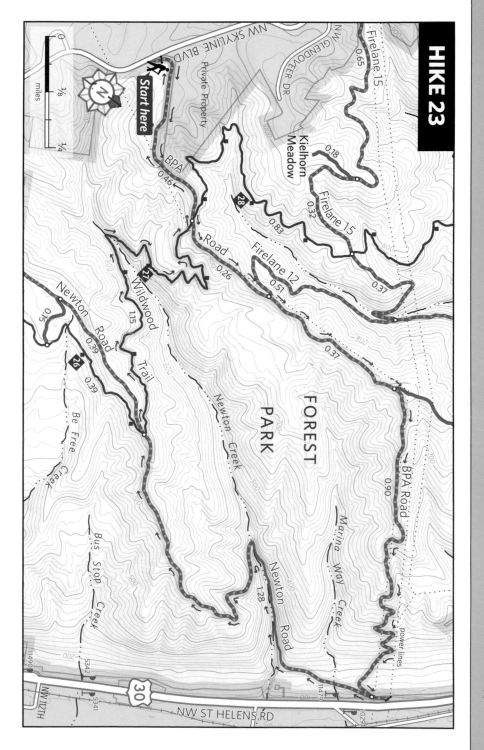

HIKE 23

Start here

NW SKYLINE BLVD

Private Property

NW GLENDOVEER DR

Firelane 15
0.65

0.18

Kielhorn
Meadow

Firelane 15
0.32

0.28

0.83

BPA
0.46

Road

0.26

Firelane 12
0.51

0.37

27

Wildwood

Newton Road
0.15

0.39
26

0.39

Be Free Creek

Trail
1.15

800

Newton Creek

FOREST
PARK

0.37

800

BPA Road
0.90

Marina Way Creek

power lines

Bus Stop Creek

Newton Road
1.28

700

11490

5342

5341

30

11479

10291

NW 112TH

NW ST HELENS RD

miles
0 1/8 1/4

N

Hike Twenty-Three

207

mountains and rivers, and travels along some of the most pristine, healthy woods and watersheds in the entire Portland park system.

To reach the trailhead, drive northwest along NW Skyline Boulevard, 5.6 miles from the intersection of NW Skyline Boulevard and NW Cornell Road. The parking area, which is just past Milepost 9 on Skyline, can accommodate up to six cars. It is somewhat difficult to see as it is off the road and near a row of mailboxes with numbers beginning at 9640. The start of the hike, BPA Road, is well marked on a large, green park gate.

More like a nice country lane than a utility access, BPA Road starts off heading slightly uphill, traversing under maple trees and alders that arch overhead. Soon the pathway begins a gentle descent, following a ridge that separates two major drainages of the Park— Miller Creek Watershed (900 acres) to the north and Newton Creek Watershed (447 acres) to the south. These two watersheds exhibit the healthiest ecosystems in the park, and are vegetated with native flowers, shrubs, and trees, and, in select parts, old-growth fir and cedar. Along the road, outstanding views of Mt. St. Helens and Mt. Rainier can be seen, as well as the winding Willamette and Columbia rivers. In June, beautiful orange tiger lilies are plentiful on the trail as well as, in spots, native Oregon iris, in light blue and lavender forms.

Continue on BPA Road for almost 2 miles, ignoring all side trails. As the path approaches U.S. Highway 30, its pitch becomes steeper and requires careful footing. When the ground is wet, it can be exceedingly slippery and, when dry, small pebbles on the hard road surface act like ball bearings. A trekking pole is helpful here. At lower elevations along the road, look for native Oregon white oak trees, which are uncommon in Forest Park. Other interesting plants can be found growing in these more dry sections of the park. Be on the lookout for oval-leaved viburnum and, in April, the beautiful white fawn lily. Also be observant for poison oak, prevalent in patches nearer the highway. BPA Road ends at an orange park gate at Highway 30. Just before reaching the gate, though, make a sharp turn to the right towards a second orange gate. This is Newton Road and the beginning of a scenic uphill portion of the loop.

Newton Road begins as a narrow trail. At 0.05 mile it crosses Marina Way Creek, and a quarter mile further, turns to ascend, following Newton Creek. The pathway climbs through the center of Newton Canyon, passing through luxuriant groves of cedar and hemlock and maple trees draped with moss. In spring and early summer, a wide variety of native birds can often be heard singing along the creek, including Western Wood Pewees, Black-headed Grosbeaks, Orange-crowned Warblers, and Swainson's Thrushes. After 1 mile, Newton Trail widens as it begins to rise more abruptly uphill. At 1.33 miles, Wildwood Trail intersects Newton Road. At the junction, turn right on Wildwood Trail.

From Milepost 26¼ to 26¾, Wildwood Trail gently meanders along the walls of beautiful Newton Canyon. Fine specimens of old-growth trees can be found here and native plants and ferns thrive.

This section is one of only a few pockets in Forest Park where true old-growth features can be observed. Under natural conditions, certain traits begin to be noticeable in forest stands that are over one hundred and fifty years old. These include the presence of huge trees that often have irregular crowns, or broken tops, and overtop the adjoining canopy. In Newton Canyon, some Douglas fir giants reach up to two hundred feet in height and eighty-seven inches at diameter at breast height. Other structural attributes indicative of old-growth habitat are the occurrence of large, standing dead trees (snags) and a prevalence of hefty dead and downed logs in various stages of decay. Snags are essential for cavity-nesting birds such as woodpeckers, and downed logs contribute to the health and nutrient level of the soil. Both of these features can be seen along this stretch of Wildwood Trail.

After Milepost 27, Wildwood Trail switchbacks several times and climbs up towards BPA Road. Along this section, the character of the vegetation of the forest changes yet again. Cedar, fir, and hemlock are reduced. The south-facing slope of Newton Canyon is predominately made up of younger maple and alder trees with a dense understory growth of elderberry, salmonberry, and other common shrubs. BPA

Road intersects Wildwood Trail just before Milepost 27½. Turn left here and complete the loop by hiking up BPA Road a half mile more to return to the parking area.

BPA Road and Firelanes 13 and 13A

DISTANCE: 3.62 miles round trip

HIKING TIME: 1½ to 2 hours

LOW ELEVATION: 473 feet

HIGH ELEVATION: 1065 feet

CUMULATIVE ELEVATION GAIN: 609 feet

DIFFICULTY RATING: Strenuous

GPS COORDINATES: 45° 35' 32.44" N 122° 48' 51.65" W
   514481mE 5048773mN

Foot traffic only on Firelanes 13 and 13A. BPA Road is open to cyclists and equestrians as well as pedestrians.

MILEAGE AND DIRECTIONS

0.00   Begin at BPA Road Trailhead, just off Skyline Blvd. Hike BPA Road.

0.46   Cross Wildwood Trail. Continue on BPA.

0.72   Intersect Firelane 12. Continue on BPA.

1.09   At junction with Firelane 13, turn left.

1.60   At intersection with Firelane 13A, turn right.

1.70   Conclusion of Firelane 13A. Retrace steps to junction with Firelane 13.

1.80   Turn right on Firelane 13.

1.91   Firelane 13 ends. Retrace steps back up Firelane 13.

2.53   Junction of Firelane 13 and BPA Road. Turn right and ascend BPA Road.

3.62   End at BPA Road Trailhead.

This hike is one for the "All Trails Challenge." It doesn't really go anywhere but down, and dead-ends above U.S. Highway 30. Presently, there are no connector trails to add some variety and to complete the trip requires retracing your steps back *up.* Like many of the east-west, bisecting roads and firelanes in Forest Park, this route extends from Skyline Boulevard (1,065 feet) towards Highway 30, and is therefore strenuous primarily due to its steepness. Yet this hike has its own rewards. For anyone desiring an outing with sweeping views of mountains and rivers on trails less traveled, and with a good workout thrown in, this is a fun one to try. The path follows under powerlines for much of its length and provides the chance to see wildlife often hidden among the trees. Be watchful for Red-tailed Hawks soaring above and Turkey Vultures congregating in the lower reaches. Tracks of black-tailed deer and coyotes are frequently observable in muddy spots along the ridge tops.

To reach the trailhead, drive northwest along NW Skyline Boulevard 5.6 miles from the intersection of NW Skyline Boulevard and NW Cornell Road. The parking area, which is just past Milepost 9 on NW Skyline, can accommodate up to six cars. It is somewhat difficult to see as it is off the road, near a row of mailboxes with numbers beginning at 9640. The start of the hike, the Bonneville Powerline Access (BPA) Road, is well marked on a large, green park gate.

BPA Road begins as a pretty, grassy lane that passes through a tree-lined corridor under a canopy of red alder trees. At first, it undulates gently, and then opens up as it approaches the powerlines. Cleared of trees to allow access for transmission poles, the road reveals in spots fine views of Mt. Rainier and Mt. St. Helens and the confluence of the Willamette and Columbia rivers. After approximately a half mile, BPA Road crosses Wildwood Trail. Stay on BPA Road, which continues down the ridgeline. This road is the separation point between two significant watersheds in Forest Park. On the left (north) of BPA Road is Miller Creek Watershed; on the right (south) is Newton Creek Watershed. Deep within these forested ravines remnant stands of old-growth trees can still be found.

A quarter mile past the intersection of Wildwood Trail, Firelane 12 intersects BPA Road on the left. Remain on BPA Road until it forks at a major junction underneath several powerlines. At this juncture, veer left on Firelane 13, and climb uphill.

Firelane 13 lies entirely within the Miller Creek Watershed. This watershed is recognized as being one of the City of Portland's premier natural assets. Its habitat and water quality conditions sustain populations of native fish and wildlife species. It furnishes clean water as well as flood control. Because they operate within a natural

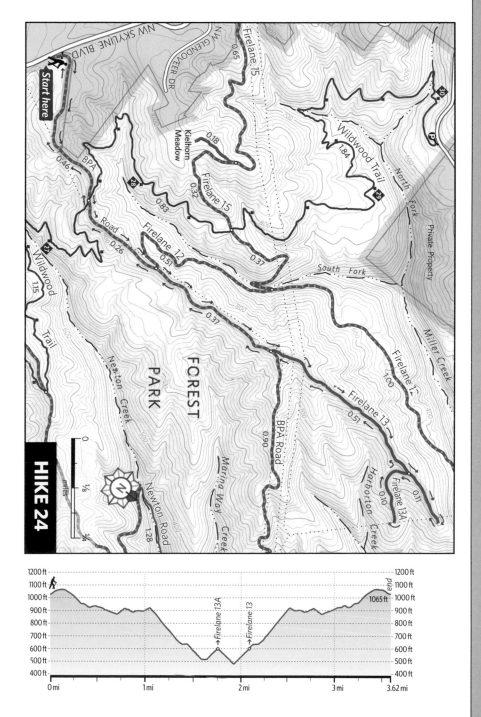

HIKE 24

Start here

NW SKYLINE BLVD

NW GLENDOVEER DR

Firelane 15   0.65

Kielhorn Meadow   0.18

0.46   BPA

28

Firelane 15   0.32

0.83

Road 0.26

Firelane 12   0.51

0.37

Wildwood Trail   1.84

North Fork

810

P

29

Private Property

South Fork

Miller Creek

21

Wildwood   1.15

Trail

Newton Creek

FOREST PARK

0.37

800

Firelane 13   0.51

Firelane 15   100

100

BPA Road   0.90

Marina Way Creek

Harborton Creek

0.10

Firelane 13A

0.11

Newton Road   1.28

0   ⅛   ¼   miles

ecosystem, the watershed's natural processes are superior to human efforts at storm water and pollution control.

> "Even at their best, technological solutions cannot replace the functions provided by habitats and species that have evolved together over millennia to create diverse, resilient, productive ecosystems. ... Native species have a reasonable chance of survival with the right hydrology, the right habitats, adequate water quality and biological diversity. With these elements functioning properly, the ecosystem itself is likely to become more diverse, complex, resilient and self-sustaining."
>
> —2005 Portland Watershed Management Plan

At the crest of the hilltop, Firelane 13 affords one of the most far-reaching overlooks in Forest Park. Even though the view is compromised by a network of powerlines, it's worth taking the time to pause at the picnic tables placed under the transmission poles to look around. Rural Sauvie Island and Mts. St. Helens, Rainier, and Adams are observable, and offset by the curving blue courses of the Willamette and Columbia rivers and Multnomah Channel. Continue

on Firelane 13, being watchful of your footing, as the trail heads sharply down the ridgeline before entering back into the shelter of trees. After a half mile, Firelane 13A trail approaches on the right.

To explore this short firelane spur, turn right and wind through a second-growth forest of Douglas fir and bigleaf maple, with rich, native understory vegetation of Oregon grape, salal, and sword ferns. Firelane 13A ends at the top of a ridge 0.5 mile from the Willamette River. Just to the south is Harborton Creek, which flows deep within the canyon, and eventually enters into Multnomah Channel.

As there is no existing trail leading from this point to Highway 30, turn around and hike back to the junction of Firelanes 13A and 13. Turn right and walk 0.11 mile further to reach the end of Firelane 13, where there is an overlook. Situated underneath cleared powerlines, this promontory reveals tremendous views of the northern end of Forest Park. Looking to the northwest, the Coast Range can be seen, and also the important forested corridor that lies between the rural mountains and Forest Park. This vantage point makes clear the link between the two, and can help one understand how wildlife can travel from what scientists call "rural reserves" into the city. This connection is a major reason why Forest Park exhibits such an unusual abundance and diversity of animals native to the Northwest.

For the return trip to the trailhead, retrace your steps back up Firelane 13 and BPA Road.

Firelanes 1, 2, and 3, Wildwood Trail, Maple Trail, and Nature Trail Loop

DISTANCE: 6.13 miles

HIKING TIME: 3 hours

LOW ELEVATION: 553 feet

HIGH ELEVATION: 984 feet

CUMULATIVE ELEVATION GAIN: 836 feet

DIFFICULTY RATING: Moderate

GPS COORDINATES: 45° 32' 53.19" N 122° 44' 41.94" W
   519907mE 5043873mN

Foot traffic only on Firelane 2 and on Wildwood Trail, Maple Trail, and Nature Trail. Firelane 1 is also open to horses and bicycles. Firelane 3 is open to cyclists and pedestrians only.

MILEAGE AND DIRECTIONS

0.00   Begin at Firelane 1 Trailhead off Forest Lane.

0.33   Turn left onto Wildwood Trail.

1.28   Intersect Chestnut Trail. Stay on Wildwood.

1.88   Cross Firelane 2. Stay on Wildwood.

1.98   Intersect Maple Trail. Stay on Wildwood.

2.79   Turn right on Firelane 3.

3.10   Turn right on Maple Trail.

3.96   Turn left on Wildwood Trail.

4.06   Turn left on Firelane 2.

4.52   Turn right on Leif Erikson Drive.

4.80   Turn right on Nature Trail.

5.73   Turn right on Firelane 1.

6.13   End at Firelane 1 Trailhead.

Firelanes are an integral part of Forest Park. Twelve in total, they run predominantly east-west down the flanks of the park, stretching from NW 53rd Avenue (Firelane 1) to the north end of the park near NW Newberry Road (Firelane 15). Other than official trucks, no motorized vehicles are allowed on them. Many are open to cyclists, some to equestrians. All are open to pedestrians, who can find great enjoyment strolling up or down their wider pathways that seem more

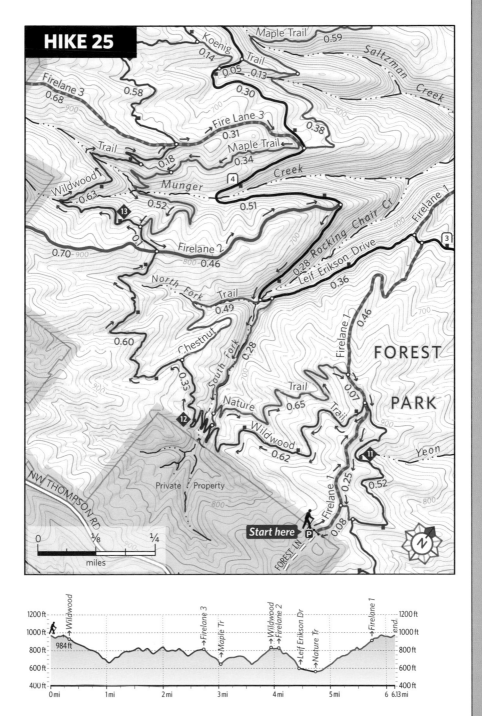

HIKE 25

Maple Trail 0.59

Saltzman Creek

Koenig 0.14 Trail 0.05 .0.13
0.30
0.58

Firelane 3 0.68
-900

Fire Lane 3 0.31
Maple Trail 0.34
0.18

Trail
Wildwood 0.63
13
0.52
Munger
4 Creek 0.51
0.38

0.70-900
Firelane 2 800 0.46
0.28 Rocking Chair Cr
Leif Erikson Drive 0.36
Firelane 1
3

North Fork Trail 0.49
0.60
Chestnut South Fork 0.28
Firelane 1 0.46

FOREST

0.35
Nature 0.65
Trail 0.07
PARK

12
Trail
Wildwood 0.62
0.25
11 Yeon

NW THOMPSON RD.
Private Property
Firelane 1 0.52

0 ⅛ ¼
miles

Start here P
FOREST LN
0.08

N

0mi 1mi 2mi 3mi 4mi 5mi 6 6.13mi

1200ft
1000ft 984ft
800ft
600ft
400ft

→Wildwood
→Firelane 3
→Maple Tr
→Wildwood
→Firelane 2
→Leif Erikson Dr
→Nature Tr
→Firelane 1
end

1200ft
1000ft
800ft
600ft
400ft

like picturesque country paths than fire roads. This loop explores a few of the southernmost firelanes, as it travels along some of the most scenic trails in the park.

To reach the trailhead, drive 2.2 miles from the intersection of NW 23rd Avenue and NW Lovejoy along NW Cornell Road (Lovejoy becomes Cornell Road beyond NW 25th) until it intersects with NW 53rd Drive. Turn right on 53rd Drive and follow it for 1.7 miles, then turn right again on NW Forest Lane, which is marked by a sign. Follow Forest Lane (which is actually the beginning of Firelane 1) until it meets a locked park gate.

Walk past the gate and head downhill on this uppermost section of Firelane 1. At 0.33 mile, the firelane intersects Wildwood Trail. Turn left and begin hiking on Wildwood, which soon takes the hiker through woods of Douglas fir and enters the beautiful Saltzman Creek Watershed.

All along this section of Wildwood, the trail is gentle and provides easy walking. Continue on the trail, passing all side trails—Nature, Chestnut, Firelane 2 and Maple trails—until Firelane 3. Just before Firelane 3, near Milepost 13¼, Wildwood crosses over Munger Creek.

Munger Creek is named after Thornton Munger (1883–1975), an influential, pioneering scientist who for many years was chief of research for the U.S. Forest Service at the Pacific Northwest Experiment Station. Munger is well known for his long-term studies of native plants and wildlife of Oregon and Washington, and his research legacy has been honored by naming the celebrated Wind River Study Area of the Washington Cascades the "Thornton Munger Research Natural Area." Along with Ding Cannon, Munger was instrumental in the establishment of Forest Park in 1948 and for twelve years served as chairman of the Forest Park Committee of Fifty. Throughout his tenure, he was a strong proponent for what today is widely referred to as "urban natural areas." Until his death, Munger worked dedicatedly to obtain private inholdings along the parks' boundaries for inclusion into, as he termed it, this "wilderness within the city."

At the intersection of Wildwood Trail and Firelane 3, turn right. Firelane 3 is part of the site of the worst fire to ever strike Forest Park. In 1951, the Bonny Slope Burn raged across Forest Park and for three days burned twelve hundred acres inside the park and even more than that to the west, where Forest Heights development is located today. After the devastation, plans for fire management were put into place and firelanes were built throughout the park to allow needed access into the park. No major fires have occurred in Forest Park for nearly sixty years.

Continue heading down Firelane 3 for a quarter mile. At its juncture with Maple Trail, bear sharply right on Maple Trail, which follows the ravines bordering Munger Creek, and continue on Maple for almost 1 mile. Maple Trail, one of only three major lateral trails running north-south between Skyline Boulevard and Highway 30 (the other being Leif Erikson Drive and Wildwood Trail), captures the spirit of Forest Park with its beauty and quiet solitude. At Maple Trail's terminus with Wildwood Trail near Wildwood Milepost 13, turn left on Wildwood and backtrack for 0.1 mile until it crosses Firelane 2.

Firelane 2 is a particularly scenic pathway open only to pedestrians. It extends on both sides of Wildwood Trail. Unfortunately, the upper portion, after slightly more than a quarter mile, comes up to privately owned property. This negates access to Skyline Boulevard and makes the trail a dead end. Park advocates hope that sometime in the future this property of exquisite conifer woods could be acquired and make an important contribution to Forest Park as well as protecting a significant portion of the Saltzman Creek Watershed headwaters.

For the loop, turn left onto Firelane 2 and hike downhill for 0.46 mile along a ridge dividing Munger Creek and the main stem of Rocking Chair Creek. Firelane 2 ends at Leif Erikson Drive. Turn right on Leif Erikson and hike 0.31 mile to the intersection of Nature Trail, coming in from above. Here, turn right onto Nature Trail, crossing the south fork of Rocking Chair Creek.

The origin of the name Rocking Chair Creek sometimes mystifies Forest Park hikers and several explanations have arisen through the years. The truth behind the name, however, is rather prosaic: it arose from a park employee's discovery, long ago, of a lone rocking chair in the creek near this spot.

For 0.28 mile, Nature Trail follows Rocking Chair Creek and ascends up the canyon. The path then levels out for 0.65 mile, ending at a large open meadow. Several new benches are placed within the grassy glade and are perfect for taking a water break or picnicking. Firelane 1 is just beyond the meadow. Conclude the loop by hiking up the firelane for 0.4 mile more and return to the parking area.

Firelane 5, Leif Erikson Drive, Cleator Trail, Wildwood Trail, and Saltzman Road Loop

DISTANCE: 4.10 miles
HIKING TIME: 2 hours
LOW ELEVATION: 627 feet
HIGH ELEVATION: 1080 feet
CUMULATIVE ELEVATION GAIN: 413 feet
DIFFICULTY RATING: Moderate
GPS COORDINATES: 45° 33' 43.62" N 122° 47' 0.05" W
    516908mE 5045420mN

Foot traffic only on Cleator Trail and Wildwood Trail. Leif Erikson Drive and Saltzman Road are open to pedestrians, cyclists, and equestrians. Firelane 5 is open to pedestrians and cyclists only.

MILEAGE AND DIRECTIONS

0.00   Begin at the Saltzman Road Trailhead. Hike Firelane 5.
0.23   Side trail to right leading to overlook. Continue on Firelane 5.
0.87   Cross Wildwood Trail. Continue on lower Firelane 5.
1.10   Turn right at the junction with Leif Erikson Drive.
1.48   Cross Saltzman Road. Stay on Leif Erikson.
2.21   Turn right on Cleator Trail.
2.45   Turn right on Wildwood Trail.
2.98   Turn left on Saltzman Road.
4.10   End at Saltzman Road Trailhead.

Walking along this very pleasant loop in the center of Forest Park is reminiscent of a stroll along country roads with the added benefit that no cars are allowed. In addition, it makes a great running

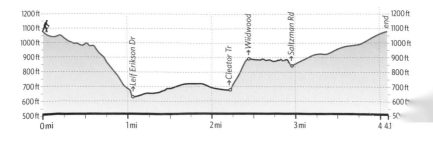

loop. Upper Firelane 5, Leif Erikson Road, and Saltzman Road are well maintained and, for most of their distances, allow easy hiking and good footing. The lower section of Firelane 5, with the help of volunteers and many cycling enthusiasts, has recently been made into a narrow single-track trail. Cleator and Wildwood trails are footpaths only, and offer a more primitive feeling. At several points along the loop, scenic viewpoints of the broad Doane Creek Watershed can be observed.

To reach the trailhead from downtown Portland, drive northwest on U.S. Highway 30 (St. Helens Road) for 7.2 miles from its intersection with Interstate 405. Continue past the St. John's Bridge and turn left at the traffic light immediately after the bridge. This is NW Bridge Avenue and the northern ramp to the bridge. Take the first right onto NW Germantown Road, and follow it for 2.1 miles until its intersection with NW Skyline Boulevard. Turn left on NW Skyline and go 1.7 miles until NW Saltzman Road. Turn left and continue for 0.1 mile more to reach the parking area.

Firelane 5 begins at a locked park gate. Pass around the gate and begin walking on a wide, graveled, all-weather road, which continues for a half mile before turning to an earthen surface. At first, the path is mostly level and wanders among a forest of approximately sixty to one hundred and twenty years of age. Some of the evergreens in this area are nearly one hundred and thirty feet tall. In woods such as these, the understory shrubs and plants tend to be diverse, as greater amounts of light are able to pass through the more open, seasonally leafless hardwood species. In addition, the higher nitrogen content of the soil under red alder makes for conditions conducive for a well-developed shrub layer.

After a quarter mile, a graveled roadway comes in from the right, extending up a steep hill. This road was originally intended to lead to a large homesite, one of many slated for development in this area. In an effort to preserve Forest Park's integrity, Metro purchased twenty-seven acres of important interior property within the park in 2000 with funds from a 1995 bond measure. At the top of this side-path is

HIKE 26

Start here

NW WIND RIDGE RD

Saltzman Road

Wildwood Trail

Firelane 5

0.87

0.69

0.23

112

15

Wildwood Tr

0.36

800

Cleator Trail 0.24

16

0.53

Saltzman Rd

0.15

0.50

0.23

Leif Erikson Drive 0.73

16

Firelane 4 0.48

0.88

Saltzman Road 0.45

Maple Creek

Maple Trail 1.28

Maple Trail

17

7

0.53

Doane Cr

600

FOREST

500

PARK

1100

1100

1000

1000

900

N

miles

0   1/8   1/4

a far overlook above the canyons that can be viewed in late fall and winter when leaves are off the trees.

Continue on Firelane 5. A second road to the right appears after another quarter mile as the firelane passes beneath a powerline. This, too, was a designated homesite but now is protected. The graveled surface of Firelane 5 ends at this spot, and the trail narrows as it descends through a scenic conifer grove. Numerous large Douglas fir trees can be seen as the road continues down the ridge. Some of these tall trees, with their stalwart, straight trunks, are approaching one hundred and twenty years old.

Wildwood Trail intersects Firelane 5 at 0.87 mile. Cross Wildwood and continue on the lower portion of Firelane 5, which no longer is a road but becomes a single-track trail for the next quarter mile. This section of the firelane is often used by mountain bikers, who helped in its construction. During wet weather, though, the pathway can be slick, and at spots exposed tree roots cross the trail surface, requiring more careful attention. At its conclusion, Firelane 5 intersects Leif Erikson Drive. A large green structure that resembles a giant dumpster is located here. In the past this was a water-retention facility for use in case of wildfire. In 1990, it was abandoned due to problems with leaking and when new water sources became available along NW Skyline Boulevard.

Turn right on Leif Erikson Drive for 0.4 mile. The road travels above Doane Creek Canyon on a level and graveled surface. Near 6¼ miles, Leif Erikson crosses NW Saltzman Road. At this intersection, a wide-spanning view of the St. John's Bridge, Vancouver Lake, Terminal 6, and the confluence of the Willamette and Columbia rivers can be seen. Here, too, is a picnic bench for those who wish to take a moment to enjoy the overlook.

Continue on Leif Erikson Drive by crossing Saltzman Road and, after a quick jog to the left on Saltzman, taking the first hard right through an open gate. Stay on Leif Erikson until Milepost 5½. Here, begin looking for the junction of Cleator Trail, which comes in from the right. Turn onto Cleator Trail, and hike the relatively

Cleator Trail was named for Fred W. Cleator (1884–1957), who worked for the U.S. Forest Service for many years as the Supervisor for Recreation for Oregon and Washington. An avid outdoorsman and ardent conservationist, Cleator left an unparalleled legacy for the Northwest. In 1928, he initiated and developed a route of trails down the spine of the Cascades in Oregon and Washington, today known as the Pacific Crest Trail. He was instrumental in the advancement of many wilderness areas within the two states. Additionally, in the 1940s he became a resolute voice to create a wilderness park in the West Hills of Portland, today's Forest Park. Working as a volunteer, he enthusiastically led groups of Mazamas, Scouts, and other groups in building trails and restoring the forest vegetation on the area's denuded, burned, and logged hillsides. Together with close friend Garnett "Ding" Cannon, Cleator worked to stimulate interest in the creation of Forest Park and was pivotal in motivating the City Club to study the issue. The City Club's resultant report in 1945—advocating for a wilderness Forest Park—was largely influenced by Cleator's steadfast support.

steep pathway that looks out over Maple Canyon as it passes through second-growth woods while steadily climbing for a quarter mile.

Cleator Trail ends at an intersection with Wildwood Trail at Milepost 15½. Presently, the trail ends here, as the upper portion soon enters private property. This land is another example of an area within Forest Park's boundaries that should be protected from development as it comprises a significant portion of the headwaters in the Doane Creek Watershed.

Turn right on Wildwood Trail and head north on the level trail for a half mile. At Milepost 16, Wildwood intersects with Saltzman Road. Turn left and continue up Saltzman. The road is graveled, well maintained, and provides good footing for walking or running. Like Firelane 5, Saltzman Road gives the appearance of an agreeable country lane as it climbs towards Skyline Boulevard. After 1.12 miles, the road reaches the Saltzman Parking Area, completing the loop.

It is important to preserve the headwaters within a watershed because they determine the integrity of an entire drainage system. What happens in the headwaters translates all the way down the stream. Keeping the headwaters of a watershed intact and in a naturally vegetated state helps to control localized flooding downstream, provides cleaner water, prevents "flashy flows" of water running off pavement, and moderates water temperature. In essence, everything that happens in a watershed's headwaters is reflected in the downstream portion of its creeks. In a short, steep drainage, such as those within Forest Park, entire streams can become degraded if headwaters lose their native vegetation and are developed. In this way, protecting the upper portions of Forest Park's streams remains a priority for the future health of the park and the Willamette River.

Tolinda Trail, Springville Road, Wildwood Trail, and Waterline Trail Loop

DISTANCE: 5.37 mile loop

HIKING TIME: 2½ hours

LOW ELEVATION: 258 feet

HIGH ELEVATION: 1068 feet

CUMULATIVE ELEVATION GAIN: 847 feet

DIFFICULTY RATING: Strenuous

GPS COORDINATES: 45° 35' 17.75" N 122° 46' 43.97" W
  517248mE 5048326mN

Foot traffic only on Tolinda Trail, Wildwood Trail, and Waterline Trail. Springville Road also allows bicycles. Leif Erikson Drive is also open to bicycles and equestrians.

NOTE: *Both Tolinda and Waterline trails are steep and can be very slippery under wet conditions. These trails may not be advisable in winter.*

MILEAGE AND DIRECTIONS

0.00 Begin at Tolinda Trailhead on Germantown Road.

0.75 Turn left on Leif Erikson Road.

1.55 Turn right on Springville Road.

1.93 Turn right on Wildwood Trail.

3.47 Turn left on Waterline Trail.

3.87 Intersect with Waterline Meadow at Skyline Blvd. Return down Waterline Trail.

4.27 Intersect with Wildwood Trail. Continue on Waterline Trail.

4.62 Intersect Leif Erikson. Turn left 120 feet. Turn right on Tolinda Trail.

5.37 End at Tolinda Trailhead on Germantown.

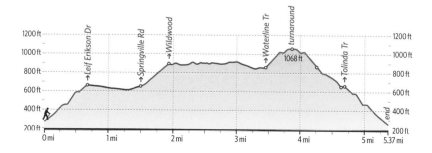

The Tolinda/Springville/Waterline Trail Loop is a fascinating hike for two reasons. One, it traverses the full width of the park, climbing all the way from lower Germantown Road near the St. John's Bridge to Skyline Boulevard and back. Two, it allows a close-up glimpse of a nearly intact, healthy watershed—Forest Park's Springville Watershed—from its headwaters to the point where it empties. While requiring some exertion and careful footing in the steepest parts, it is a worthwhile route through deep coniferous woods and along clear flowing streams, as well as offering the chance to see the largest meadow, maintained and mowed by Portland Parks, within Forest Park.

To reach the trailhead, drive northwest on U.S. Highway 30 (St. Helens Road) for 7.2 miles from its intersection with Interstate 405. Continue past the St. John's Bridge and turn left at the traffic light immediately after. This is NW Bridge Avenue and the north ramp to the bridge. Take the first right onto NW Germantown Road and follow it for 0.3 mile. The parking area is on the left by a fire hydrant and a park gate. Be sure not to block this gate as it is used by official vehicles.

Begin the hike by walking around the locked gate and heading uphill. The trail starts out fairly gently, climbing along the side of a ridge hugging Springville Canyon, and at first is well maintained and partially graveled. Groves of large middle-aged conifers line the ravine while Springville Creek flows in the canyon bottom a hundred or more feet below. As with many trails that border Highway 30 and other major traffic routes, invasive species such as ivy and blackberry, escaping from urban areas, have entered the canyon in its lower reaches and are degrading the health of the native vegetation. Attempts to combat these destructive species are perpetually ongoing.

After a switchback, the trail approaches a level clearing. This is the site of the old Camp Tolinda—a Camp Fire Girls camp that operated from 1948 until the 1970s. Today, it is no longer used and young cedar trees have been planted as revegetation efforts. All along this bench in June, the pink blossoms of hundreds of native fireweed emblazon the

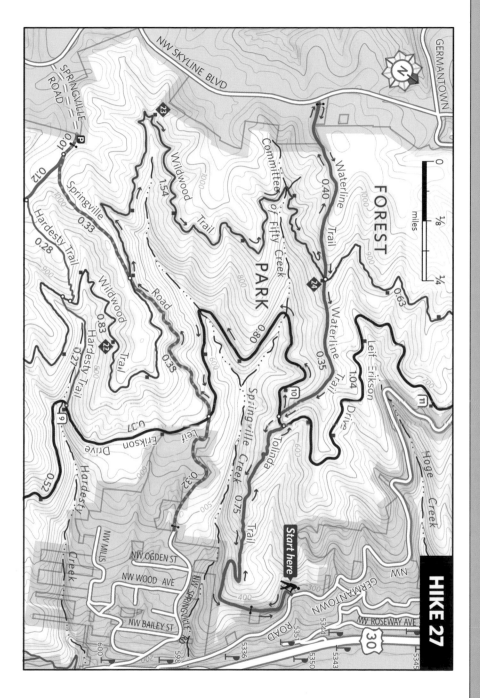

NW SKYLINE BLVD

GERMANTOWN

SPRINGVILLE
ROAD

FOREST

PARK

Committee of Fifty Creek

Wildwood Trail 1.54

Springville 0.33

Hardesty Trail 0.28

Wildwood Trail 0.83

Hardesty Trail 0.27

Road 0.38

Waterline Trail 0.40

0.63

Leif Erikson Drive 1.04

Waterline Trail 0.35

Springville Creek 0.80

Leif Erikson Drive 0.27

Hardesty 0.52

Toliada 0.32

Springville Creek Trail 0.75

Hoge Creek

NW MILLS

NW OGDEN ST

NW WOOD AVE

NW BAILEY ST

NW SPRINGVILLE RD

NW GERMANTOWN

NW ROSEWAY AVE

Start here

HIKE 27

30

miles

0   1/8   1/4

23

24

P 0.01

0.12

10

11

6

22

trailsides. Further up, showy displays of six-foot-tall Columbian lilies can be seen in early summer.

After the clearing, the route becomes more steep as it enters the middle of the park. Before long, ivy declines, eventually disappearing completely, as healthy assemblages of native sword ferns, Oregon grape, and salal grow vigorously beneath the tall evergreens. Smaller but noteworthy plants such as native waterleaf and piggyback plants also proliferate trailside. Numerous birds can be heard calling from the woods of lush Springville Canyon, the species varying at different times of the year. Bird watchers can delight in hearing Olive-sided Flycatchers, Downy and Hairy Woodpeckers, Brown Creepers, Pacific-slope Flycatchers, Black-headed Grosbeaks, Western Tanagers, American Goldfinches, Pine Siskins, Wilson's Warblers, Winter Wrens, and perhaps even a Pygmy Owl.

At 0.67 mile, Tolinda Trail ends at Leif Erikson Drive. Turn left on Leif Erikson, and walk until the intersection with NW Springville Road. Fine views into the throat of deep Springville Canyon follow the entire length of Leif Erikson, where mature, tall, straight-limbed Douglas firs predominate. Turn right at Springville Road and for slightly more than a quarter mile head up the gently ascending pathway. Be on the lookout for white dogwoods blooming alongside the road in springtime. Pairs of Red-tailed Hawks (photo page 69) are often observed flying over this part of the park. At the juncture of Springville Road and Wildwood Trail, turn right on Wildwood.

This section of Wildwood Trail, from Milepost 22½ to 24, meanders exclusively through the 695-acre Springville Creek Watershed. The headwaters to this drainage, stretching to Skyline Boulevard, can be seen as the trail curves in and out of ravines made by tributaries to Springville Creek. At the wetter rivulet areas, red elderberry and salmonberry bushes proliferate, as well as birds that prefer a more moist habitat, such as Wilson's Warblers (photos page 73), a jaunty, bright yellow bird that, because of black markings on the top of its head, looks to be wearing a black beret.

At Wildwood Milepost 24, turn left onto Waterline Trail. This ridge-line trail is the dividing line between Springville Creek Watershed, to the south, and Linnton Creek Watershed, to the north. The path follows Committee of Fifty Creek and ends at its headwaters, near Skyline Boulevard.

Committee of Fifty Creek is named after the civic organization that, in 1946, began a plan of action to establish Forest Park. Led by Ding Cannon and Thornton Munger, the Committee of Fifty endeavored to follow through on the City Club of Portland's recommendations in a 1945 report supporting the creation of a six-thousand-acre primitive park for Portland. After months of dedicated work, the group met with success and the park was at last established in 1948. Without the involvement of the City Club and the Committee of Fifty, Forest Park would not be here today.

From this vantage point along Waterline Trail, the health of the Springville Creek Watershed can be comprehended by understanding several key features. For the most part, the area has virtually full forest cover, with only small pockets of private development near the road. This lack of development aids in preventing pollutants from entering the stream flow. Too, the umbrella of cover helps to reduce the effects of erosion and works to mitigate flooding from seasonal rainfall. This helps to protect lower areas from damaging floods as well as providing the Willamette River with cleaner inflow. In addition, the vegetation of the Springville watershed is predominately native and in good condition—factors that help to maintain biodiversity. All of these contributions play an invaluable role in the City of Portland's work to improve the watershed health of the entire city.

Walk 0.4 mile to the top of Waterline Trail. Here, several side paths lead up to a water reservoir situated in an extensive, open field. This attractive spot is the largest grassy meadow in Forest Park; it is well worth the time to stop at one of the picnic tables to enjoy the setting.

Continue the hike by returning down Waterline Trail. This pathway can be slippery in sections and has several steep pitches that, when wet, are more difficult to navigate; trekking poles can very helpful in such parts. At the intersection of Wildwood Trail, continue on lower Waterline Trail until the intersection with Leif Erikson Drive.

Waterline Trail ends here. To return to the Tolinda Trailhead, turn left and walk 120 feet to access Tolinda Trail, which takes off downhill and to the right. After a little more than a half mile, Tolinda Trail ends at Germantown Road Parking Area, completing the loop.

Lower Firelane 1, Wildwood Trail, Chestnut Trail, and Leif Erikson Loop

DISTANCE: 5.19 miles

HIKING TIME: 2½ hours

LOW ELEVATION: 43 feet

HIGH ELEVATION: 943 feet

CUMULATIVE ELEVATION GAIN: 1149 feet

DIFFICULTY RATING: Strenuous

GPS COORDINATES: 45° 33' 15.66" N 122° 43' 59.32" W
520828mE 5044569mN

Foot traffic only on Wildwood Trail and Chestnut Trail. Firelane 1 and Leif Erikson Drive also allow both horses and bicycles.

NOTE: *If access to Lower Firelane 1 is a problem, this loop can be made in reverse by starting at the top of Upper Firelane 1, located off NW 53rd Drive and Forest Lane. (For directions, see Hike 25.)*

MILEAGE AND DIRECTIONS

0.00   Begin at Lower Firelane 1 Trailhead off Highway 30. Hike Lower Firelane 1.

1.43   Cross Leif Erikson Drive. Continue on Firelane 1.

1.89   Intersect Nature Trail. Continue on Firelane 1.

1.96   Turn right onto Wildwood Trail.

2.91   Turn right on Chestnut Trail.

3.40   Turn right on Leif Erikson Drive.

3.76   Turn left on Lower Firelane 1.

5.19   End at Lower Firelane 1 Trailhead.

For those wishing to get in shape for summer hiking in the mountains, this little-traveled loop provides good conditioning, for it climbs nearly nine hundred feet in less than two miles. But it also offers the chance to explore a section of Forest Park where there are no other trails and yields some of the finest year-round, panoramic views in the entire park. Additionally, more large mammals may use this important travel corridor than any other southern route in Forest Park. The chance to see hawks, coyotes, and black-tailed deer is perhaps greater here than any other close-in pathway in Forest Park.

Presently, there is no parking available at the trailhead, although Portland Parks and Recreation has future plans to create an official park entrance here. One can easily access this area by bus, however, or be dropped off at the beginning of Lower Firelane 1. To reach the trailhead from downtown Portland, drive northwest on U.S. Highway 30 (NW Yeon Avenue) until its three-way intersection with NW St. Helens Road and NW Kittridge Avenue. Turn left onto NW St. Helen's Road, then immediately right beside a chain-link fence by Brazil Electric Motors (4315 NW St. Helen's Road). Or, by bus take TriMet #17 from downtown and disembark at the bus stop at the intersection of NW Yeon and Kittridge avenues. From here, proceed carefully across the crosswalk and look for the parking lot of Brazil Motors. The trailhead to Lower Firelane 1 is just north and at the back end of the parking lot where a steep track leads up the slope near a park gate.

The hike begins along a rocky roadway that rises sharply with several steep switchbacks until it reaches a powerline. At this intersection, the pathway immediately levels out and begins to follow under the powerline, paralleling US Highway 30, for slightly over 1 mile. These lower, eastern-most reaches of Forest Park have an industrial feel and, being so close to the city, sometimes evince home sites used by transients. The vegetation along the highway is severely degraded with large tracts of invasive weeds, predominantly English ivy, Himalayan blackberry, non-native clematis, and English holly. These destructive plants escape from the city and begin to take hold, requiring constant eradication to try to keep them in check. Fortunately, a model new

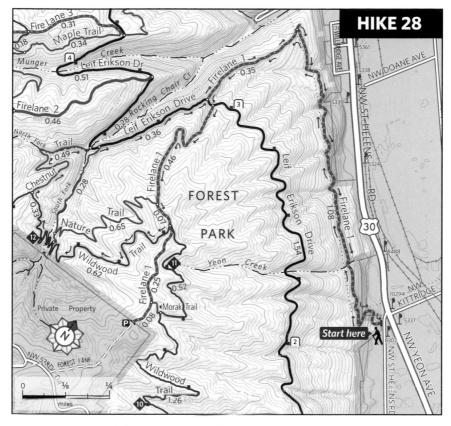

program, initiated by Portland Parks and Recreation, is generating much-needed help. In a collaborative effort, the Federal Emergency Management Agency, Portland General Electric, City of Portland Bureau of Environmental Services, and Portland Parks are working together to clean up these degraded sites surrounding the powerline by replanting with native species, with the shared goals of fire reduction, powerline access, and habitat restoration.

For the first mile, Lower Firelane 1 is wide and pleasant on which to walk. It rises and falls moderately as it crosses several intermittent creeks—most notably Yeon Creek—and winds along ravines within the Willbridge Watershed. Being an important corridor pathway, it is a great place to look for game. Abundant evidence of black-tailed deer tracks and droppings and coyote scat signifies its use by lots of mammals.

Hike Twenty-Eight

Black-tailed deer frequent Forest Park, but their tracks are generally more visible than the animals themselves. These deer are not herd animals and seldom form large associations. Rather, they occur in small family groups or small groups of bucks. Antlers shed by bucks are sometimes found alongside the firelanes.

Noise and clamor from the industrial area is a constant companion as well, but the wide-ranging views from this low shoulder make the trip well worth it. Along the route, all four of the major mountains—Mt. Rainier, Mt. St. Helens, Mt. Adams, and, further up the trail, Mt. Hood—are visible, as well as a panorama of Portland, from the US Bank Building ("Big Pink") downtown, through the industrial area, Swan Island, University of Portland, to the Burlington and St. John's bridges and beyond.

At 1.1 miles, Firelane 1 makes an abrupt ninety-degree turn to the left as it ends at a promontory directly above Rocking Chair Creek Canyon. Leaving the powerline, the trail follows a ridge separating two watersheds, Saltzman Creek and Willbridge. The character of the firelane changes and becomes more natural; sword ferns cover the forest floor underneath bigleaf maple trees, western hemlock trees, and large Douglas fir. Slightly over a quarter mile further, Firelane 1 crosses Leif Erikson Drive. Stay on Firelane 1, and go uphill,

continuing to gain elevation, sometimes steeply. After one-half mile, pass the Nature Trail junction coming in on the right. Continue on Firelane 1 a short distance more until its intersection with Wildwood Trail. For anyone desiring a rest, this is the place. Four new picnic tables are placed here at the uppermost part of this loop. From here on, it's nearly all downhill. After a break, turn right on Wildwood Trail and begin heading north, for 1 mile.

This section of Wildwood Trail, from Milepost 11¼ to just before 12¼, wends in and out of numerous coniferous ravines, all a part of the scenic Saltzman Creek drainage. Just past Milepost 11¾, the trail crosses South Fork Rocking Chair Creek. From this point, the trail climbs uphill, out of the ravine, until it reaches Chestnut Trail, a quarter mile further.

Turn right onto Chestnut Trail. This short trail is narrow and rocky in spots, but highly characteristic of native Northwest forests with its array of plants and wildflowers. It descends relatively quickly and can be slippery when wet after rain. For much of the way, Chestnut Trail follows North Fork Rocking Chair Creek. The trail ends at Leif Erikson Drive. Turn right on Leif Erikson by a picnic table and the well-known American chestnut tree for which Chestnut Trail was named.

Follow Leif Erikson for slightly under a half mile on an exceptionally nice part of the drive as it overlooks the steepest and most impressive section of Rocking Chair Creek Canyon. On the uphill portion, large outcroppings of basalt border the road and in places the walls are punctuated with abundant growths of licorice ferns. At the junction with Lower Firelane 1, turn left. Firelane 1 descends sharply. As with many of the more precipitous trails in Forest Park, walking uphill, although strenuous, is easier. The same trail going downhill can be more difficult. Bare slopes can be slippery, if wet, and provide less-secure footing. Trekking poles can be helpful on these downhill slopes.

At the intersection with the powerline, continue on Lower Firelane 1, following beneath the powerline. A mile further, the firelane drops down to St. Helen's Road, completing the loop.

Hoyt Arboretum

DISTANCE: 2.58 miles

HIKING TIME: 1½ hours

DIFFICULTY RATING: Easy

GPS COORDINATES: 45° 30' 56.52" N 122° 42' 57.42" W
     522185.7mE 5040280mN

Foot traffic only on all trails in Hoyt Arboretum.

MILEAGE AND DIRECTIONS

0.00   Begin at Visitor Center. Hike Overlook Trail.

0.53   Turn left on Maple Trail.

0.60   Turn left on Hawthorne Trail.

0.77   Turn right on Cherry Trail. At intersection with Wildwood Trail, jog left for 20 yards, then left again on the continuation of Cherry Trail.

0.98   At upper intersection with Wildwood Trail, turn left on Wildwood Trail.

1.03   Turn right on Holly Trail. Hike Holly Trail to Fairview Boulevard.

1.13   Cross Fairview Blvd., and turn right by picnic shelter on Spruce Trail. Hike Spruce Trail.

1.55   Turn left on Wildwood Trail (between Milepost 2½ and 2¾).

1.81   Turn left on White Pine Trail. Cross Fischer Lane and continue on White Pine.

2.31   At intersection with Creek Trail, turn right.

2.39   Turn left on Hemlock Trail.

2.45   Turn left on Fir Trail.

2.58   End at Fairview Boulevard and Visitor Center.

Hoyt Arboretum is a 185-acre, living museum featuring trees and plants collected from all parts of the globe. Established in 1928 jointly by the U.S. Forest Service, Portland Parks, and community leaders including Thornton Munger, its peaceful, natural setting, through which the southern-most section of Wildwood Trail traverses, is an important native laboratory and conservator of the earth's biodiversity. Today, the arboretum showcases more than eight thousand individual trees and shrubs, including many rare

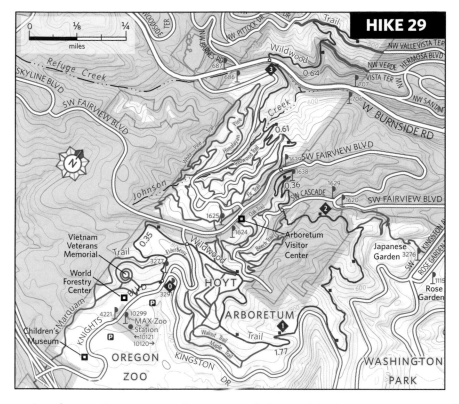

and endangered specimens from around the world. The temperate climate of western Oregon makes this one of the few places where such a remarkable variety of trees can grow. Over six thousand of the arboretum's trees and shrubs are labeled, denoting common and scientific names and native habitats. As our planet continues to lose native species to extinction, Hoyt Arboretum plays an invaluable role in furthering scientific understanding, safeguarding valuable genetic material, and preserving diversity on a global level.

To reach the arboretum, travel U.S. Highway 26 from downtown Portland. Take the Oregon Zoo exit and continue past the zoo on SW Knights Boulevard. At Knights' intersection with SW Fairview Boulevard, turn right and go 1/8 mile further to the Arboretum Visitor's Center. Hoyt Arboretum can also be reached by Max Line Rail to the Washington Park Station, or by TriMet bus 63, which stops in front of the Visitor Center.

The arboretum, with over twenty trails covering twelve miles, is an exceptional place to walk for people of all abilities. Open meadows alternate with groves of widely diverse assemblages of trees. Since the first tree was planted in 1931, everything within the arboretum has been organized taxonomically, in groupings of specific plant families. Varieties of maple trees, for example, are all planted in one location, while specimens of oaks are assembled in another. In general, on the south-facing slopes east of Fairview Boulevard, deciduous trees predominate. West of Fairview on the north-facing ravines, conifers make up the landscape.

At every season of the year, the arboretum offers something new to appreciate. In spring, flowering trees in the Magnolia Collection, together with numerous varieties of cherry and dogwood trees, set the hillsides abloom. In summer, the Conifer Collection, with its hundreds of pines, firs, cedars, spruces, sequoias, and hemlocks, provides welcome shade on a warm day. In fall, exquisite crimson, orange, and yellow leaves highlight the Maple Collection, where maples, oaks, beeches, and ashes create some of the most spectacular scenery in all of Portland. In winter, the Holly Collection, with

splashes of bright red berries, showcases over one hundred and forty varieties of holly.

While a myriad of routes can be chosen to explore the arboretum, for an easy, 2½-mile loop that captures some of its diversity begin at the Visitor Center and hike up Overlook Trail. At the top of the hill, next to a water tank, turn right and continue on Overlook Trail as it meanders down open meadows and reveals wide vistas. Near the bottom of the slope, at the intersection with Maple Trail, turn left onto Maple Trail and enter the arboretum's Maple Collection.

This important collection contains over sixty different species of maples, many of which are threatened globally. In partnership with the North American Plant Collections Consortium (NAPCC), Hoyt Arboretum is working to collect specimens of all of the world's maples in an attempt to preserve their vital, though diminishing, genetic material.

At the junction of Maple Trail with Hawthorn Trail, turn left on Hawthorn Trail, which wanders through many colorful varieties of hawthorn trees. Soon the trail intersects with Cherry Trail. Turn right here and follow Cherry Trail up the hill to the water tank, where it merges with Wildwood Trail.

Turn left on Wildwood and walk across the top of the slope, taking a moment to pause at the viewpoint, which on a clear day displays Mts. Rainier and Adams. At the junction with Holly Trail turn right, and descend towards Fairview Boulevard through a field exhibiting numerous varieties of holly.

At Fairview, cross the road and head towards the large covered picnic shelter, where Spruce Trail begins. Head north on this trail, which travels through the arboretum's Conifer Collection, which features one of the largest assemblages of coniferous trees in the world, with over two hundred and forty species collected from six continents.

Spruce Trail ends at a junction with Wildwood Trail near the end of Bray Lane. Turn left onto Wildwood Trail and proceed to the newly built Redwood Overlook. Situated among a magnificent grove of tall, straight-trunked redwoods, this peaceful oasis is a new addition to the arboretum. Hoyt Arboretum Friends, a non-profit group supporting the park, generously contributed to the development and construction of this lovely site. It is well worth taking a moment here to reflect on the stalwart redwoods and sequoias that one day will grow into giant trees.

Continue on Wildwood Trail as it curves down the ravine to the canyon bottom, where it crosses over a bridge above Johnson Creek. Beyond this point, the vegetation is now maintained as a natural area and highlights plants native to the Douglas fir region of western Oregon. At Wildwood Trail's junction with White Pine Trail, turn left onto White Pine. This trail crosses Fischer Lane and continues on the other side. Abundant displays of sword fern cover the upper hillsides and graceful vine maples drape over the trail in many spots. Remain on White Pine as far as Creek Trail. Here, turn right, then turn left at an intersection with Hemlock Trail, where there is a second bridge crossing.

After passing over the creek, Hemlock Trail comes to a junction with Fir Trail. Turn left onto Fir Trail. This path leads back to the picnic shelter and, immediately beyond that, to Fairview Boulevard and the Visitor Center, completing the loop.

"Hoyt Arboretum is a place where the wonder and beauty of the complex plant kingdom can be brought home to people of all ages. ... It inspires knowledge, appreciation, reverence, and responsible action on behalf of all the interlocking components of ecosystems."

—Dan Moeller, Portland Parks and Recreation

Along the hills northwest of Portland "there are a
succession of ravines and spurs covered with remarkably
beautiful primeval woods ... It is true that some
people look upon such woods merely as a troublesome
encumbrance standing in the way of more profitable use
of the land, but future generations will not feel so and will
bless the men who were wise enough to get such woods
preserved. Future generations, however, will be likely to
appreciate the wild beauty and the grandeur of the tall fir
trees in this forest park ... its deep shady ravines and bold
view-commanding spurs, far more than do the majority
of the citizens of today, many of whom are familiar with
similar original woods. But such primeval woods will
become as rare about Portland as they now are about
Boston. If these woods are preserved, they will surely come
to be regarded as marvelously beautiful."

John Charles Olmsted and Frederick Law Olmsted, Jr.,
Report of the Park Board, Portland, Oregon, 1903

Bridge to the Future

Sixty years ago, a group of community-oriented individuals set out to do something big for their city. Motivated by their love of Oregon's outdoors and inspired by a long-standing vision, they strove for a goal larger than themselves—one that considered the Portland of the future.

Led by Ding Cannon, Thornton Munger, and Fred Cleator, these dedicated people worked to preserve a forest that stretched from downtown Portland and extended towards the rural Coast Range. They clearly understood that, as their city grew, areas of wildness and natural beauty would become more scarce. They recognized also the human need for places offering solace and refuge, peace and rejuvenation.

All Portlanders today benefit from their devotion to this dream. Their efforts gave us a priceless gift—Forest Park. Today, Portland, Oregon, reigns as the only metropolitan area in the nation that offers its citizens a wilderness … in the heart of its city.

For its solitude, beauty, and unspoiled naturalness, Forest Park is unequaled as a city park. Located within a region of over a million people, the park maintains over one hundred and seventeen species of native birds and fifty-three species of mammals that live and range throughout its borders. Scores of native plants bring the western coniferous forest ecosystem right into the center of our city. Eleven natural watersheds act to provide clean water to a thirsty and ailing Willamette River. And, after sixty years of careful, conservative management, Forest Park still remains restorative and inspiring, and concordant with the founders' original intent.

But for this privilege to continue to exist—and indeed it is a privilege—several things are necessary. We are at a pivotal point in the park's history, standing on a bridge that reaches out from the past and crosses over to the future.

Great challenges are currently facing the park; our responses will determine their outcome. If Forest Park is to retain its abundance of native wildlife, it is essential that we preserve large blocks of unbroken interior forest habitat. That means maintaining Forest Park's North Unit for its high resource values, in spite of growing recreational demand. Equally important, it will be necessary to insure that the park is not one day surrounded on all sides by urban sprawl. If the corridor of natural habitat that presently connects the park to rural areas of the Coast Range is eliminated, the wildlife diversity that we know today in Forest Park will dramatically decline.

Private holdings within the park's boundaries continue to threaten its integrity, especially the health of Forest Park's watersheds. These areas need to become a part of the park, as was originally intended in the master plans drawn up by the Olmsted Brothers, Robert Moses, the City Club, the Forest Park Committee of Fifty, the City Council, the Oregon Parks Foundation, and the Forest Park Natural Resources Management Plan. In addition, the battle to eradicate detrimental invasive species is critical if Forest Park is not to one day become an ivy forest.

Perhaps the greatest challenge, though, is how to preserve Forest Park's intrinsic wilderness qualities—those things that allow inspiration, quiet reflection, the chance to partake of natural beauty— while addressing the increasing demand for all kinds of recreation within the park.

It's a philosophical question, really. Do we, as a community, want Forest Park to become a recreation capital or remain foremost as a wilderness? How much do we value its native wildlife and vegetation? Are we willing to make some sacrifices to preserve its primitive nature, to keep its resources wild and free?

The choice is now ours. We can remain on the bridge and watch the future unfold. Or, we can step out and walk toward it with a renewed vision. Protecting Forest Park for the next sixty years, keeping its ecological functioning high and its wilderness spirit intact, will take hard work. It will require dedication and a deeper understanding than ever before that this place is unique among all city parks in the country.

For its naturalness, beauty, and remarkable history, Forest Park is unquestionably Portland's quiet treasure. It is a native place that defines who we are as Oregonians. Looking to the past, we can learn from the people who strove for decades to create Forest Park.

These founders did not shy away from the challenges. Rather, they fought to leave us an unparalleled heritage. When I pause to consider all they accomplished, and the priceless resource they gave us freely, I realize something:

We are not entitled *to* this gift. Rather, we are entrusted *with* it. Now it's our turn to pass it on.

History will show: did we?

"Today and in the future, our challenge lies in allowing Forest Park its natural progressions while protecting its resources— treading lightly upon it as we learn from its wildness and marvel at its beauty."

—Elizabeth Patte

BIBLIOGRAPHY

Adams, L.W. and L.E. Dove. 1989. *Wildlife Reserves and Corridors in the Urban Environment: a Guide to Ecological Landscape Planning and Resource Conservation*. National Institute for Urban Wildlife, Columbia, MD.

Adams, L.W. and D.L. Leedy, eds. 1987. *Integrating Man and Nature in the Metropolitan Environment*. National Institute for Urban Wildlife, Columbia, MD.

Bennett, E.H. *The Greater Portland Plan*. Portland, 1912.

Burgess, R.C. and D.M. Sharp, eds. 1891. *Forest Island Dynamics in Man-dominated Landscapes*. Springer-Verlag, New York.

Cline, S.P., et al. "Snag Characteristics in Douglas Fir Forests, Western Oregon." *Journal of Wildlife Management*, 44.1980: 773-86.

Davis, A.M., and T.F. Glick. "Urban Ecosystems and Island Biogeography." *Environmental Conservation*, 5. 1978: 299-304.

Diamond, J.M. 1975. "The Island Dilemma: Lessons of Modern Biogeographic Studies for the Design of Natural Preserves." *Biological Conservation*. 7:129-146.

Forest Park Committee. 1976. "A Management Plan for Forest Park." (As further revised by Council action Nov. 10, 1976, and amended by Friends of Forest Park, Dec. 21, 1989.) Portland, OR.

Franklin, J.F., et al. *Ecological Characteristics of Old-growth Douglas Fir Forests*. USDA Forest Service General Technical Report. PNW-118. 1981.

———, et al. *Natural Vegetation of Oregon and Washington*. USDA Forest Service General Technical Report. PNW-8. 1980.

Harris, L.D. 1984. *The Fragmented Forest—Island Biogeography Theory and the Preservation of Biotic Diversity*. University of Chicago Press.

———. 1988. "Landscape Linkages: the Dispersal Corridor Approach to Wildlife Conservation." *Transactions of the North American Wildlife Natural Resource Conference*. 53.959-607.

Hitchcock, C.L., and A. Cronquist. *Flora of the Pacific Northwest*. Seattle, 1978.

Houle, M.C. 1990. "Wild About the City: Phase One of the West Hills Wildlife Corridor Study." Prepared for the Multnomah County Division of Planning and Development.

Keil, B. *Guide to the Roads and Trails of Forest Park*. Portland, 1973.

Lewis, M., and W. Clark. *The Lewis and Clark Expedition*. Vol. 3, Edited by Nicholas Biddle. New York, 1961.

MacClintock, L., R.F. Whitcomb, and B.L. Whitcomb. 1977. "Island Biogeography and 'Habitat Islands' of Eastern Forests. Evidence For the Value of Corridors and Minimization of Isolation in Preservation of Biotic Diversity." *American Birds*. 31:6-12.

Mackintosh, G. ed. 1989. *Preserving Communities and Corridors.* Washington, D.C.

Mannan, R.W., et al. "Use of Snags by Birds in Douglas Fir Forests, Western Oregon." *Journal of Wildlife Management,* 44. 1980: 787-97.

Maser, C., et al. *Natural History of Oregon Coast Mammals.* USDA Forest Service General Technical Report. PNW-133. 1981.

Meslow, E.C. "The Relationship of Birds of Habitat Structure—Plant Communities and Successional Stages." *Proceeding of the Workshop on Nongame Bird Habitat Management in the Coniferous Forests of the Western United States.* Edited by R. DeGraff. USDA Forest Service General Technical Report. PNW-64. 1978: 12-18.

Moses, Robert. *Portland Improvement.* Report to the Portland City Council. Portland, 1943.

Munger, T.T. *History of Portland's Forest Park.* Portland, 1960.

Newton, M., et al. "Role of Alder in Western Oregon Forest Succession." *Biology of Alder.* Edited by J.M. Trappe, et al. Pacific Northwest Forest and Range Experiment Station. 1967: 73-84.

Noss, R.F. 1987. "Protection Natural Areas in Fragmented Landscapes." *Natural Areas Journal.* 7:2-13.

Olmstead, J.C., and F.L. Olmstead, Jr. *Report of the Park Board.* Portland, 1903.

Pintarich, Dick. "The Portland That Might Have Been." *Oregon Magazine.* Aug. 1979: 53-60.

Portland Parks and Recreation; Bureau of Planning. 1995. "Forest Park: Natural Resources Management Plan." Adopted by City Council February 8, 1995.

Robbins, C.S., et al. *Birds of North America.* New York, 1983.

Soule, M. 1986. "Conservation Biology—the Science of Scarcity and Diversity." Sinauer Assoc. Sunderland, Mass.

Sullivan, R. 1989. "Tying the Landscape Together: the Need for Wildlife Movement Corridors." Cooperative Extension Service, University of Florida.

Trimble, D.E. "Geology of Portland, Oregon and Adjacent Areas." *Geological Survey Bulletin.* 1119. 1963.

Warren, C.E. et al. "Conceptual Frameworks and Philosophical Foundations of General Living Systems Theory." *Behavioral Science,* 24. 1979: 296-310.

Wilcove, D.S. 1987. "From Fragmentation to Extinction." *Natural Areas Journal.* 7: 23-29.

Wilcox, B.A. and D.D. Murphy. 1985. "Conservation Strategy: the Effects of Fragmentation on Extinction." *American Naturalist.* 125: 879-887.

Wilson, E.O. 1988. *Biodiversity.* National Academy Press. Washington, D.C.

INDEX

250